THE POSTWAR EVOLUTION OF
DEVELOPMENT THINKING

The Postwar Evolution of Development Thinking

Charles P. Oman

and

Ganeshan Wignaraja

St. Martin's Press   New York

© OECD Development Centre 1991

First published in the United States of America in 1991

Printed in Great Britain

ISBN 0–312–07186–8 (cloth)
ISBN 0–312–07185–X (paper)

Library of Congress Cataloging-in-Publication Data
Oman, Charles Pennington.
The postwar evolution of development thinking / Charles P. Oman
and Ganeshan Wignaraja.
p.   cm.
Includes bibliographical references (p.   ) and index.
ISBN 0–312–07186–8 (cloth). —ISBN 0–312–7185–X (pbk.)
1. Economic development.   2. Dependency.   I. Wignaraja, Ganeshan,
1962– . II. Title.
HD75.046   1991
338.9—dc20   91–27768
                                                   CIP

To Sunthari and Poona
To Isabel and Wallace
To the memory of Jane

CONTENTS

Acknowledgements

The authors are grateful to Louis Emmerij, President of the OECD Development Centre, for the inspiration and support he provided, without which this book would not have been written. They are also grateful to Keith Griffin, Professor and Chairman of the Department of Economics at the University of California, Riverside, for his continuous encouragement and support.

Many thanks go to Albert Fishlow, Hans Singer, Henri Bretaudeau (who also provided several World Bank documents), Winston Fritsch, Ian Goldin and Howard White for their comments on a first draft of the study, and to Gladys Ambort for research assistance on Part II. A special note of gratitude also goes to Sandra Lloyd for her cheerful and tireless efforts in processing the manuscript.

Preface

In a period when discussions about the alleged crisis in development thinking and practice abound, it is important to take some distance and examine where we stand. This is the purpose of the series 'Economic Choices before the Developing Countries' which the OECD Development Centre has launched and of which Keith Griffin's book, *Alternative Strategies for Economic Development*, was the first to appear. Griffin's study was concerned with the practice of development and looked at how countries have been able to reach a given set of economic and social objectives by pursuing one or several development strategies.

The present volume is the indispensable companion to the Griffin book in that it examines the theoretical highlights of post-World War II thinking in the field of economic and social development. In a sense, Keith Griffin looked at the practice and kept theory explicitly in the background; Charles Oman and Ganeshan Wignaraja look at the theory and keep the practice explicitly in the background.

Just as the late 1970s and early 1980s ushered in a new orthodoxy in economic policy thinking in the OECD region, so the 'neoclassical resurgence' – as the authors of the present book call it – threw into series question some of the very foundations of post-war development thinking. This questioning was reflected in the titles of such provocative works as 'The Birth, Life and Death of Development Economics' by Dudley Seers, 'The Rise and Decline of Development Economics' by Albert Hirschman, and *The Poverty of Development Economics* by Deepak Lal. While a growing number of development writers argued for a multidisciplinary approach to the problems of underdevelopment, the thrust of much of the critique of development thinking by mainstream economists was that it tended to underestimate the importance for developing countries of key lessons from the advanced countries: encourage private initiative and let markets do their job.

Many crucial issues raised in the development literature nevertheless remain unresolved. A recent illustration of this is Joseph Stiglitz's *Americal Economic Review* article of May, 1989, which explores the causes and consequences in developing countries of 'market failures and the failure of private, non-market solutions', especially in knowledge and information, learning by doing, and capital markets. Of course, the rather simple dichotomy that some drew in the 1980s between the role of the private sector and that of the State – which sometimes even appeared as a dichotomy between good and bad – has always been viewed as naïve by those who have really reflected on the question. Thus, for example, Deepak Lal notes approvingly that orthodox economists since John Stuart Mill have been critical of the doctrine of *laissez-faire*, and agrees with Keynes that the important thing for governments is not to do things which individuals are doing already, to do them a little better or a little worse, but to do things which at present are not done at all.

Today, the relevance of development theory, far from fading, is taking on new proportions. Beyond the large majority of the world's population living in the developing countries, this growing relevance applies to much of Eastern Europe and the Soviet Union, whose development problems now loom large on the horizon. It also increasingly applies at the international level to the OECD region, where the slowdown of productivity growth since the mid-1970s, and especially the acceleration of economic globalisation in the 1980s and the simultaneous rise of 'strategic' national and regional trade policies and protectionist pressures, all highlight the relevance of the indivisibilities, complementarities, externalities and economies of scale to which development thinking has given so much attention.

This is, therefore, an important book which is being published at a particularly timely moment. It brings out the wealth of ideas, experiences and controversy that have emerged during the more than forty-five-year evolution post-war development thinking, which all too often is lost sight of, or even forgotten, in the rush to grapple with 'new' issues and problems. Moreover, this book does so in a way that is unique in its unified, yet comprehensive, coverage of Latin American structuralist, dependency and Marxist views, as well as the multiple strands of more orthodox development thinking and practice, and their critics. It also does so in a multidisciplinary fashion, which is crucial in a period where, as the authors note, 'With the renewal of democracies still fragile, there is also considerable awareness that, in the final analysis, economic policies must depend as much on political considerations and their ability to build social consensus as on their strict theoretical coherence'.

I believe that this book will be a useful tool for a broad range of policy advisors and policy makers concerned with the problems associated with less-than-smoothly functioning markets in the global economy of the coming years, as well as for economists, political scientists and other students and practitioners in the field of development *per se*.

Louis Emmerij
President
OECD Development Centre
February 1990

Introduction

Development thinking and development practice are in a state of flux. There are of course fundamental differences – ideological, theoretical, methodological – among different schools of development thought. Those differences could be the healthy result of, and should contribute to, informed debate. More disconcerting is the fact that one must seriously question how well development practice today is informed by such debate – and even how well informed the debate itself is. The relationships among diverse strands of development thinking that have emerged during the postwar period often appear today poorly understood, ill perceived, lost in a forest of development literature where attention usually focuses on only one or a few trees. And, as a result, there appears to be an increasing isolation of development practice from development theory, of development policy from development research, of current debate from past experience.

The purpose of this book is to provide an overview of the evolution of postwar development thinking, and practice, in a way that keeps the trees from hiding the forest. Its purpose is thus not to explore the details of any particular strand of development thinking, but to bring out the relations among the more important strands, and to shed some light on how these strands relate to the broad course of development policy and practice since the Second World War.

Our survey is divided into two parts. Part I covers what we call orthodox development thinking. It comprises four chapters, each focusing on a major theme: capital accumulation and industrialisation; dualism, agriculture-centred development and the green revolution; open-economy development and the neoclassical resurgence; and reformist development thinking. Part II, which looks at heterodox development thinking, is in turn divided into two chapters: the Latin American structuralist and dependency schools; and Marxist development thinking.

Our focus on the postwar period reflects the fact that it is only since the end of the Second World War that analysts and policy-makers have extensively and explicitly focused on the causes of, and barriers to, growth and development in what were once categorised as 'backward' areas, subsequently referred to as the 'underdeveloped', 'less developed' or 'Third World' countries, and now widely referred to as 'developing' countries. It is, however, important to note that several events during

1

the first half of this century and during the immediate postwar period contributed significantly to the great interest in Third World development that has emerged since the War.

One was the disruption of world trade during the Depression and War years of 1914–1945, which induced a transition to what came to be called inward-oriented growth or import-substituting industrialisation in some developing countries, notably in Latin America. An important result was the emergence there of 'new' groups of local elites whose material interests were directly tied to the local production of manufactures for the local market, and who, therefore, pursued policies they hoped would promote the modernisation and development of their national economies much more actively than had their landlord and merchant-capitalist predecessors at the head of the local power structure. Two examples of this were Peronism in Argentina and the Cardenas period in Mexico.

Another factor was the restructuring of alliances among the industrialised countries and the creation of international organisations during and immediately after the War. The Allied Powers explicitly declared their adhesion – e.g., in the first Allied Declaration of 1941 – to the principle that the only sure basis of peace was the enjoyment of economic and social security by free people, and they committed themselves to establishing a world order that would pursue this objective once the War was over. One important result was the establishment of the United Nations at the 1945 San Francisco Conference, where the goal of creating a world order promoting economic and social development was reaffirmed. It is interesting to note that of the 51 countries that participated in the Conference, only 10 or 12 were developed countries and a majority of the remainder were Latin American countries.

Another factor of major importance was of course the postwar break-up of the colonial empires and the attainment of political independence in much of Africa and Asia. As the process of decolonisation advanced and as local elites in the newly independent countries established themselves in the seat of local political power, or struggled among themselves in attempting to consolidate that power, promises of economic prosperity were made to mobilise local supporters and defeat rival factions to gain control of the state. The need for strategies to attain economic and social development that would accompany political independence thus emerged as a primary preoccupation in much of Africa and Asia in the 1950 and 1960s.

The postwar period of decolonisation also witnessed a marked increase in international tensions between developed capitalist and socialist countries. The 'Cold War', as this tension was called in the 1950s and early 1960s, and the concern on the part of the dominant capitalist countries that conditions of social and economic under-development left poor countries 'ripe' for Communist revolution – a concern exacerbated by the 'loss' of China in 1949, and again by that of Cuba in 1959 – thus contributed to the increased interest shown by the developed countries in the development problems of the Third World. This concern was in part reflected, at the policy level, in 'Point IV' of the Truman Administration's 1949 foreign-policy programme, in the United Kingdom's 1950 'Colombo Plan' and, a decade later, in the Kennedy Administration's 'Alliance for Progress' in Latin America, for example. It was also reflected in the creation of the Development Assistance Committee of the OECD in 1960/61, and two years later of the OECD Development Centre, as well as in the reorientation of the focus of World Bank programmes toward the Third World, and in numerous multilateral technical and financial aid programmes carried out under the auspices of the United Nations.

As the postwar rehabilitation of Europe and Japan progressed and international trade gained new vigour, many private organisations based in OECD countries also became increasingly interested in the problems of and prospects for development in the Third World. The phenomenal postwar growth of the OECD economies was notably accompanied by the emergence of numerous multinational corporations that played an increasingly active role in expanding trade flows and capital movements not only among the developed countries but also between these countries and the Third World. Many of these corporations increasingly looked to the latter region not only as a traditional source of raw materials but also as a market for their products (capital goods, including technology, as well as consumer and intermediate goods, and armaments), and in some cases as a base for direct investment in local import-substituting industries. Possibilities for and barriers to growth and development in the Third World thus attracted increasing private-sector interest, largely because of its local-market potential, but also because of a growing interest in promoting local political stability and avoiding labour unrest (in production of primary export products as well as in manufactures for the local market).

Finally, a factor which undoubtedly contributed to the growth of worldwide concern over the problems of poverty and human suffering prevalent in so many Third World countries was the vast increase in the availability of information on world poverty. Largely responsible for this dramatic increase were, on the one hand, the revolutions in communication techniques (notably television) and, on the other, the work of various international and multilateral organisations which for the first time began to collect systematic data on economic conditions throughout the Third World after the War. We shall discuss some of this work in Part I, notably in the chapter on reformist development thinking.

PART I
Orthodox Development Thinking

Orthodox Development Thinking

Our survey of orthodox development thinking is divided into four chapters. Chapter 1 reviews the capital-accumulation and industrialisation theories that constituted the dominant current of orthodox development thinking during the immediate postwar period and up to the early 1970s. Increased capital accumulation and industrialisation were perceived by many writers and policy-makers to have been the vehicle by which the developed countries historically achieved sustained growth and development, and were thus widely seen as the road whereby the less-developed countries could achieve development. Indeed, while the 'dual economy' models of the 1950s and 1960s stressed the co-existence, in underdeveloped countries, of 'modern' capitalist industrial and 'traditional' rural subsistence sectors, they too pointed to capital accumulation and industrialsation as the road to development – with the rural sector providing the surplus labour and part of the capital required for industrialisation.

It was only in the late 1960s and particularly during the 1970s that the heavy emphasis on industrialisation was partly superseded by a focus on agriculture and the need to develop the rural sector in its own right, to which we turn in Chapter 2. One cause of this shift in emphasis was increasing disillusionment with the strategies and policies of import-substituting industrialisation as many countries reached the limits of the 'easy' phase of substitution, and as growth was increasingly constrained by severe inefficiencies in industry, dependence on food imports and balance-of-payments deficits. Another cause was the advent of the 'green revolution' production techniques and their apparent, if controversial, applicability to the conditions of small rural producers.

The origins of the neoclassical resurgence, which is the subject of Chapter 3, actually go back to the development of mainstream marginalist economic analysis and particularly to international trade theory and the concept of comparative advantage. It was in the late 1960s and early 1970s, however, that criticisms of import-substituting industrialisation strategies by neoclassical economists arguing for more open-economy approaches to development began to make their full weight felt. And it is particularly during the 1980s that the neoclassical emphasis on the market mechanism and 'getting prices right' came to dominate development debates. This neoclassical resurgence was reinforced by the critique of Keynesian policies and the move towards 'supply-side economics' in dominant policy circles in much of the OECD region during the 1980s. It also largely coincided with the debt crisis and promotion by the World Bank and IMF of 'structural adjustment' policies in much of Latin America and Africa – at a time when the success of some East Asian developing countries' export-led industrialisation strategies reached spectacular proportions.

The late 1960s and particularly the 1970s also witnessed the emergence of what may be called reformist development thinking, reviewed in Chapter 4. Critical of the heavy emphasis on growth and industrialisation of the 1950s and 1960s, but also of the neoclassical approach to development, the reformist strand of orthodox development thinking brought important light to bear on the problems of poverty, growing inequality of income distribution and 'basic human needs'. Practically from the outset, however, reformist development strategies met considerable opposition both from important aid donors and from some developing-country governments. By the beginning of the 1980s, reformist development thinking was therefore increasingly overshadowed not only by the neoclassical resurgence but by the proponents of agriculture-centred development as well.

Finally, and rather recently, the neoclassical approach has in turn come under increasing criticism from within the orthodox literature. With growing protectionist pressures in OECD countries and the continuation of the debt crisis (and its social and political as well as economic consequences) notably in Latin America, with the prolonged food crisis in Africa (at a time when global food surpluses are also an issue) and with growing OECD protectionism forcing some of the Asian manufacturing-export-led 'success stories' of the 1970s and 1980s to rethink their development strategies as well, the focus is increasingly turning once again to industrialisation- and agriculture-based development strategies. Renewed attention is also being given to the domestic market, while policy-makers seek to avoid the pitfalls of the 'inward-oriented' strategies of the 1950s and 1960s.

1 Capital Accumulation and Industrialisation

An early strand of orthodox development literature presented the view, derived essentially from classical and neoclassical trade theory and the free-trade doctrine of 'comparative advantage',[1] that in general underdeveloped countries should (continue to) specialise in the production of raw materials and primary products for export in order to finance imports and growth. Jacob Viner and Gottfried Haberler, for example, argued in the 1950s for such a strategy.[2] Their reasoning emphasized the theoretical benefits to be derived from trade, and focused empirically on the development experiences of such countries as Denmark, Australia and New Zealand. Those experiences were purported to show that specialisation in the production of primary products, even a single agricultural commodity, can lead to rapid increases in productivity and capital accumulation, and that such production for export can serve as an 'engine' of growth and development.

The theme of trade as an engine for growth will be pursued in our chapter on open-economy development. What is important here is to point out that the view that underdeveloped countries should concentrate on primary exports was widely disputed not only by heterodox writers (cf. Chapter 5) but also within the orthodox literature of the 1950s and 1960s. Many writers argued that there had been secular changes in international income elasticities of demand for primary products, especially agricultural goods, since Denmark, Australia and New Zealand first attained development. Even more important, early orthodox critics of the relatively 'purest' defenders of free trade focused on the latter's failure to examine more closely the specific nature of the *internal* problems of capital accumulation in the less developed countries.

Emerging from this criticism, a major strand of the orthodox development literature that caught the attention of development specialists and policy-makers in both the developed and developing countries during the 1950s and 1960s focused on *industrialisation* as a, if not the, requisite of development. Many shared the view, implicitly if not explicitly, that the developed countries were rich because they were industrialised, and that much of the Third World was poor because it

9

remained heavily based on subsistence agriculture. The importance of agriculture in development tended to be ignored, moreover, because, as Theodore Schultz pointed out in 1964, the agricultural sector was commonly thought to be enveloped by tradition and prejudice that would hamper its own modernisation, and because of a widespread wish on the part of policy-makers to promote and build industries that carried the image of modernisation.[3]

THE ROSTOWIAN VIEW OF GROWTH, INDUSTRIALISATION AND AID

One of the most widely discussed studies of development to highlight the key role of industrialisation was that of W.W. Rostow, elaborated during the 1950s and published in 1960 as *The Stages of Economic Growth, a Non-Communist Manifesto*.[4] Frequently referred to as the 'take-off' theory, Rostow's stages – he portrayed development as an essentially linear (as opposed to dialectical) historical process consisting of five consecutive stages – are well known by now, as are many of the major criticisms of his theory. Despite widespread agreement with many of these criticisms, however, the view remains deeply embedded in development thinking that countries pass, at different times, through a series of comparable stages of development, that there are fundamental similarities in this process, and that today's less developed countries can more or less follow (and are following) in the footsteps of today's more developed countries.

Rostow's study is also noteworthy because of its unusual scope (he presented it as nothing less than a manifesto) and its considerable influence on development policies, involving both the formulation of 'aid' programmes (most notably that of the United States) and the design of development strategies in some areas of the Third World.[5] Particularly important for our purposes, it brought together or at least touched upon many of the ideas and policies developed or analysed more extensively by other authors during the 1950s and 1960s.

Thus, in addition to its focus on industrialisation, an important aspect of Rostow's study is its view, explicit or implicit, of the relationships between economic growth and overall societal development, and between capital investment and economic growth. Regarding the growth-development relationship, Rostow's position reflects the approach prevalent in orthodox development thinking at least until the 1970s – and to a considerable extent still today – which considers the two as virtually inseparable, if not equivalent, and concentrates on requirements for and obstacles to *growth*. This growth-centred orientation is undoubtedly the result of several factors, but above all it reflects the widely accepted notion – not inconsistent, by the way, with a Marxist view of history and social change – that revolutionary increases in society's material production capacity are the fundamental (though not necessarily the unique) requirement of global societal development.

Moreover, in order to achieve this increase in production capacity, Rostow, like many orthodox economists of the 1950s and 1960s, subscribed to the notion put forward by Simon Kuznets, Albert Hirschman and others of the *leading sector*. This notion states that at different moments or periods of industrial growth, different sectors within industry grow considerably faster than the economy as a whole and give dynamism to the rest of the economy.[6]

Rostow's view of economic take-off and the concept of the leading sector were also fed, and then reinforced, by the work of Gerschenkron on Europe's growth experience during the 19th century. Gerschenkron argued that differences in the level of economic growth among countries made it possible to classify them according to their degree of backwardness, and that the more backward a country's economy, the more likely was its industrialisation to start discontinuously as a sudden 'great spurt' and to proceed at a relatively high rate of growth of manufacturing output.[7]

A second important reason for the growth orientation found in the orthodox development literature can be put quite simply: growth lends itself to quantitative measurement, whereas other concepts of development are often thought to be amorphous, difficult to grasp and impossible to measure. So in their striving for mathematical rigour, many development analysts trained in the positivist tradition find it most convenient to focus on growth.[8]

Regarding the relationship between investment and growth, here again Rostow's approach was representative of much of the orthodox development literature of the 1950s and 1960s, in that it reflected the direct influence of the post-Keynesian growth models. In the West, the Great Depression of the 1930s aided the spread of Keynesian methods of analysis. Even though the unemployment resulting from a lack of aggregate demand during recessions in developed economies was different from the unemployment problem found in underdeveloped economies, Keynesian techniques influenced policy in the latter group of countries as well. In particular, they provided a conceptual basis for national demand management and other forms of state intervention.

The most important post-Keynesian growth model adopted for developing countries was the Harrod–Domar model, developed during the 1930s and 1940s to clarify the delicate balance between income, savings, investment and output required to *maintain stable* growth and full employment in a (developed) capitalist economy.[9] It was nevertheless used by many development economists to attempt to identify savings and investment rates needed to *achieve* self-sustained growth in a developing (capitalist) economy. Indeed, already in 1951, a major UN report on *Measures for the Economic Development of Under-Developed Countries* emphasized the need for capital accumulation:

> In most countries where rapid economic progress is occurring, net capital formation at home is at least 10 per cent of the national income, and in some it is substantially higher. By contrast, in most underdeveloped countries, net capital formation is not as high as 5 per cent of the national income, even when foreign investment is included. (...) How to increase the rate of capital formation is therefore a question of great urgency.[10]

W.A. Lewis advanced a similar view in his *Theory of Economic Growth* published in 1955,[11] and Rostow picked it up in his description of the conditions leading to development, arguing that a decisive characteristic of his third stage, the key 'take-off' period, is 'a rise in the rate of productive investment from, say, 5 per cent or less to over 10 per cent of national income (or net national product)'.[12]

This aspect of the Rostowian *cum* Harrod–Domar approach to development analysis is of particular relevance not only because of its widespread influence on orthodox development thinking in general during the 1950s and 1960s, but also because of the major role it played in the design – or perhaps the justification – of US aid policy during the same period. Specifically, this approach gave rise to, or at least supported, the politically attractive notion that a massive dose of aid and foreign capital to less developed countries that were ready for 'take-off' – Rostow argued that the take-off period generally lasts (only) about 20 years – would rapidly bring a recipient country to a point where aid would no longer be needed.

Rostow was heavily criticised, within the orthodox literature, for overstating his case. Many authors argued that in the history of developed and developing countries alike, it is impossible to identify any unique and relatively short historical phase as the take-off period.[13] Nevertheless, in the actual practice of aid, certain marked tendencies can be largely attributed to the Rostow *cum* Harrod–Domar approach. First, aid was often seen as part of a short, sharp effort to surmount one crucial hurdle. This in turn gave rise in some cases, notably in the US aid programme, where Rostow's influence was greatest, to an all-or-nothing approach, and to a rather bland optimism. The 1969 Pearson Report, which was a major and comprehensive study purporting to evaluate the developed countries' international development-assistance operations and was cast in an analytical mould that clearly owed much to Rostow, exemplifies such optimism.[14] At least one leading analyst thus argued, in 1974, that another result was 'to impede perception of the limitations on the aid-giver's role which would facilitate a more precise and selective identification of the purposes that aid can usefully serve in different situations. The danger is that attention will be focused on things that aid in most cases probably cannot do, like transforming an entire economy, and diverted from things that it perhaps can do, like meeting some specific and limited need'.[15]

Furthermore, when unreasonable expectations were not fulfilled, this optimism often gave way to excessive pessimism. And all along, aid agencies remained in confusion about their role during Rostow's second stage – during which the pre-conditions for take-off are put in place.

THE TWO-GAP MODEL

In addition to the relatively widespread application of the Harrod–Domar model to development planning, the late 1950s and early 1960s witnessed a slowing of growth and industrialisation in many underdeveloped countries (see also Chapter 5). Several empirical studies were then undertaken to test the hypothesis that significant increases in and/or high rates of domestic savings were closely correlated with rapid industrial growth. In failing to confirm this hypothesis – the correlation was found to be positive and significant in some cases, but insignificant in others, and negative in a few[16] – the results of these empirical studies in turn led to the development of the 'two-gap' model.

In essence, the two-gap model hypothesises that whereas in the very early stages of industrial growth insufficient savings may stand as the principal constraint on the rate of domestic capital formation, once industrialisation gets well under way the principal constraint may no longer be domestic savings per se, but the availability of foreign exchange required to import capital equipment, intermediate goods and perhaps even raw materials used as industrial inputs. The foreign-exchange gap may thus supersede the savings gap as the principal development constraint.

The two-gap model proved to be particularly relevant for many countries in Latin America and South Asia that attempted to industrialise during the 1950s and 1960s by following a policy of import-substituting industrialisation (ISI). This strategy tended to be based on the production of consumer goods for the home market as a substitute for imports. At a later date, as part of the ISI strategy, attempts were made by some countries to substitute home production for imports of intermediate and capital goods. (The ISI strategy entailed the use of import and exchange controls and an extensive reliance on planning machinery and other forms of state intervention in production, distribution and exchange.) Therefore in the stage of ISI where an economy does not produce its own capital goods and many of its industrial inputs, there is a substantial increase in demand for imports (and hence in foreign-exchange requirements) leading to balance-of-payments difficulties for many developing countries.

The two-gap model represented, it was commonly agreed within the orthodox development literature, a significant improvement of the highly simplified initial view of the savings-investment-growth relationship in a developing country. Regarding its implications for the role of aid, furthermore, the two-gap model essentially reinforced those of Rostow's approach, in the sense that both tended to focus aid users' (donors' and recipients') attention on the need for investment resources which could be supplemented through aid. These features are clearly captured by the pioneering 1962 Chenery–Bruno model and by the more complete Chenery–Strout model published in 1966.[17]

In actual aid practice, however, just as the simplified savings-gap approach to aid justification required an assumption that the marginal savings rate is significantly higher than the average savings rate,[18] so the foreign-exchange-gap approach required an assumption that the rate of growth of exports would eventually, if not immediately, exceed the rate of growth of imports. Without these assumptions, the recipient's need for aid could continue – even grow – indefinitely. When there was cause to doubt the validity of these assumptions in the case of any particular recipient country (as was most frequently the case according to empirical studies), however, donors tended in fact to see aid not as an instrument to fill gaps but as a way to influence the recipient to change fiscal policy and to introduce other measures to raise savings, or export promotion, or both. ('Policy dialogue' between aid donors and recipients, which became very much the fashion during the 1980s, thus actually dates back to this period.)

'TRICKLE-DOWN': SAVINGS, ACCUMULATION AND INCOME DISTRIBUTION

Much of the orthodox development literature refrained during the 1950s and 1960s from looking very deeply into the factors that determine how a society's product is distributed among its members, i.e. that determine who benefits from growth. This neglect of income distribution might have resulted from the lack of reliable statistics needed to undertake such analysis in most developing countries. A closer examination nevertheless suggests that the neglect can be explained to a significant extent by a set of beliefs regarding the operation of a 'trickle-down' mechanism, as well as by the importance attached to increased savings as a requirement for 'take-off'.

For example, one important strand of thought, whose proponents included Walter Galenson and Harvey Leibenstein (1955), held that a highly unequal income distribution was necessary for savings that would facilitate investment and hence growth.[19] The basic premise was that the rich save and invest a higher proportion of their incomes while the poor spend their income on consumption goods. Given that GNP growth rates are a function of the percentage of national income saved, the more a country's income distribution is skewed in favour of the upper income strata, the greater will be the savings and hence growth rates. Furthermore, the more growth occurs, the more income will trickle down to lower income strata via the market mechanism. If large inequalities persisted, Keynesian-type solutions were argued to be possible, via taxes and subsidy programmes.

This line of reasoning was reinforced by Simon Kuznets' analysis, also published in 1955, of the relationship between per capita income levels and income distribution during the process of economic growth, known as the Kuznets U-shaped-curve hypothesis.[20] According to this hypothesis, there is an historical tendency for inequality first to increase, then to level-off and eventually to decline during the course of economic growth. During the early period of development there is a large low-income agricultural sector and a modern industrial high-income sector. As industrialisation proceeds labour moves from the agricultural sector to the industrial sector, which acts as a factor to reduce inequality in the long run. But in the short run the tendency is for inequality to increase because the variance of incomes within sectors is high (for example, because of a greater proportional accumulation of assets by the rich than by the poor) and because of a rise in the mean income differential between the two sectors. Once a sufficient proportion of the total population is in the urban sector and placed in wage employment, the tendency for inequality to rise is checked and tends to be reversed as the low-income groups gain political influence.

Although Kuznets derived this hypothesis from the historical experience of a few developed nations, it was generally thought also to hold for the developing countries. It was therefore widely assumed in the orthodox literature that in the long run growth would result in higher incomes for everyone, rich and poor alike. Only in the 1970s did Kuznets' theoretical and empirical position come under increasing criticism, by the reformist school, as we shall see in Chapter 4.

The neglect of income distribution may also have been a result, unintended or otherwise, of views put forward by a number of important theorists whose common denominator was recognition that it could be extremely difficult to start growth in very backward economies. 'Igniting' a process of industrialisation was thus a central concern for these theorists, whose work can be labelled by catch phrases: Rosenstein-Rodan (big push), Nurkse (balanced growth), Hirschman (unbalanced growth, backward and forward linkages) and Perroux (growth poles), as well as Rostow (take off), Gerschenkron (great spurt) and others. The focus of these authors on inter-industry relations within the industrial sector constituted a major part of orthodox development thinking from the mid-1940s right up to the 1970s.

THE FOCUS ON INTER-INDUSTRY RELATIONSHIPS

Big Push

The man generally identified as the first modern development writer was a pioneer of the study of inter-industry relationships and their implications for growth: as early as 1943, Paul Rosenstein-Rodan emphasized the importance of 'discontinuities' and pecuniary external economies in industrial development.[21] He argued that investment decisions are interdependent and that due to the limited size of the market characteristic of underdeveloped economies, on the one hand, and the competitive pressures on investors to take advantage of economies of scale in production, on the other, investment projects are often too risky for individual investors in underdeveloped countries. Rosenstein-Rodan was therefore one of the first to come out in favour of the 'big push' development strategy, involving government planning to co-ordinate and provide incentives for simultaneous investment in several complementary industries that would yield substantial increases in national production and simultaneously increase the size of the domestic market.[22]

Rosenstein-Rodan also argued for major public investments in social overhead capital. He concluded that due to their indivisibilities and significant externalities in creating profitable investment opportunities, such investments in social overhead capital or infrastructure would have to precede directly productive investments by the private (or public) sector. This view was of course adopted by many multilateral and national development aid and lending agencies following the War, notably including the World Bank.[23]

Rosenstein-Rodan's view of the importance for the development process of pecuniary and technological externalities was also a precursor of important strands of orthodox analysis. Tibor Scitovsky, in particular, clarified the distinction between pecuniary and non-pecuniary external economies and their significance for development, notably the pecuniary externalities of investment in the capital-goods sector that affect investment in consumer-goods production.[24] Rosenstein-Rodan's view of the importance of technological externalities, due especially to the risk for individual investors of less than full appropriability of returns to their investments in the training of workers and other such human-capital formation, likewise foreshadowed a major strand of orthodox thinking – generally associated with the name of Theodore Sahultz[25] and others (cf. Chapter 2).

Balanced Growth

In 1952, Ragnar Nurkse picked up Rosenstein-Rodan's theme of the 'vicious circle of poverty' and developed it further in defense of a strategy of 'balanced growth'.[26] Nurkse dissected the vicious circle as follows: on the demand side, domestic market size is limited because incomes are low, reflecting low productivity levels that are in turn due to the low level of domestic capital formation; and the incentive to invest (the demand for capital) is constrained by the limited size of the market. On the supply side, the circular relationship runs from the low income level to the small capacity to save, hence a lack of capital, and so to low productivity and low incomes.

In contrast to the straight-forward neoclassical approach (which would hold that the condition of relative capital scarcity characteristic of underdeveloped economies should imply high marginal returns to, and thus attract, capital investment), Nurkse emphasized along with Rosenstein-Rodan the constraint placed on investment and hence overall growth by the limited size of the market characteristic of such economies. After noting that exports on the world market provided a crucial source of demand-sustaining growth during the 19th century in many of today's developed countries, he argued that possibilities for today's underdeveloped countries to break out of the 'vicious circle' by similarly relying on world market demands for their exports were very limited.[27]   The solution Nurkse proposed was a synchronised and simultaneous application of capital throughout industry in order to bring about a generalised expansion of the market; i.e. he proposed a strategy of 'balanced growth'.

In at least one important respect, furthermore, Nurkse's approach differed sharply with the Rostowian doctrine. Whereas the latter portrays the underdeveloped countries as following in the path already taken by the developed countries, and basically ignores the possibility that the existence of the more advanced countries could have seriously detrimental effects on the development efforts of the less developed,[28] in his analysis of the savings constraint Nurkse drew attention to an important aspect of the relations between the two groups of countries:

> It seems to be a common view that the capacity for domestic saving in underdeveloped countries depends on an initial increase in productivity and real income...and that some form of outside help – say, foreign investment – is required to bring about this initial improvement and so break the vicious circle. This theory begins to look a bit shaky as soon as we realize that it is not only the absolute but also the relative level of real income that determines the capacity to save. Although the absolute level of even the poorest countries has risen, it is doubtful whether saving has become any easier; on the contrary, it may have become more difficult for them, because there has occurred at the same time a decline in their relative income levels in comparison with those of the economically advanced countries.[29]

Applying what Duesenberry called the 'demonstration effect',[30] Nurkse argued that despite large differences in income levels between developed

and underdeveloped countries, consumers in the latter often seek to
emulate consumption standards in the rich countries. The result is lower
marginal propensities to save in today's underdeveloped countries than
was historically the case when the advanced countries were at similar
income levels. Pointing out that the demonstration effect tends to
undermine savings capacities that are already negatively affected in
underdeveloped countries by the vicious circle of poverty, Nurkse
therefore rejected the traditional view that prosperity spreads from the
more to the less developed countries.

Nurkse took his analysis even further by pointing out that 'the almost
universal countermove' of less developed countries has been to restrict
imports, especially of so-called luxury and semi-luxury goods, but that
such import restrictions generally attack only the surface of the
problem. They fail to resolve the problem, first, because capital goods
and industrial inputs imported under a strategy of import substitution
often respond to consumption patterns heavily influenced by the
demonstration effect – 'the country's capital supplies, scarce as they are,
and painfully brought into existence, will be sucked into relatively
unessential uses'. And second, they fail because the demonstration
effect tends to operate through an upward shift in the general
consumption function and not in the import-consumption function
alone.

Nurkse concluded his analysis of the implications of the demonstration effect by commenting on two possible alternatives. One is 'far more
radical forms of isolation than luxury import restrictions', for which he
cited two historical examples: 'It is well known that Japan, in the early
course of her industrialisation, imitated the Western World in
everything except consumption patterns... The other instance of radical
isolation is Soviet Russia's iron curtain...'.[31] In raising isolationism as a
possible strategy for countries seeking development in the 20th century,
Nurkse was in a curious way foreshadowing in the early 1950s the call
made by some Third World economists in the 1970s for 'delinking', (to
which we return in Chapters 4 and 5). Nurkse's reaction to this
possibility was similarly a forerunner of that of many orthodox
development specialists today:

That this might be a possible and perhaps a necessary solution is
a disquieting thought, and one naturally turns in search of an
alternative. Could it be that the alternative lies in unilateral
income transfers or, in plain English, gifts from rich to poor
countries?[32]

More recent proposals to create some kind of 'second Marshall Plan' for the Third World are also reminiscent of Nurkse's question. Nurkse's answer ran as follows:

> Suppose we have a model, then, where on the one hand international income disparities open up gaps in the balance of payments and on the other unilateral income transfers come in to fill these gaps. Is this a sufficient and satisfactory solution to the problem of capital formation in the poorer countries? Clearly it is not... No permanent basis will be created within the country for higher living standards in the future... The upshot is that external resources, even if they become available in the most desirable forms, are not enough. They do not automatically provide a solution to the problem of capital accumulation in underdeveloped areas. No solution is possible without strenuous domestic efforts...[33]

Whereas many Third World economists would increasingly call for profound *structural* changes, both within less developed countries and internationally (cf. Chapters 4 and 5), Nurkse himself emphasized the need for strenuous efforts in the field of *public finance* as the best way to counteract the demonstration effect and bring about the required level of domestic savings in underdeveloped countries. In limiting his attention largely to the role of public finance, as opposed to structural change, Nurkse's position again foreshadowed that adopted by many orthodox writers, notably the IMF, in more recent years.[34]

Nurkse's analysis of the implications for development of the 'demonstration effect' was largely uncontested within the orthodox literature. The major criticism came from heterodox writers arguing, as we shall see in Part II, that the principal obstacle to development is to be found not in the nature of consumption patterns per se, but in the capitalist nature of *production* today both in underdeveloped countries and internationally. Among orthodox writers, the main subject of debate was Nurkse's call for balanced growth. Several authors in fact called specifically for 'unbalanced growth'.

Unbalanced Growth and Linkage Effects

One of the most influential contributors to this debate was Albert Hirschman, who argued in 1958 that the deliberate creation of *disequilibria* is the best way of achieving development.[35] In many ways Hirschman agreed with Nurkse, e.g. on the limited nature of investment capacity as the principal obstacle to development and on the 'complementary' nature of investments. But Hirschman further argued that a key characteristic of most underdeveloped economies is the weakness of their inter-industrial linkages, leading him to the conclusion that the best strategy is to concentrate investments in those industries with the greatest number of linkages.[36] He thought the best candidates to be those roughly half-way along the production process, whose products serve as inputs to other industries ('forward linkages') and whose needs for inputs create demand for the products of still others ('backward linkages'). In other words, whereas Nurkse's balanced-growth approach reflected the notion that the less dynamic sectors of the economy would hold the potentially dynamic ones back, Hirschman's argument for unbalanced growth reflected the notion that the more active sectors would pull the more passive ones forward.[37]

If the balanced-growth doctrine stressed *markets* as the main limitation on growth, Hirschman's version of the unbalanced-growth doctrine also pointed up scarcity of entrepreneurial and managerial decision-making as an important obstacle to growth in many of today's less developed countries:

> This is the major bone that I have to pick with the balanced growth theory: its application requires huge amounts of precisely those abilities (entrepreneurial and managerial abilities) which we have identified as likely to be in very limited supply in underdeveloped countries... In other words, if a country were ready to apply the doctrine of balanced growth, then it would not be underdeveloped in the first place.[38]

Hirschman further argued that since the number of investment projects that could be undertaken simultaneously in an underdeveloped economy is constrained primarily by the scarcity of entrepreneurship and management skills, the great advantage of a strategy of unbalanced growth would be to create highly profitable investment opportunities by generating external economies and linkage effects from which other industries stood to benefit – thereby *inducing* investment decisions, both economising and stimulating an expansion of 'our principal scarce resource, namely, genuine decision making'.[39]

In the realm of policy implications, two major points emerged from the balanced- versus unbalanced-growth controversy. First, whereas Nurkse's balanced-growth approach implied a need for investments in agriculture along with industry, Hirschman's analysis suggested a concentration of investment in key large-scale industrial projects, namely those likely to have the largest number of linkages. In concentrating his attention on industrial investments, Hirschman felt – and here his views may have reflected those contained in the 'dual economy' models discussed below – that agriculture in general and peasant agriculture in particular had relatively few linkages with the rest of the economy. In any case, Hirschman's unbalanced-growth doctrine had a major impact on development practice, as reflected during the late 1950s and early 1960s in the concentration of orthodox development policy and analysis – including aid programmes – on *large-scale industrial* projects in many less developed countries.

The second major policy implication concerned the role of state planning. The balanced- and unbalanced-growth doctrines both called attention to the indivisibilities ('lumpiness') and complementarities (external economies) of investment, and as such called for a type of co-ordination which market forces, if left to themselves, would not likely succeed in bringing about. Although balanced growth as advocated by Nurkse was conceivable under either private or public coordination, the importance he attributed to external economies – and hence to the difference between social and private costs and benefits – clearly called for government planning. Similarly, unbalanced growth as propounded by Hirschman, which looked to the State to induce and repair disequilibria, called for planning if it was to be effective in practice.

In emphasizing the need to stimulate investment *decisions* as the key to successful development, furthermore, Hirschman's analysis foreshadowed the shift in orientation of the major aid donors from their initial focus on the savings and foreign-exchange 'gaps', to a tendency to focus on purported weaknesses in developing countries' institutions, particularly their public and private administrative systems, as the crucial obstacle to development. One result was an increase in aid donors' support for development of local administrative, managerial and entrepreneurial skills in developing countries.

This shift of emphasis also led, by the mid-1960s, to an emphasis on the identification and appraisal of investment projects[40] and on other administrative measures as crucial concomitants of the effective utilisation of aid. The net result was a generalised call by aid donors and international financial institutions – of which the World Bank was a conspicuous example – for Third World governments to develop national 'Plans' as a condition of aid.[41]

Growth Poles

Finally, an important contributor to the study of inter-industrial relationships and their implications for development whose work is unfortunately less known in the Anglo-Saxon development literature, but who was among the first to develop the notion of 'growth poles', is François Perroux. Perroux's analysis, as published in 1955,[42] can be summarised as follows: First, industry as a whole generally consists of certain dynamic subsectors or 'propellant industries' which, through various types of linkages and external economies, are largely responsible for inducing growth in other industries, and, if large or powerful enough, in the economy as a whole. Second, the interaction of industries is often *destabilising*, in particular because of its non-competitive or, more precisely, its oligopolistically competitive nature. According to Perroux – and here his position was a forerunner of the arguments to be made by Hirschman and others in favour of unbalanced growth – the destabilising action of individual industries taken in isolation can be a propellant for growth when, over a longer period, the dominant firm raises the productivity of the industry and achieves an efficient accumulation of capital superior to that which would have been the case in an industry operating under a more competitive regime.

And third, Perroux argued that due to greater proximity and human contacts, *territorial concentration* adds its specific effects to the structure of industry and the nature of growth:

In a complex industrial 'pole' which is geographically concentrated and growing, economic activities are intensified...Collective needs emerge...and link themselves up. Site rents are added to business profits. Various types of producers, entrepreneurs, skilled workers and industrial labour are formed, influence each other, create their traditions, and eventually share common interests. (...) To these intensifying effects are added the effects of regional disparities. The growth of the market in space, when it comes from the linking up of industrial poles, is quite *the opposite of growth equally shared*; it operates through concentrations of the means of production in points of growth from which then radiate arrows of exchange. The national economy appears now as a combination of relatively active groups (propellant industries, geographically concentrated poles of industry and activity) and relatively passive groups (impelled industries, regions dependent on geographically concentrated poles). The former induce into the other phenomena of growth.[43]

In looking at the significance of regional disparities, and in concluding that the dynamic 'growth poles' induce growth in their 'dependent' regions, Perroux's analysis parallels in important respects that developed by other authors in terms of the 'dual economy' models, to which we turn our attention shortly.

But, in explicitly recognising the oligopolistic nature of capital in the predominant sectors or 'poles' of the economy, both at the national and international level, Perroux explored another important facet of economic growth that was otherwise given little attention in the orthodox literature, namely the rise of conflict between growth regions produced by poles of growth and politically organised territories:

> Insofar as national and nationalistic policies persist in a world in which they are overtaken by technology and the development of economic life, wastes are sustained which, even in the absence of violent conflicts, constitute brakes on growth and from which come quasi-public oligopolistic struggles which endanger prosperity and peace.[44]

In looking at the relationship between economic growth and 'quasi-oligopolistic struggles', public and private, which 'endanger prosperity and peace', Perroux touched on a subject that would be increasingly emphasized in international fora by Third World spokesmen, and whose direct relevance to the evolution of North–South relations would only begin to make itself fully evident in the decade of the 1970s.

INDUSTRIALISATION ISSUES SINCE THE 1960s

The emphasis in the early orthodox literature on industrialisation and on the non-linear aspects, or discontinuities, of capital accumulation and of the development process – starting with Rosenstein-Rodan (1943) and running through Nurkse (1952), Perroux (1955), Hirschman (1958), Rostow (1960) and the two-gap model – had a tremendous impact on development thinking and practice in the two decades following the Second World War. It favoured a strong policy bias in many developing countries towards industrialisation (and to a lesser extent towards industrial programming) and 'underwrote' reliance in a considerable number on the 'trickle-down mechanism' to distribute the benefits of growth to the poor.

Of course, industrialisation had already advanced considerably in parts of Latin America prior to the emergence of this literature. In the larger countries of the region (notably Argentina and Brazil), which were largely cut off from their major export markets and sources of manufactured imports during the War and Depression years of 1914–45, market forces had already given rise to import-substituting industrialisation, particularly in the production of consumer goods. Moreover, with the emergence of 'structuralist' development thinking in the 1950s, there was strong support for a policy bias in favour of industrialisation and industrial programming among heterodox development thinkers as well (cf. Chapter 5), particularly in Latin America.

But the promotion of import-substituting industrialisation as a development strategy went far beyond Latin America in the 1950s and 1960s. Some countries, such as India, pursued a strategy of expanding a core of basic industries including heavy metals, chemicals and large-scale power projects on the grounds that these industries had the maximum backward and forward linkage effects. The priority accorded to heavy industry and large-scale power generation projects – reflecting the influence of P.C. Mahalanobis[45] – also contributed to the spread of macro-economic or highly aggregate-level planning, and to a growing role for public-sector enterprise.

Other countries, more numerous, focused initially on consumption-goods industries that often included assembly of imported inputs, and later turned to the promotion of basic heavy industries.

Thus, in the 1950s and 1960s, ISI strategies dominated the industrial drives not only in most of Latin America (Mexico and the Andean countries had also begun to pursue ISI) but also in much of Asia, including South Korea, Taiwan and the Philippines as well as India and Pakistan (and China). The early to mid-1960s also saw the beginnings of ISI strategies in some African countries (Ghana, Zambia, Kenya and Nigeria).

Foreign Direct Investment and Multinational Corporations

In virtually all these countries, tariff and non-tariff import barriers were one of the main policy instruments used to promote ISI. This in turn led to considerable debate on protectionism and the 'infant-industry' argument, to which we return in Chapter 3.[46] But it is also noteworthy that while some countries (e.g. India, later Korea) restricted foreign investment, other countries, notably in Latin America, pursued ISI policies in conjunction with relatively liberal treatment of foreign direct investment (FDI).   The result, in Latin America, was to attract substantial flows of FDI and a rapidly growing presence of multinational corporations in local manufacturing during the 1950s and 1960s.

As ISI ran into growing difficulties both in Latin America and in other developing countries, however, the result was the emergence of considerable debate on the role of FDI and multinational corporations, particularly in the late 1960s and early 1970s.   This debate focused on such issues as the role of multinational firms in international technology transfer and the 'appropriateness' of the technologies they employ in developing countries, their use of transfer-pricing techniques and other means to transfer financial surpluses abroad, their 'denationalisation' of local industry and, more generally, their threat to 'national sovereignty'.[47]

These concerns contributed to the creation of the United Nations Centre on Transnational Corporations, for example.   They were also germane to the Andean Pact's 'Decision 24', which limited foreign ownership of investments in member countries to minority positions. But, more generally, it was during the late 1960s and early 1970s that many developing countries introduced policies to regulate FDI and the behaviour of foreign investors.   These policies included, with widely varying degrees of scope and emphasis: the establishment of government boards for screening and registering FDI, the demarcation of sectors or specific industries where foreign investment was forbidden or restricted, limitations on overseas remittances of profits and royalties, restrictions on foreign takeovers of local firms, local-integration and/or export-performance requirements, and restrictions on foreign equity ownership to minority shares.

One result has been a growing importance since the early 1970s of reduced- or non-equity forms – the 'new forms' – of investment by multinational corporations in developing country industries.[48]   Another result, made possible by the recycling of 'petrodollars' from 1973 to 1982, was a rapid growth of borrowing on international financial markets by developing countries, some of which undoubtedly found it easier and cheaper (real interest rates were very low during much of the 1970s) to pursue debt-financed industrialisation strategies than to negotiate with multinational corporations for new flows of direct investment.

Indeed, with the multinationals tending to adopt lower profiles in the developing countries during the 1970s, and particularly because of the rapid growth in the volume of borrowing, the debt phenomenon tended to overshadow discussion of FDI in the development literature by the late 1970s. Only since the mid-1980s has much attention been given again to FDI as an important source of industrial assets (particularly such intangible assets as technology, organisational know-how and access to export markets), as well as financial capital, for many developing countries. Now, however, while the developing countries (many, not all) are liberalising their policies, sometimes in competition with one another, in efforts to attract more FDI, many of the potential foreign investors are more reluctant to risk large sums in industrial projects in developing countries.[49]

ISI vs. EOI

It was also in the late 1960s and early 1970s that ISI strategies began to come under heavy criticism from some leading orthodox writers. Particularly important in this regard was the work undertaken for the OECD Development Centre by Little, Scitovsky and Scott, published in 1970.[50] This study, which looked at the industrialisation experience of six countries (Brazil, India, Mexico, Pakistan, the Philippines and Taiwan), argued that ISI strategies lead to significant inefficiencies, discourage exports, exacerbate unemployment and worsen the foreign-exchange problem. The thrust of their policy recommendations, which set the tone and direction of the neoclassical resurgence that would gain full force a few years later (cf. Chapter 3), was that governments should rely more on markets and the price mechanism, reduce administrative controls and promote internationally competitive export activities.

The 1960s and early 1970s were also the period when Taiwan and South Korea joined Hong Kong and Singapore – the four are variously referred to now as the Asian NICs, NIEs, the Four Little Dragons or the Four Tigres – in adopting export-oriented industrialisation strategies. The relative success of these strategies has been cause for an important group of orthodox economists to hold them up as proof of the benefits of export-oriented industrialisation (EOI) based on market principles.[51]

While the critique of ISI strategies that inhibit exports is now widely accepted, even among heterodox writers, their historical and political significance should not be overlooked. In many countries, notably but not only in Latin America, ISI strategies that were strongly biased against agriculture in favour of industry (generally to the detriment of exports as well) have played a crucial role in the struggle by certain groups of emerging industrialists, financiers, etc. – 'modernising elites' to use Rostow's term – to gain or consolidate positions of local economic *and political* power vis-à-vis powerful land-owning classes whose interests and behaviour were often inimical to industrialisation or even to a modernisation of their own traditional primary-product export activities. Indeed, it can be argued that for political as well as economic reasons, in countries where a traditional land-owning elite remained powerful (notably in Latin America), ISI has been a necessary, though not sufficient, condition for industrial development.

Noting the importance of ISI in the early period of industrialisation in Taiwan and Korea as well as the rapid growth of industrial exports by Latin America in the 1980s, a number of authors have thus stressed that ISI and EOI strategies should not be seen as substitutes.[52] Moreover, as we explain further in our chapter on open-economy development strategies, some policy prescriptions in favour of EOI have also come under criticism within the orthodox literature.[53]

Indigenous Technological Capability

Against the background of many developing countries' ISI programmes 'running out of steam' in the 1960s and 1970s, and of growing competition among developing countries in the 1980s to export manufactured products in the face of rising protectionist pressures in the developed countries, the question of indigenous technological capacity in developing countries has also taken on new importance in the orthodox literature in recent years.[54] Looking at the extent to which imported manufacturing technology is adapted, modified or improved by local firms, a number of studies in Latin America and Asia have painted a picture rather different from the stereotyped image of technologically dependent countries relying largely on unadapted and often 'inappropriate' imported technologies.

Detailed analyses of corporate technological capacities in Brazil, South Korea, Taiwan and India, for example, have found that successful local firms often make major investments to learn new skills and absorb new knowledge at an early stage of industrialisation, i.e., before a base of competence exists in their country in industries that may be relatively mature in developed countries. They have also found that the development of local technological capabilities requires a long process of learning, based partly on production experience ('learning by doing'), partly on importing technology and know-how in the form of capital goods and consultants, and partly on a conscious process of investment in knowledge-creation through experimentation, training and R&D. Since learning involves organising knowledge in particular sequences (e.g. training and education, search and experimentation), the learning process can itself be learned.

These studies also provide empirical evidence that enhanced indigenous technological capabilities lower production costs through better choice and management of technology, often lead to improved output quality and a greater range of product designs, and permit cheaper subsequent expansions of plant and equipment. These benefits in turn affect a country's overall productivity growth rates, the relative success of its industrialisation process, the flexibility of its economic structure, and its ability to compete in international markets. With the acceleration of technological change and technological mastery requiring the effective deployment of a constant stream of new technologies, these studies conclude, the development of indigenous technological capability (which does not imply self-sufficiency) has become even more crucial for sustainable industrialisation in developing countries.

Regional Integration

Support for EOI strategies and, more recently, for development of indigenous technological capability have not been the only reactions in the orthodox development literature to the problems of ISI. Along with some heterodox writers, a number of orthodox writers began already in the early 1960s to call for more economic integration among regional groups of developing countries to overcome the major constraint on ISI which they saw as insufficient demand in individual countries to achieve an efficient level of output in ISI industries.[55] This problem could be solved, they argued, by the creation of a customs union or free trade area at a regional level that combined markets through the removal of internal tariff barriers and made economies of scale in production realisable. They further argued that if internal specialisation within the union was based on comparative advantage, a more rational pattern of regional production and trade would also result, and that over time, with the full realisation of scale economies, these ISI industries would be able to export to countries outside the union.

The widespread acceptance of the view of the benefits to be derived from regional integration was reflected in the formation of such major economic groupings as the Latin American Free Trade Association (1961), the East African Community (1967), the Association of South East Asian Nations (1968), the Andean Common Market (1969) and the

Caribbean Community and Common Market (1973). The move to integrate on a regional basis often has been seriously hindered in practice, however, by problems ranging from a lack of physical and commercial infrastructure required for significantly increased trade and a failure of supply to respond to the enlarged market, to the tendency for some countries to benefit more than others from the union.[56] As a result, most of these arrangements have failed to meet original expectations, some having been abandoned and others toned down.

Experience suggests that future unions must be sufficiently cohesive and capable of coordinating industrial, trade, and perhaps monetary policies, but above all of ensuring an equitable distribution of the benefits and costs of integration among member countries. The political impetus for regional integration nevertheless remains strong, as illustrated by the recent establishment of the South Asian Association for Regional Cooperation and the agreement between Brazil and Argentina. The strengthening of regional economic groupings in Europe, North America and Pacific-Asia, combined with the acceleration of economic globalisation, also point to regional integration as a re-emerging issue as we move into the 1990s. For many developing countries seeking to retain, or to eke out, a share of global industrial markets in the face of rapid technological change, intense international competition and growing protectionist pressures in the OECD region, regional integration may become indispensable.

Notes and References

1.   The notion of comparative advantage or comparative cost was of course first elaborated by David Ricardo in the 19th century within the framework of the labour theory of value. In the early decades of this century, E.F. Heckscher and B. Ohlin developed the neoclassical version of trade theory, one of whose major conclusions was that free trade induced a tendency towards relative factor price equalisation internationally. This latter aspect of neoclassical trade theory was further developed in the late 1940s by P.A. Samuelson. The original articles are: E.F. Heckscher, 'The Effect of Foreign trade on the Distribution of Income' in *Readings in the Theory of International Trade*, American Economic Association, 1950 (translated from Swedish original, 1919); B. Ohlin, *Interregional and International Trade*, Harvard University Press, Boston, 1933; P.A. Samuelson, 'International Trade and the Equalisation of Factor Prices' in *The Economic Journal*, Vol. LVIII, No. 230, London, June 1948; and P.A. Samuelson, 'International Factor – Price Equalisation Once Again' in *The Economic Journal*, Vol. LIX, No. 234, London, June 1949.

2. In support of the doctrine of development through free trade, see for example J. Viner, *International Trade and Economic Development*, the Free Press, 1952; and G. Haberler, *International Trade and Economic Development*, Cairo, 1959.

3. T.W. Schultz, *Transforming Traditional Agriculture*, Yale University Press, New Haven, 1964.

4. Rostow's 'take-off' theory appeared in its first published formulation in an article entitled 'The Take Off into Self-Sustained Growth', in *Economic Journal*, March 1956.

5. Regarding the influence of Rostow's doctrine on US aid policy, it is noteworthy that Rostow himself served as President of the United States National Security Council under the Kennedy and Johnson administrations, and that US aid was very closely tied to its overall strategic policy during this period. (On the latter point, see J. White, *The Politics of Foreign Aid*, London, 1974, Chapter VI). Regarding the direct influence of Rostow's doctrine on Third World development thinking, an interesting example is provided by Nasser's reported enthusiasm for Rostow's work and its influence on the First Plan of the United Arab Republic, elaborated in 1959-1960 (Olivier Carré reports that Nasser's socialism was characterised by 'an optimism for which W.W. Rostow's manual (which Nasser had read with gusto and asked all his collaborators to read and meditate) was largely responsible', cf. O. Carré, 'Utopies socialisantes en terre arabe d'orient' in *Revue Tiers-Monde*, Vol. XIX, no. 75, 1978).

6. See for example, S. Kuznets 'Quantitative Aspects of the Economic Growth of Nations', in *Economic Development and Cultural Change*, various issues, especially part II: 'Industrial Distribution of National Product and Labour Force', July 1957 Supplement; A. Hirschman, *The Strategy of Economic Development*, Yale University Press, New Haven, 1958; and H. Giersch, 'Stages and Spurts of Economic Development' in H. Dupriez, ed., *Economic Progress*, Louvain, 1955.

7. See A. Gerschenkron, 'Economic Backwardness in Historical Perspective' in B. Hoselitz, ed., *The Progress of Underdeveloped Areas*, Chicago, 1952; 'Social Attitudes, Entrepreneurship, and Economic Development' in *Explorations in Entrepreneurial History*, October 1953; 'Notes on the Rate of Industrial Growth in Italy, 1881-1913' in *The Journal of Economic History*, December 1955; and especially *Economic Backwardness in Historical Perspective*, Harvard University Press, Cambridge, 1962.

8. It has also been argued that the dominant industrialised countries' interest in the Third World reflects not so much a concern for the welfare of the masses of the people living there as it does a desire to promote an expansion of world markets and investment possibilities, hence the preoccupation with growth as opposed to more 'amorphous' concepts of development. This argument, however, is rarely found within the orthodox literature.

9. R.F. Harrod, 'An Essay in Dynamic Theory' in *Economic Journal*, April 1939; and E.D. Domar, 'Capital Expansion, Rate of Growth and Employment' in *Econometrica*, April 1946.

10. The authors of this report include W.A. Lewis (UK), T.W. Schultz (US), A. Baltra Cortez (Chile), D.R. Gadgil (India) and G. Hakim (Lebanon).

11.   G. Allen and Unwin, London.

12.   W.W. Rostow, *The Stages of Economic Growth: A Non-Communist Manifesto*, Cambridge University Press, Cambridge, 1960, p. 39. Much more recently, Sen has argued that the countries with more rapid income growth have indeed been those with higher savings rates and more rapid industrialisation. In reviewing this literature, Stern highlights the problems in establishing a causal relationship or even a significant positive correlation between savings and growth rates, but argues that the data do point to such a relationship between investment and growth rates. Cf. A.K. Sen, 'Poor, Relatively Speaking' in *Oxford Economic Papers*, Vol. 35, No. 1, 1983; and N. Stern, 'The Economics of Development: A Survey' in *Economic Journal*, Vol. 99, September 1989.

13.   More generally, critics have attacked Rostow on his contention that history can be seen as a sequence of stages through which all countries must pass. See G. Ohlin, 'Reflections on the Rostow Doctrine' in *Economic Development and Cultural Change*, July 1961; A. Fishlow, 'Empty Economic Stages?' in *Economic Journal*, March 1965; and S. Kuznets, 'Notes on the Stages of Economic Growth as a System Determinant' in A. Eckstein, ed., *Comparison of Economic Systems*, University of California Press, Berkeley, 1971.

14.   *Partners in Development*, Report of the Commission on International Development (chaired by L. B. Pearson), Praeger, New York, 1969.

15.   White (1974), *op. cit.*, p. 117.

16.   On the savings-growth issue, see, for example, H. S. Houthakker, 'On Some Determinants of Savings in Developed and Underdeveloped Countries' in *Problems of Economic Development*, International Economic Association, 1965. See also D.W. Johnson and J.S.Y. Chin, 'The Savings-Income Relation in Underdeveloped and Developed Countries' in *Economic Journal*, June 1968.

17.   Chenery and Strout saw foreign aid as being used not only to accelerate the rate of investment during a Rostow-type take-off period, but also to provide the basic pre-conditions for the transition to self-sustaining growth – including skills, modern technology and new institutional arrangements. In addition, they split the transition process into three phases each with a single constraining factor. These constraining factors are the skill limit, the savings limit and the foreign-exchange limit. See H.B. Chenery and A. M. Strout, 'Foreign Assistance and Economic Development' in *American Economic Review*, September 1966; H.B. Chenery and M. Bruno, 'Development Alternatives in an Open Economy: the Case of Israel' in *Economic Journal*, Vol. 72, 1962. A critical look at this model is presented by H. Bruton, 'The Two Gap Approach to Aid and Development: A Comment' in *American Economic Review*, 1969, and by K. Griffin, 'Foreign Capital, Domestic Savings and Economic Development' in *Oxford Bulletin of Economics and Statistics*, 1970.

18.   If insufficient savings is assumed to be the principal obstacle to growth and aid is expected to overcome this obstacle, then as national income grows total savings should increase rapidly if the *marginal* savings rate is significantly greater than the (relatively low) average rate of savings.

In this case, as national income grows domestic savings can soon replace aid as the primary source of investment resources required to sustain growth; and as growth continues the initial resource transfer may even be reversed (i.e., the 'aid' may be paid back). If, on the contrary, domestic savings do not increase substantially as a proportion of national income, then aid may be required indefinitely to sustain growth. For a detailed explanation of the economic theories used to justify aid see, for example, R.F. Mikesell, *The Economics of Foreign Aid*, Weidenfeld and Nicolson, London, 1968.

19. Probably the earliest paper which expounded these views is W. Galenson and H. Leibenstein, 'Investment Criteria, Productivity and Economic Development' in *Quarterly Journal of Economics*, August 1955.

20. S. Kuznets, 'Economic Growth and Income Inequality' in *American Economic Review*, Vol. 45, March 1955.

21. P.N. Rosenstein-Rodan, 'Industrialisation of Eastern and South Eastern Europe' in *Economic Journal*, Vol. 53, 1943. In subsequent papers, Rosenstein-Rodan complemented his analysis of the 'discontinuities' of industrial expansion with that of its 'indivisibilities', i.e., the importance of economies of scale. See in particular, 'Notes on the Theory of the Big Push' in H.S. Ellis and H. Wallich, eds., *Economic Development for Latin America. Proceedings of a Conference held by the International Economic Association*, St. Martin's Press, New York, 1961. See also P. Rosenstein-Rodan, ed., *Capital Formation and Economic Development*, MIT Press, Cambridge, 1964, and 'Natura Facit Saltum: Analysis of the Disequilibrium Growth Process' in G. Meier and D. Seers, eds., *Pioneers in Development*, Oxford University Press for the World Bank, New York, 1984.

22. Recent work by Murphy, Schleifer and Vishny has shown how these views can be formalised and developed. It demonstrates, for example, the importance of income distribution and population size in generating demand large enough to make manufacturing viable, and that a 'big push' can move an imperfectly competitive economy with multiple equilibria from a 'bad' equilibrium to a better one. See K.M. Murphy, A. Schleifer and R. Vishny, 'Industrialisation and the Big Push' and 'Income Distribution, Market Size and Industrialisation', NBER Working Papers No. 2708 and No. 2709, 1988.

23. Rosenstein-Rodan went to the World Bank in 1947, where he became the Assistant Director of the Economics Department and Head of the Economic Advisory Staff.

24. T. Scitovsky, 'Two Concepts of External Economies' in *Journal of Political Economy*, April 1954.

25. See for example, T. Schultz, 'Capital Formation by Education' in *Journal of Political Economy*, December 1960.

26. R. Nurkse, 'Some International Aspects of the Problem of Economic Development' in *American Economic Review*, May 1952.

27. See especially *ibid*. For an orthodox critique of this particular aspect of Nurkse's argument, see I. B. Kravis, 'Trade as a Handmaiden of Growth: Similarities between the Nineteenth and Twentieth Centuries' in *Economic Journal*, December 1970.

28.   As mentioned above, in fact, to the extent that Rostow's study looks at relations between more and less developed countries, it holds that 'external intrusions...literal or figurative' of the latter by the former made, 'in the general case in history', a decisive contribution to the development of the less advanced society. See Rostow (1960), *op. cit.*

29.   Nurkse (1952), *op. cit.*, p. 577.

30.   J.S. Duesenberry, *Income, Saving and the Theory of Consumer Behaviour*, Cambridge, 1949.

31.   Nurkse (1952), *op. cit.*, p. 582.

32.   *ibid.*, p. 582.

33.   *ibid.*, pp. 582–583.

34.   Given the notable differences between Nurkse's views and those generally defended by the IMF, for example on the viability today of relying on exports to finance development, the similarity between Nurkse's argument on the role of public finance and the position frequently adopted by the IMF in its negotiations with Third World governments may at first glance appear surprising, even paradoxical. It should be remembered, however, that in proposing a strategy of balanced growth Nurkse was centring his attention on what he thought was required for development in a private enterprise economy, and in this fundamental respect his approach coincided with that of the IMF.

35.   A.0. Hirschman (1958), *op. cit.* See also A.O. Hirschman, 'A Dissenter's Confession: The Strategy of Economic Development Revisited' in Meier and Seers, eds., *Pioneers in Development, op. cit.*

36.   Various attempts at quantifying 'backward' and 'forward linkages' are presented in 'The Symposium on Linkage Effect Measurement' in *Quarterly Journal of Economics*, Vol. 90, No. 2, May 1976. For a more recent statement of Hirschman's views on linkages and industrialisation in Latin America, see A.O. Hirschman, *Essays in Trespassing: Economics to Politics and Beyond*, Cambridge University Press, New York, 1981, Chapter 4.

37.   It has been argued that Nurkse's assumptions more accurately reflected conditions in South Asia, whereas Hirschman's assumptions were more representative of conditions in Latin America. See for example, P. Streeten, 'Balanced versus Unbalanced Growth' in *Economic and Political Weekly*, April 20, 1973, p. 670; and K.N. Raj, 'Linkages in Industrialisation and Development Strategy: Some Basic Issues' in *Journal of Development Planning*, No. 8, 1975.

38.   Hirschman (1958), *op. cit.*, pp. 53–54.

39.   In his critique of development economics as a whole, Deepak Lal has in turn criticised the view that entrepreneurship is in short supply in developing countries as not only wrong but contributing to paternalistic attitudes that fail to understand the potential power of market forces in developing countries. See D. Lal, *The Poverty of Development Economics*, Institute of Economic Affairs, London, 1983.

40.   Along these lines, a major contribution of the OECD Development Centre was I.M.D. Little and J.A. Mirrlees, *Manuel of Industrial Project Analysis in Developing Countries*, OECD Development Centre, Paris, 1969. This subject will be discussed further in Chapter 3.

41. The early planning models were based on the input-output techniques developed by Leontief (cf. W. Leontief, *The Structure of the American Economy 1919–1929*, Harvard University Press, Cambridge, 1941) and were concerned with the feasibility or consistency of different sectoral targets (see for example, H.B. Chenery, 'Inter-regional and International Input-Output Analysis' in T. Barma, ed., *The Structural Interdependence of the Economy*, John Wiley & Sons, New York, 1956). Capital requirements and growth were then introduced, and dynamic input-output models came to be used in many planning commissions around the world (see for example, C.R. Blitzer, P.B. Clark and L. Taylor, *Ecnomy-Wide Models and Development Planning*, Oxford University Press, Oxford, 1975).

42. F. Perroux, 'Note on the Concept of Growth Poles', *Economie Appliquée*, Vol. 8, 1955. See also F. Perroux, *L'economie du XXè siecle*, Presses universitaires de France, Paris, 1961.

43. Perroux (1955), *ibid.*, pp. 287–288 (emphasis added).

44. *ibid.*, pp. 288–289 (emphasis in original).

45. P.C. Mahalanobis, 'Some Observations on the Process of Growth of National Income' in *Sankhya*, Vol. 12, Pt. 4, September 1953; and 'The Approach of Operational Research to Planning in India' in *Sankhya*, Vol. 16, Pts. 1 and 2, December 1955. See also P. Streeten, 'Development Dichotomies' in Meier and Seers, *op. cit.*, pp. 355–358.

46. For a detailed account of the various theoretical arguments for protection, including infant industry protection, domestic distortions in commodity markets and distortions in factor markets, see W.M. Corden, *The Theory of Protection*, Oxford University Press, London, 1971.

47. See particularly R. Vernon, *Sovereignty at Bay: the Multinational Spread of US Enterprises*, Basic Books, New York, 1971; C. Kindleberger, ed., *The International Corporation*, MIT Press, Cambridge, 1970; and S. Lall and P. Streeten, *Foreign Investment, Transnationals and Developing Countries*, MacMillan, 1977. For a recent review of both orthodox and heterodox views on the role of multinational corporations in development, see R. Jenkins, *Transnational Corporations and Uneven Development: The Internationalisation of Capital and The Third World*, Methuen, London, 1987. See also, T. Moran and contributors, *Investing in Development: New Roles for Private Capital?*, Transaction Books for the Overseas Development Council, New Brunswick, 1986, and United Nations Centre on Transnational Corporations, *Transnational Corporations in World Development Trends and Prospects*, United Nations, New York, 1988.

48. The 'new forms' of investment include joint ventures, licensing, management and production-sharing contracts, international sub-contracting and turnkey operations. For an overview of the trends, causes and implications of the new forms of investment see C. Oman, *New Forms of International Investment in Developing Countries*, OECD Development Centre, Paris, 1984, and C. Oman, *New Forms of Investment in Developing Country Industries: Mining, Petrochemicals, Automobiles, Textiles, Food*, OECD Development Centre, Paris, 1989.

49. See C. Oman (1989), *ibid.*

50.   I.M.D. Little, T. Scitovsky and M.F.G. Scott, *Industry and Trade in Some Developing Countries*, Oxford University Press for the OECD Development Centre, London, 1970.

51.   See for example, B. Balassa and Assoc., *Development Strategies in Semi-industrial Economies*, Johns Hopkins University Press, Baltimore, 1982; and A.O. Krueger, 'Trade Policy as an Input to Development' in *American Economic Review*, papers and proceedings, May 1980.

52.   See for example, I. Adelman, 'Beyond Export-led Growth' in *World Development*, vol. 12, No. 9, 1984. See also H.W. Singer, 'Industrialisation: Where do we stand? Where are we going?' in *Industry and Development*, No. 12, 1984.

53.   W.R. Cline, 'Can the East Asian Model of Development be Generalised?' in *World Development*, Vol. 10, No. 2, 1982; C.H. Kirkpatrick and F.I. Nixson, eds., *The Industrialisation of Less Developed Countries*, Manchester University Press, 1983; and R.M. Kavoussi, 'International Trade and Economic Development: The Recent Experience of Developing Countries' in *The Journal of Developing Areas*, April 1985.

54.   See for example, C. Dahlman and L. Westphal, 'Technological Effort in Industrial Development' in F. Stewart and J. James, eds., *The Economics of New Technology in Developing Countries*, Frances Pinter, London, 1982; C. Dahlman, B. Rose-Larson and L. Westphal, *Managing Technological Development: Lessons from Newly Industrialising Countries*, World Bank Staff Working Paper No. 717, Washington D.C., 1985; J. Enos and W.H. Park, *The Adoption and Diffusion of Imported Technology in the Case of Korea*, Croom Helm, 1987; J. Katz, ed., *Technology Generation in Latin American Manufacturing Industries*, MacMillan, London, 1987; A. Amsden, *Asia's New Giant: South Korea and Late Industrialisation*, Oxford University Press, New York, 1989; and S. Lall, *Learning to Industrialise*, MacMillan, London, 1987, and *Building Industrial Competitiveness: New Technologies and Capabilities in Developing Countries*, OECD Development Centre, Paris, 1990.

55.   Details of the economic arguments behind the call by orthodox writers for regional integration among developing countries can be found in P. Robson, *The Economics of International Integration*, London, 1972, and M. Carnoy, ed., *Industrialisation in a Latin American Common Market*, Brookings Institution, Washington, D.C., 1972. One of the most influential early studies was J. Viner, *The Customs Union Issue*, Carnegie Endowment for International Peace, New York, 1950.

56.   For a comprehensive survey of the problems of various regional integration arrangements, see C. Vaitsos, 'Crisis in Regional Cooperation among Developing Countries: A Survey' in *World Development*, Vol. 6, 1978.

2 Dualism and Agriculture-centred Development

While many development writers focused on industry and inter-industry relations within the industrial sector, another group that had a major impact on development thought and policy during the 1950s and 1960s focused on inter-*sectoral* relations. The latter's work gave rise to the so-called 'dual-economy' models, in which an essential characteristic of underdevelopment is seen to be the existence in a country of both a 'modern' capitalist sector and a backward 'traditional' sector. According to these models, as development takes place the modern sector expands and the traditional sector shrinks; development is achieved when dualism vanishes. The early literature, like that discussed in the preceding chapter, tended to see industrialisation as the road to development and overcoming dualism. Later dual-economy analyses gave more attention to the development and modernisation of agriculture in its own right.

DUALISM: STATIC AND DYNAMIC MODELS

Following Hayami and Ruttan, we can classify dual-economy models as either 'static' or 'dynamic'.[1] Their main difference lies in the degree of interaction between the two sectors: whereas such interaction is limited in the 'static' models, the 'dynamic' models emphasize an increasing degree of interaction.

Dualism was first analysed in a static framework as a sociological phenomenon, by Boeke in 1953.[2] Boeke analysed the failure of liberal economic policies in Indonesia, adopted under the Dutch colonial regime in 1870, to improve the welfare of the native population. He argued that attempts to transform the local society by a modernisation process based on Western institutions and technology were doomed to failure because 'social needs' (such as custom and tradition) were predominant in Indonesia, whereas economic needs essentially determine economic activity and institutions in the West. Thus, technological change in Indonesian agriculture via new inputs would simply lead to increased population growth, for example. Boeke's analysis lent support, again, to policies favouring heavy industrialisation at the expense of agriculture.

Of the many criticisms of Boeke's analysis, that of Higgins, in 1956, was among the most important.[3] Higgins rejected Boeke's concept of sociological dualism, pointing out that his empirical observations were inaccurate, and argued that 'technological dualism' was a more useful concept.[4] He saw the modern sector as consisting of highly organised mines and plantations using imported labour-saving or capital-intensive technology, and the traditional sector as made up of unorganised subsistence agricultural producers using labour-intensive production methods. Higgins saw expansion of the modern sector depending on its export demand, and, more importantly, he saw only limited linkage effects (via demand for labour or products) that would benefit the traditional sector, with increases in capital stock the only way to absorb labour from the traditional sector. He thus saw the modern sector constituting a virtual enclave in the developing country. This in turn led to discussion of 'enclave dualism', a concept developed for example by Hla Myint.[5]

The Lewis model

The 'dynamic' dual-economy models proved far more influential, however. Seldom, in fact, has a single article been so instrumental to shaping development thinking as the dual-economy model elaborated by W. Arthur Lewis in his 'Economic Development with Unlimited Supplies of Labor', published in 1954.[6] Lewis, like Rostow and others, argued that the key to economic development is rapid capital accumulation in industry, and that the central problem in the theory of economic development is to understand the process by which a community which was previously saving and investing 4 or 5 per cent of its national income or less, converts itself into an economy where voluntary saving is running at about 12 to 15 per cent of national income or more. But in contrast to those authors and policy-makers whose attention focused primarily on industry itself (i.e. on intra-sectoral relations), Lewis focused primarily on inter-sectoral relationships.

Lewis' model was set in a classical economic framework and comprised two sectors, a 'capitalist' or 'modern' sector and a 'subsistence' or 'traditional' sector. The distinguishing features of the former are the hiring of labour and the sale of output for profit, whereas those of the latter are self- or family-employment and a *marginal* productivity of labour approximately equal to zero. Due to the non-capitalist nature of institutional arrangements in the 'traditional' sector (e.g., workers may retain ownership of the land), however, workers in this sector collectively consume their total product, i.e., each member has an income roughly equal to the *average* product of labour. Wages in the capitalist sector are determined by labour's income in the non-capitalist ('subsistence') sector, since the former sector expands by drawing labour from the latter (though capitalist wages normally have to be somewhat higher than subsistence earnings in order to induce labour to migrate and to cover the cost of migration). At the existing level of wages in the capitalist sector, then, the supply of labour is assumed to be perfectly elastic ('unlimited') due to the low marginal productivity of labour ('disguised unemployment') in the subsistence sector.

The key to economic expansion, according to Lewis' dual-economy model, is the use of the capitalist surplus, which is assumed to be re-invested in the capitalist sector and thus to create new capital. As the capitalist sector expands (wages remaining constant), labour migrates from the subsistence sector into wage employment, the capitalist surplus becomes even larger, there is further reinvestment of profits, and so on. As national income (and aggregate labour productivity) grows with the progressive absorption of labour into the modern sector, the share of profits in national income increases, and since the major source of savings is profits, savings and capital formation also increase as a proportion of national income. The capitalist sector continues to expand until the emigration of surplus labour from the traditional sector is complete (i.e., 'disguised unemployment' is eliminated), at which point capital accumulation has caught up with the supply of labour and wages begin to rise; i.e., when the marginal product is equal in the capitalist and non-capitalist sectors, the analysis then becomes the same as in the usual neoclassical one-sector economy.

Lewis' dual-economy approach stimulated considerable debate in the orthodox development literature of the 1950s and 1960s. Two important shortcomings of the Lewis-type approach were perceived to be: i) its assumption that whatever the capitalist sector produced it could sell, and ii) that it took for granted the demand side of the investment process as well, in assuming the existence of a capitalist class which would mobilise surpluses, reinvest profits, and demonstrate the entrepreneurial skills required for the process of economic expansion envisioned by Lewis.[7] Regarding the first point, the potential problem of insufficient aggregate demand was a primary focal point of the advocates of balanced growth, as discussed above. Similarly, regarding the second point, the analysis of behaviour in the capitalist sector was given ample attention by the advocates of unbalanced growth.

Although these are notable weaknesses, much of the controversy surrounding Lewis' analysis stemmed from the widespread impression that it assumed 'disguised unemployment' (in the sense of zero marginal productivity of labour) in the rural sector. This assumption was condemned as unrealistic because it implied that labour can be withdrawn at anytime without loss in output even if no technological change were to take place. Lewis argued that he did not rest his model on the assumption of disguised unemployment and that all he meant by 'unlimited supplies of labour' was an excess supply of labour at an exogenously given wage.[8] He did, however, use the special case of zero marginal product of labour in examples and believed it to hold in some developing countries, notably Jamaica and India.

Ranis and Fei

Building on the initial assumptions of Lewis, Ranis and Fei published a more detailed model of the process of modernisation of a labour-surplus economy within a neoclassical framework in 1961.[9] Their model showed that a process of excess labour transfer from the traditional sector to the modern sector results in the full development and commercialisation of a developing-country economy. They followed Lewis by assuming both the presence of surplus labour and the exogenous determination of wages, but they extended his analysis to give agriculture a greater role in promoting industrialisation. They introduced the possibility of innovation and technical progress in agriculture – which serve to shift the production function in agriculture upwards and thus raise output – thereby pointing to the importance of increasing agricultural productivity even before the transfer of surplus labour to industry is complete.

Ranis and Fei also developed the hypothesis that part of the savings required for growth, as well as 'surplus labour', is supplied by agriculture. The generation of savings from the agricultural sector rests crucially on the role played by rural landlords: movement of surplus agricultural workers to industry results in a reduction in total rural consumption (assuming that the agricultural workers left behind do not increase their consumption by an amount equal to that which was previously consumed by the departing labour) and a large proportion of the agricultural surplus arising from the emigration of labour accrues to the landlords, who are assumed to appropriate the surplus and make the savings available to the industrial sector. The landlords may also use some of the savings for investment to raise agricultural productivity, which would contribute to a rise in agricultural surplus.

Overall, industrial profits remain the main component or source of funds for industrial expansion, and these profits will constitute an increasing share of the value of industrial output, since wage rates are assumed not to rise. From the process of saving in the rural sector described above, capital accumulation in the industrial sector will be supplemented to a considerable extent by the agricultural surplus. The rate at which surplus labour can be transferred from the agricultural to the industrial sector is a function of the rate of population increase, the growth of industrial capital stock (determined by the growth of profits in industry and the agricultural surplus) and the nature of technical progress in agriculture.

External trade, foreign borrowing and aid (soft loans or even grants) play only a secondary role in the process of growth described by Ranis and Fei. They, like Lewis, emphasized the role of capital accumulation in the promotion of industrialisation. But they went further in stressing the interdependence of agriculture and industry in the evolution of the dual economy; and they recognised the dynamic impetus provided by technological change, especially in agriculture.

The Ranis and Fei model stimulated a great deal of response in the development literature. One criticism was that they failed to make a distinction between wage labour and family-farm-based labour. Consistent with its neoclassical approach, the logic of the model implies a rural structure with land owned or at least controlled largely by landlords and peasants providing wage labour.

Another criticism was that the role of prices and money in the process of development was neglected. Money in itself is not a simple substitute for capital in an aggregate production function. Many economists have since pointed out that money and physical capital are complementary to one another in the process of development (in particular, credit policies have been shown to play an important part in easing bottlenecks in the growth of agriculture and industry).[10]

Third, the generation of savings in the rural sector as portrayed by Ranis and Fei is very dependent on the role played by the landlord. It may be incorrect to portray the landlord as eager to save (rather than engage in conspicuous consumption), eager to transfer these savings to industry (even though the growth of industry could eliminate his power and position), and eager to innovate (assuming that he has the knowledge required to do so).[11]

And fourth, like Lewis, Ranis and Fei were criticised for assuming that the marginal product of labour is zero in their first phase of economic expansion.

The Lewis and Ranis–Fei dual-economy models have nevertheless had a tremendous impact on development theory and policy. For a start, during the 1960s there emerged an extensive theoretical and empirical debate over the meaning and existence of 'surplus labour', as evidenced in the discussion over whether or not the marginal productivity of labour in subsistence agriculture is really zero.[12] This questioning of the notion of surplus labour did not prevent it from being increasingly adopted as a basis for development and aid policy, however.[13]

Second, in looking at the urban or capitalist-sector side of the picture, many argued – in a fashion not unlike Hirschman's argument on the lack of entrepreneurial and managerial skills as the primary obstacle to growth – that even if an unlimited supply of unskilled labour were assumed to exist, in most underdeveloped countries skilled labour is in very short supply.[14] This in turn led to numerous studies and projections of education and manpower needs in developing countries (one of the more sophisticated models was that published in 1965 by Tinbergen and Bos).[15] Partly in reaction to the hitherto excessive concentration in development thinking on the need to accumulate physical capital, and following studies showing that output often grew faster than could be explained by the rate of growth of physical capital and labour inputs alone, increasing attention was thus given within the orthodox literature, and by some of the major aid donors, to the need for investments in 'human capital'.[16]

These debates led in turn to a broadening of the use of the term 'capital' in the orthodox development literature. Capital formation had normally been equated with such readily quantifiable productive resources and goods as land, durable equipment, commodity stocks and foreign claims.   But since the 1960s, 'capital stock' has been reinterpreted broadly in some of the literature to include the body of knowledge and skills possessed by people and the capacity and training of the people to use their knowledge base efficiently.   Hence it is now widely accepted that outlays on education and informal training (as well as improvements in health and nutrition) directly contribute to productivity by raising the quality of the population, and that this investment will continue to give a future return in terms of higher output and less waste of resources.

Third, the theoretical framework developed by Lewis and Ranis–Fei provided the basis for subsequent dual-economy models. In 1967, for example, Jorgenson extended the boundaries of neoclassical growth theory to analyse the problems of developing countries.[17] His dual-economy model assumed the existence of surplus labour, but in the less restrictive sense that while the institutional wage in agriculture (the average product) is greater than the marginal product of labour, the latter is not necessarily zero. He also assumed that factor-neutral technological progress takes place in agriculture. His policy conclusions pointed to the importance both of accelerating the rate of technological progress in agriculture, and of measures to lower the rate of population growth in reducing poverty and unemployment.

Another extension, in 1972, was the Kelly, Williamson, Cheatham (KWC) model.[18] In contrast to Jorgenson, the KWC model assumes that agriculture as well as industry use both production factors, capital and labour. And whereas Jorgenson assumes a Cobb–Douglas production function for both sectors,[19] in the KWC model the elasticity of substitution between capital and labour is assumed to be less than one in industry and equal to or greater than one in agriculture. Leaving aside the more detailed technical features of the two models, the main advantage of the KWC model is that while it analyses dualism in terms of production technology (like Jorgenson), it also considers demand conditions and different patterns of population increase exhibited by the two sectors. Critics point out, however, that it lacks an analysis of institutional factors that strongly influence the course of development, such as the role of the state, and that it insufficiently tackles the issues of income distribution, employment and consumption gains that emerge from the development process it describes.

Fourth, the work of Lewis and Ranis–Fei pointed up the fact that although a labour transfer in the direction of the modern capitalist sector was taken for granted, little was known about the actual process of migration and the implications of very high rates of rural-urban migration for the pattern of urbanisation in the Third World. This deficiency in the literature was partly corrected by the construction of a theory of rapid rural-urban migration in the context of high rates of urban unemployment by Harris and Todaro in 1970.[20] Stimulated by the dual-economy analysis, the Harris–Todaro migration model and the pressing problems of urbanisation – such as rising urban unemployment, and the inability of city administrations to provide proper infrastructure and adequate levels of services – other analysts turned to the important topics of the management of cities[21] and, in particular, the role of the so-called informal sector as an entry point for potential migrants. We return to the literature on the informal sector, notably that produced by the ILO's World Employment Programme, in Chapter 4 on *Reformism*; suffice it here to note that the wave of literature on inter-sectoral relations led to an 'about turn' in the late 1970s, in the sense that policy recommendations switched from promoting a more rapid rate of rural–urban migration, to favouring rural development in the widest possible sense as it became obvious that cities could no longer cope with increasing waves of migrants from the countryside.[22]

It is also noteworthy that most of the dual-economy models have been set in the framework of a closed economy. Thus, not only do they point to industrial-led growth in the 'modern' sector as the route to the absorption of surplus labour and hence to development, it can be argued that their closed-economy focus tended to encourage countries to look inwards and to pursue import-substituting strategies of industrialisation.

Finally, while the dual-economy models (notably Ranis–Fei) point to the usefulness of output growth in agriculture as well as in industry, their emphasis is very much on extracting resources – labour, savings and economic surplus – from agriculture for the benefit of industry. They pay little attention to the mechanisms required to actually extract the surplus, or to the difficulties of sustaining the production of the surplus in the face of such extraction via deteriorating terms of trade for agriculture, etc. In short, what these models do not include is a mechanism of development of the agricultural sector as such.[23] From about the mid-1960s, the agricultural sector – notably traditional 'subsistence' or peasant agriculture – was increasingly given an equal and sometimes dominant role in the orthodox literature, and in development policy.

THE CASE FOR INSTITUTIONAL CHANGE: REDISTRIBUTIVE LAND REFORM

Another major defect of the dual-economy models is that they portray the rural sector as a homogeneous, colourless entity consisting of unorganised subsistence farms. This unitary view of the agrarian structure of developing countries remained dominant during the 1950s and 1960s, but it was not the only orthodox view. During the early 1950s there also emerged a strand of thinking that studied the different forms of land tenure and ownership in agriculture.

One of the earliest studies pointing to the existence in the developing countries of a diversity of patterns of land tenure – commercial ownership, owner occupation, feudal tenant-landlord systems – was the United Nations report on *Land Reform: Defects in Agrarian Structure as Obstacles to Economic Development*, published in 1951. Also, in 1955, an important lecture by a leading proponent of land reform, Warriner, singled out 'land systems in which the large estate is the predominant form of tenure as in need of reform'.[24] Warriner identified three types of land tenure and economic organisation associated with large estates: the latifundio system characteristic of Southern Europe and Latin America, which is managed by salaried officials and worked by labourers, squatters and share croppers; plantation estates owned by a company with foreign capital and management employing very intensive methods of cultivation; and share-cropping arrangements characteristic of Asia where large landowners lease small units to tenant cultivators on the basis of a share contract.

It was probably the Latin American latifundios that came under the heaviest criticism for their lack of economic efficiency. In 1961, for example, as a direct result of pressure from a broad coalition of industrialists, peasants and others opposed the feudal system of exploitation and inefficiency, the Punta del Este Charter of the Organisation of American States was adopted as a basis for policy dialogue. The Charter called on all the countries of the continent to pass anti-feudal land reform laws. Two years later, in 1963, a comprehensive study sponsored by the Canadian International Development Agency (CIDA) on land tenure problems in Argentina, Brazil, Chile, Colombia, Ecuador, Guatemala and Peru found that the latifundio-minifundio system discouraged the adoption of new agricultural technologies and was to 'blame for the disquiet in rural areas and the perpetuation of social injustice'.[25] This study helped stimulate further research into the causes of economic inefficiency prevalent in the Latin American latifundio system and fueled interest in subsequent research on the degree of economic efficiency of share-cropping in Asia as well.[26]

Although studies emphasizing the economic inefficiency of the large estates became more common from the 1960s, the obstacle of economic inefficiency was not the only motivating factor behind the land-reform movement either in Asia or Latin America. Many of the more conservative advocates, for example, saw land reform as a minimal concession towards political stability and the continuation of the status quo. These advocates often saw the redistribution of land as a means of diffusing social unrest in the countryside in order to reduce pressures for more radical social change.

There were others in the liberal economic tradition who stressed the importance of allocative efficiency in agriculture. Dorner, for example, in a book published in 1972, presents an argument that hinges on the factor proportions in a capital scarce economy and the need to develop agriculture with as many labour-intensive methods as possible.[27] He further argues that labour-intensive agricultural development was more likely to be achieved on small family-sized farms under good tenure conditions than on large estates that emphasize the use of capital against labour, or under very insecure tenure as in the case of share-cropping.

Small family farms were also a key element in the so called 'populist case' for land reform. The origins of Populism can be traced back to the 19th century,[28] but in the postwar context Lipton's 1977 critique of 'urban bias' in Third World development has been very influential.[29] Lipton's influence derives from his analysis of anti-agricultural, pro-industrial development patterns in many Third World countries as the result of urban bias in the development policies adopted by their governments. Further, Lipton argues that in the situation of capital scarcity facing most developing countries, peasant agriculture (consisting of small family farms) uses capital more efficiently than industry. These arguments are used by Lipton to support the case for a policy bias in favour of small-farm-oriented peasant agriculture.

Empirical observations of an inverse relationship between holding size and output per acre in traditional agriculture were also used by Berry and Cline, in a book published in 1979, to strengthen the populist case for land reform.[30] They inferred from the existence of this relationship that the productivity of small farms (created by land reforms) is the same as that of existing farms of equal size, and that the twin goals of greater productivity and equity can be achieved by subdividing large farms.

Finally, in contrast to the writers who have focused more on the economic efficiency argument for land reform in Latin America, studies on Asia, notably the 1977 ILO study on *Poverty and Landlessness in Rural Asia*, have pointed to inequality in land ownership as the major cause of rural income differentials. They have also stressed that neither the green revolution nor the land reforms to date have had a substantial impact on the incomes of the poorest farmers or the landless labourers. Thus, in Asia, equity rather then efficiency concerns have been the principal thrust of the case for redistributive land reform as part of a wider development strategy designed to uplift the living standards of the extremely poor.[31]

The evidence on land reform

The empirical evidence on redistributive land reforms is mixed.[32] Taiwan, South Korea and Egypt have been cited as cases where an effective redistribution of land ownership was combined with better agricultural productivity, higher output and improvement in income distribution relative to the pre-reform period. The improvement in income distribution was greater in Taiwan and South Korea than in Egypt. On the other hand, evidence from Chile, Mexico, Peru and Venezuela suggests that the land reform on balance acted to stimulate agriculture output but that agricultural productivity on the new small farmers was below that of the big private farms (especially in the case of Mexico). In Latin America, as in the case of South Asia, the land reforms reached some of the poor, but did not benefit all of this group. Moreover, in some countries, e.g. Iraq and Bolivia, land reform was accompanied by a sharp and persistent fall in output.

The mixed success of land reforms has led to their criticism by radicals, reformists and conservatives alike. Writers on the left tend to view land reforms as meaningless without a political revolution and to argue that the larger and more successful pre-reform farmers tend to benefit disproportionately while marginal farmers and the landless gain little or nothing.[33] At the other extreme, conservatives, although they may favour land reform, prefer to leave it to industrialisation and urbanisation to pick up the 'surplus labour' rather than supporting social change beyond the partial dismantling of the large estates.[34] Between these extremes, reformists often attribute the mixed success of land reforms to the failure of ensuring equal access by all farmers to inputs (such as credit) and extension services.

Be that as it may, in many countries today land reform may have become 'a dead policy issue'. In his comprehensive analysis of land reform in Latin America, de Janvry explains why: first, the political alliance for land reform that must be able to oppose the established capitalist class in agriculture is not able to do so in most countries; second, the efficiency and equity gains that characterise anti-feudal reforms have been exhausted; and third, the purchasing power and domestic demand created by the land reform is no longer important as a macro-economic consideration. In response, Bromley has argued that the main reason for the decline of land reform as a policy issue need not be simply expressed in terms of class conflicts over the control of land but can be explained by other factors. The most important of these, in his view, is the advent of new technologies in agriculture and the multitude of new economic opportunities provided by them, which 'combine to render – in many instances – land ownership quite irrelevant'.[36] In any case, the diminished attention generally given to the significance of land reform as a key to enhanced productivity brings us back to the broader issue of the modernisation of agriculture, which is now receiving considerable attention in the development literature.

THE MODERNISATION OF AGRICULTURE

One of the most important early articles to focus on agricultural development was that published in 1961 by Johnston and Mellor.[37] Their article pointed out that economic development leads to a substantial increase in the demand for agricultural products, so that failure to expand food supplies can seriously impede growth. They also emphasized that rising net cash incomes of the farm population can be important as a stimulus to industrial expansion.

Johnston and Mellor's classic article was also important because it brought forward the issue of technological change as an integral part of agricultural modernisation. Using historical evidence from Japan (1881–1920) and Taiwan (1901–1940) which showed technological progress to have been the major factor responsible for increased production and yields in basic food crops in those countries,[38] they pressed hard the case for complementarity between agricultural and industrial growth in development.

The swing towards greater emphasis on agriculture was fueled by other studies as well. One was that of Kuznets, published in 1965, which pointed to agriculture's historical contribution to economic development in terms of a production contribution, a market (demand) contribution and a factor contribution.[39] But it was probably Schultz's 1964 publication, *Transforming Traditional Agriculture*, which studied the efficiency of peasant agriculture, that had the greatest impact.[40] Drawing on empirical studies undertaken by others on Guatemala and India,[41] Schultz's main purpose was to explain the pattern of resource allocation by 'traditional' agricultural producers and to assess the possibilities for transforming traditional agriculture by investment.

Schultz summarised the *a priori* view of traditional agriculture held by many economists as one of farming as a way of life based on long established folkways, with people in poor rural tradition-bound communities being essentially idle if not lazy (i.e., preferring leisure to work), prone to indulge in wasteful consumption rather than saving (illustrated for example by elaborate marriage ceremonies) and, more generally, allocating resources inefficiently. Schultz countered this view by arguing that peasant farmers are 'poor but efficient': following a long period of trial and error they had discovered how to allocate their scarce resources efficiently given the state of available technology. Further, they are calculating economic agents who consider the marginal benefits and costs associated with different combinations of resources and production techniques. They remain poor, he argued, because of limitations on the quantity and quality of resources at their disposal.

The main policy conclusions derived from Schultz's work (sometimes referred to as the Schultz–Hopper hypothesis) were that traditional agriculturalists could not increase their output except by introducing technical innovations, and – equally important – that as efficient resource allocators they *would* introduce those innovations, if appropriate to local conditions.

The Schultz–Hopper hypothesis has been the subject of considerable debate. Many criticisms have centred on the choice of a neoclassical model to represent the behaviour of peasant farmers. In particular, it has been argued that the perfect competition model underlying the analysis cannot adequately reflect the behaviour of peasant farmers in developing countries, who are conditioned by high degrees of uncertainty and considerable institutional restrictions. In these circumstances of risk and uncertainty a peasant farmer is argued to be risk averse.[42]

Other orthodox economists have praised Schultz and Hopper for putting forward the case that in order to achieve rapid productivity and growth of agricultural output, technical change is essential. Some of these economists have nevertheless criticised Schultz and Hopper for not going far enough in their analysis. Hayami and Ruttan, who are representative of this view, argued in 1971 that the existence of a high-yielding technology is by itself an insufficient condition for achieving higher output growth, and that there has been a lack of understanding among agricultural economists of the interconnections between technological change and the institutions necessary to achieve the economic gain.[43] To fill this gap, Hayami and Ruttan constructed an induced-development model that sets out the conditions for the successful transmission of agricultural technology among countries. The central conclusion of this model is that technology transfer in the

context of agriculture is preferable via the development of loca
experimental station capacity (i.e. research, development and diffusior
capabilities) rather than transfers in the forms of specific techniques and
physical inputs.

Moreover, Hayami and Ruttan stressed that the development of
agricultural research stations should take place mainly in the public
sector but be guided by the market and not the planning system.
'provided that prices efficiently reflect changes in demand and supply of
products and factors and that there exists effective interaction among
farmers, public research institutions and private agricultural supply
firms'.[44] The implications of their work were that there should not only
be a well developed public-sector research infrastructure for agriculture,
but that agricultural research should not take place in isolation from the
field. The agricultural research system itself should be decentralised and
farmers should be organised into 'farmers' associations' to provide the
fundamental elements of effective and mutually reinforcing interaction.[45]
Like Mellor and Johnston (and other neoclassical free-trade-oriented
economists, including Little, Balassa, and Krueger), Hayami and Ruttan
drew heavily on the historic experiences of Japan, Taiwan and South
Korea. In particular, they used insights gained from the experience of the
transfer of rice production technology from Japan to South Korea and
Taiwan during the inter-war period.[46]

The Green Revolution

During the 1960s, aid donors as well as private foundations, notably the
Rockefeller and Ford Foundations, increasingly emphasized the need
for funding agricultural research in developing countries. Several
important international research centres were set up in response to their
efforts, including notably the International Rice Research Institute
(IRRI) in the Philippines in 1959, and the International Centre for
Maize and Wheat Improvement (CIMMYT) in Mexico in 1963. These
institutes were successful in developing new high-yielding dwarf
varieties of rice and wheat that have since been adopted by a number of
Third World countries, particularly Mexico, India, Sri Lanka,
Bangladesh and the Philippines. The technological breakthrough in
agriculture was thus achieved in the form of a 'green revolution'.

The term 'green revolution' refers to almost any package of modern
agricultural technologies introduced into the developing countries.
New seeds constitute the foundation of the green revolution. These
seeds require careful management plus relatively high and regular

amounts of fertilizers, pesticides and water. Byres, for example, argues that the attractiveness of the techniques derives from their being: a) labour-absorbing, thereby creating new employment opportunities; b) land-saving, thereby producing a substantial increase in output, without any increase in surface area, and possibly even with a decrease; c) scale-neutral, thereby generating an output increase on any size of holding, with no bias towards larger cultivators; and d) economical in scarce capital resources.[47]

The availability of these 'miracle' seeds, as they have been called, has had an important impact on the theory and practice of development economics. In particular, they have provided the means to carry out the modernisation of agriculture in a wide range of developing countries. The extraordinary features of these seeds meant that they could more than double yields per hectacre of rice and wheat, thereby significantly increasing the rate of growth of agricultural output. In pure economic terms, this implied at the very least a contribution to developing countries' self-sufficiency in food, enhancement of their exporting capacity in primary commodities (especially staple products), a larger agricultural surplus to finance development and, through all of these, more rapid rates of national economic growth.[48] Proponents of the green revolution (including Johnston, Mellor and Ruttan) have also argued that the new technologies are an important instrument of social and political progress. All classes of farmers, they argue, can benefit directly (including poor peasants with small farms, middle and rich peasant and capitalist farmers), and via the increased output, an additional demand for labour provides more wage employment for large numbers of rural landless labourers.[49] Thus, many pro-green-revolution economists have come to see technical process as a clear alternative to land reform and the transformation of rural institutions.

This orthodox position on the wide-ranging benefits from the green revolution has been attacked by a number of less orthodox critics who raise questions about its social and ecological effects. In effect, these critics say that the package may have brought economic gains in terms of increased output growth but that this has been accomplished at the cost of social upheavals in peasant societies. Thus, Griffin, Spitz and Cleaver, among others, argue that those farmers with the advantages of land and capital were the first to adopt the new seeds and have benefitted most,[50] because the new technology is scale-neutral but not resource-neutral (i.e. farmers require prior assets or access to funds in order to purchase the inputs). These writers emphasize the need for policies of land reform and other extension services (notably credit and advice) as an essential pre-condition to agricultural modernisation.

It has further been argued, for example by Byres, that the greater use of biochemical inputs (new seeds, fertilizers, pesticides) and a regulated flow of water have been accompanied by a rapid mechanisation of agriculture (tractors, threshers, seed drills, mechanical pumps for irrigation and combine harvesters), which has in turn contributed to unemployment and poverty among landless labourers.[51]   Other economists, notably Lipton, have drawn attention to the unequal regional and national distribution of the green revolution technologies due to the fact that they require highly favourable environmental conditions (a controlled supply of irrigation and particular types of soils) in order to produce the high yields. This means that they are restricted to parts of Asia (notably India, Pakistan and the Philippines) and parts of Latin America (especially Mexico) and that within these countries they can only be used in certain regions.[52]

Finally, in addition to failing to improve the lot of the poor, the green revolution is argued to have caused ecological problems. Biswas cites two examples of this: the increased use of pesticides, herbicides and chemical fertilizers has led both to contamination of the soil and to the destruction of wild life; and the increased use of pesticides has encouraged the development of stronger pests which in turn calls for more powerful pesticides.[53]

Although the green revolution has proved to be controversial, it has nevertheless formed the basis for many rural development strategies implemented during the 1970s. Particularly noteworthy in this regard is the major new emphasis given by the World Bank as of about 1973, under MacNamara, to directly attacking poverty in the countryside through rural development programmes.[54]   Under the Bank's 'redistribution with growth' approach – which we pick up again in Chapter 4 – it was felt that institutional reform (notably redistributive land reform) accompanied by a new style of integrated rural development projects and supported by increased Bank lending for rural development should contribute significantly to solving rural poverty in a relatively short period of time. The institutional reforms would benefit both the landless labourers and the submarginal farmers. But the likelihood of political obstacles to institutional reform meant that attention was switched to the upper fringe of the target group: the small farmers.

Small farmers in developing countries were seen by the Bank to be at a number of disadvantages: in their limited access to credit and extension advice, in facing relatively high risk and uncertainty, and in their limited access to other production factors that further reduced their ability to take advantage of the opportunities associated with the new technologies. To overcome these disadvantages the integrated rural development projects were to combine green-revolution technologies with infrastructure and support services – electricity, roads, education, family planning and nutrition – and apply them to an entire region.[55] It was hoped that adoption of the new technologies by the small farmers would in turn increase the demand for labour – increased prices of labour-competing farm machinery were also called for – thereby raising wages and incomes for the lower segments of the target group (marginal farmers and landless labour) and improving income distribution as well.[56] Keynesian multiplier effects were also seen as contributing to increased incomes, output and a general rise in rural prosperity.

In a critique of the rural development programmes of the 1970s, especially the 'integrated' projects of the World Bank and the FAO, Ruttan argued in 1984 that they were accompanied by a shift from communal organisation to direct delivery of agricultural inputs and other services through bureaucratic implementation.[57] There were some early successes in the mid-1970s due to the high concentration of human resources in organising and managing the projects – which Ruttan praised for achieving equity in distributing the fruits of growth in favour of the rural poor and under-priviledged social classes – but these efforts could not be sustained for very long by the fragile administrative and technical services that exist in many developing countries. Once donor assistance was withdrawn, many of the pilot projects that had been set up were never replicated. Ruttan therefore argued for the importance of building up existing local organisations as an alternative to centrally co-ordinated bureaucratic systems of input delivery. He also criticised the attempts to generalise a particular pilot project to the regional and national levels, arguing that individual projects should have been tailored to the needs and resources of specific rural areas.

Two further aspects of Ruttan's article are significant for our purposes. First, it constituted an important recognition by a leading orthodox agricultural economist of the institutional complexities of rural development, and of the difficulties posed by the process of agricultural modernisation. These concerns were further confirmed in a 1986 study by Quizon and Binswanger on the effects of the green revolution on income distribution in India – probably the most important case study of the green revolution strategy – which found that, without institutional reforms, the trickle down mechanism works very slowly to reduce poverty: average rural incomes rose by only about two per cent over the 20-year period from 1960–61 to 1980–81.[58] Second, similar concerns over bureaucratic 'top-down' delivery of rural development and technological change were a central concern during the 1970s of many proponents of 'bottom-up' rural development strategies centering on grass-roots participation of the poor in the process of development.[59]

The 'Second Green Revolution' and the Revival of Agriculture

The emphasis given by the World Bank to rural development during the 1970s coincided with the increasing criticism by orthodox economists of ISI strategies, as noted earlier. While much of that criticism focused on the inefficiencies created within the 'modern' sector by the trade and monetary policies and the regulatory environment characteristic of ISI strategies during the 1950s and 1960s, another effect of ISI policies was to turn the terms of rural-urban and agriculture-industry trade within countries against agriculture, often radically so.[60] The increasing emphasis given in the orthodox literature and by policy-makers, including the World Bank, to rural development and the modernisation of agriculture thus reinforced the criticism of ISI strategies.

Following the proliferation in the late 1970s and early 1980s of orthodox literature in favour of EOI strategies (which we discuss in Chapter 3), a number of orthodox writers have nevertheless been formulating macroeconomic development strategies with agriculture, not industry, as the engine of growth. Mellor, Adelman and Johnston, and Clark, among others, have argued that now that the green revolution has proved that technological advance is possible in agriculture, and that this advance has contributed to the production of considerable marketable surpluses as well as to a growth in demand and incomes, the rural sector has the potential for playing the role of the leading sector.[61] They argue that the development efforts of governments should thus focus on the design and implementation of an agriculture- and employment-based strategy of economic growth.

One of the leading proponents of this strategy, Mellor, argues for example that an agriculture- and employment-based strategy of economic growth has three basic elements. First, the pace of agricultural growth must be accelerated despite the limitation of fixed land area. He sees technological change (encompassing cash- as well as food-crops, and drought- and pest-resistant varieties of seeds) overcoming constraints to agricultural growth and allowing low-income countries to use the most powerful element of growth: technological progress. Second, he sees domestic demand for agricultural output growing rapidly, despite inelastic demand, through accelerated growth in employment (more precisely, increased demand for labour), which is facilitated by the indirect effects of agricultural growth itself. Third, he sees the demand for goods and services produced by low-capital-intensity processes increasing, facilitated by the technology-based increase in agricultural income.[62]

Recent studies have also drawn attention to the stabilising role of agriculture during the crisis of the 1980s. In their comparative analysis of Latin American growth trends, de Janvry and Sadoulet for example show that whereas prior to the crisis agricultural growth rates lagged behind those of industry and GDP, the reverse has been true during the 1980s. This leads them to propose capitalising on a relatively dynamic and resilient agricultural sector as an important element of a strategy for economic recovery.[63] A study of macroeconomic policies and agricultural performance in Brazil also points to policy biases in favour of industry since the 1950s as having contributed to the crisis of the 1980s, and argues that agriculture has moderated the crisis by bolstering the trade surplus (despite declining commodity prices) and exerting a downward pressure on food prices and inflation while supporting rural employment and incomes.[64]

The revised green-revolution strategy has even been given more favourable reviews by some critics of the original green revolution. For example, in his recent book on *Alternative Strategies of Economic Development*, Keith Griffin argues that the revised strategy represents a shift in emphasis from landlord-biased to peasant-biased technology because it stresses the importance of cash-crops and pest- and drought-resistant seeds that serve to enlarge the land area and the types of cultivator covered by the strategy.[65] Moreover, he points out, the government is allocated a greater role in supplying and financing rural infrastructure, agricultural research, input supply systems and education. This is in contrast to the original green revolution, whose proponents saw it as a mechanism of economic and social change with only the 'hidden hand' of the market guiding it.

Griffin does argue, however, that the major weakness of the original strategy still applies to the revised strategy: 'it tries to substitute technical change and agricultural expansion for institutional reforms and direct measures to improve the distribution of income and productive assets in rural areas'.[66] It is nevertheless significant that whereas the original green revolution was situated in parts of Asia and

Latin America, the revised strategy is specifically geared to Africa and parts of Asia other than Central or South Asia, because of the highly unequal patterns of land tenure in the latter regions.[67]

The development of 'social accounting matrices' (SAMs) in the 1980s has facilitated the development of quantitative analyses of the relationship between land tenure and agricultural performance.[68] Moreover, by adding a calorie dimension to the SAM, Adelman and Taylor have constructed a 'food accounting matrix' (FAM) which illustrates the trade-offs between production and distribution goals within agriculture, and the trade and fiscal implications of alternative agricultural policies. It also illustrates the rural-urban development trade-offs, and the direct and indirect effects of global development policies on the agricultural sector. In their prototype application of the FAM to Mexico, Adelman and Taylor show that a unimodal strategy favouring peasants and small farmers would be an improvement over the currently prevailing 'bimodal' strategy which aims to favour both small and large farmers but in fact favours the latter.[69]

It has also been pointed out, finally, that whereas the agricultural and employment strategy is based on the central role of technological inputs and government services, the importance of 'incentive-' or 'wage-goods' in an agricultural strategy must not be overlooked. Along these lines a recent empirical study by Berthelemy and Morrisson has demonstrated a statistically significant relationship between the supply of manufactured consumer goods (whether imported or locally produced) and the output of cash-crops in 12 Sub-Saharan African countries.[70] These findings support the proposition that farmers should not only have access to the means of production but also have the incentive, in the form of access to non-farm consumer goods, to increase marketed output.

For a number of years now, Western aid agencies and national planning bureaus in some developing countries have been increasingly devoting resources to this sector, and nearly all developing countries have some form of agricultural and rural development policy in operation at present.[71] It has become fashionable to talk of the eventual achievement of self-reliance in food by the developing countries provided they follow the appropriate policies.[72]

Sadly, however, while the technological revolution in agriculture has been of central importance, the recognition of the importance of agriculture is also in no small part due to the food crisis in sub-Saharan Africa. While access to food may be thought of as a basic human right, it seems that the food shortages and the resulting death and malnutrition were necessary to make many sit up and recognise the ultimate importance of promoting agriculture – namely to feed people. Moreover, this tragic food crisis and the resulting human misery appear to result not from any global shortage of food, but from insufficient purchasing power or access to food stocks by the affected populations. The tragic irony is that this can happen at a time when immense food surpluses are a major international problem as well.[73]

Notes and References

1. Y. Hayami and V.W. Ruttan, *Agricultural Development: An International Perspective*, Johns Hopkins University Press, Baltimore, 1971, p. 17.
2. J. H. Boeke, *Economics and Economic Policy of Dual Societies as Exemplified by Indonesia*, Institute of Pacific Relations, New York, 1953.
3. B. Higgins, 'The Dualistic Theory of Underdeveloped Areas' in *Economic Development and Cultural Change*, January, 1956. In addition, many Dutch economists have explored the defects in Boeke's work. Some of their views can be found in Dutch Scholars, *Indonesian Economics: The Concept of Dualism in Theory and Policy*, Van Hoeve Publishers, The Hague, 1961.
4. Higgin's views on technological dualism are contained in B. Higgins, *Economic Development*, Norton, New York, 1968.
5. Myint went beyond Higgins in stressing the importance of the capital market as a basis for enclave dualism. In his model, the modern sector has more favourable access to capital (and at better terms) than the traditional sector. Hence, he argues, it adopts more capital intensive techniques and registers higher labour productivity in comparison with the traditional sector. H. Myint, *The Economics of the Developing Countries*, Hutchinson Library, London, 1964.
6. In *The Manchester School of Economic and Social Studies*, May 1954. See also W.A. Lewis, 'Development Economics in the 1950s' in G. Meier and D. Seers, eds., *Pioneers in Development*, Oxford University Press for the World Bank, New York, 1984.
7. A comprehensive survey of these and other defects in the Lewis model will be found in A. Dixit, 'Themes of the Dual Economies: A Survey' in J. Mirrlees and N. H. Stern, eds., *Models of Economic Growth*, MacMillan, London, 1971.
8. For a clarification of this point, consult W.A. Lewis, 'Unlimited Labour: Further Notes', in *The Manchester School of Economic and Social Studies*, January 1958.
9. G. Ranis and J. Fei, 'A Theory of Economic Development' in *American Economic Review*, September 1961. See also their book, *Development of the Labour Surplus Economy: Theory and Practice*, Irwin, Homewood, 1964.

10.   The role of prices and money in growth and the issue of financial repression are both important in the process of broadening the base of the commercial sector and the outward spread of the monetarised economy. For a more detailed description and analysis of these issues, see U. Tun Wai, 'Interest Rates Outside the Organised Money Markets in Underdeveloped Economies', in *IMF Staff Papers*, Vol. VI, No. 1, November 1957; R.I. McKinnon, *Money and Capital in Economic Development*, Brookings Institution, Washington, D.C., 1973; A. Bhaduri, 'On the Formation of Usurious Interest Rates in Backward Agriculture', in *Cambridge Journal of Economics*, 1977; and J.D. Von Pischke, D.W. Adams and G. Donald, eds., *Rural Financial Markets in Low-Income Countries: Their Use and Abuse*, Johns Hopkins University Press, Baltimore, 1983.

11.   In the context of Latin America, Griffin has pointed out, 'urban development has been financed largely by private savings out of the surplus appropriated by the landowning class. There is no modern capitalist class which is distinct from the traditional, feudal landowning class. On the contrary, there is a considerable overlap of the urban industrial and professional groups and the large landlords.' He further argues that the consequences of this monopoly economic structure is to lead both to a low degree of economic efficiency in all the sectors (including agriculture) and to a highly unequal distribution of income. K. Griffin, ed., *Financing Development in Latin America*, MacMillan, London, 1971, p. 4.

12.   See in particular, T.W. Schultz, 'The Doctrine of Agricultural Labour of Zero Value' in his *Transforming Traditional Agriculture*, Yale University Press, New Haven, 1964, and A.K. Sen, 'Surplus Labour in India: A Critique of Schultz's Statistical Test' (with reply and rejoinder) in *Economic Journal*, March 1967. See also A.K. Sen, 'Peasants and Dualism with or without Surplus Labour', in *Journal of Political Economy*, October 1966; and M. Desai and D. Mazumdar, 'A Test of the Hypothesis of Disguised Unemployment', in *Economica*, Vol. 37, 1975.

13.   See for example R.F. Mikesell, *The Economics of Foreign Aid*, Weidenfeld and Nicolson, London, 1968.

14.   Lewis took this problem into consideration, but largely discounted it on the assumption that training facilities could be created in the capitalist sector without major difficulty. In making this assumption, Lewis may have underestimated the significant external economies inherent in training (be it formal or on-the-job-training) which lead to an under-allocation of private resources to such training.

15.   J. Tinbergen and H. C. Bos, 'A Planning Model for the Education Requirements of Economic Growth', in OECD, *Econometric Models of Education*, Paris, 1965. A critique of the system of formalised education is provided by I.D. Illich, *Deschooling Society*, Harper and Row, New York, 1971.

16.   One of the first to develop the notion of human capital was T.W. Schultz, 'Capital Formation by Education', in *Journal of Political Economy*, December 1960. See also J. Simmons, 'Education for Development Reconsidered', in *World Development*, Nov./Dec. 1979; J. Hallak and

F. Caillods, eds., *Education, Work and Employment*, UNESCO, Paris, 1980; and T.W. Schultz, 'Education Investments and Returns' in H.B. Chenery and T.N. Srinivasan, eds., *Handbook of Development Economies*, Elsevier Science Publishers, North Holland, 1988.

17. D. Jorgenson, 'Surplus Agricultural Labour and the Development of the Dual Economy', in *Oxford Economic Papers*, Vol. 19, No. 3, 1967. See also D. Jorgenson, 'The Development of a Dual Economy' in *Economic Journal*, Vol. 71, 1961. Jorgenson claims that his model is superior not only because of its greater technical precision but also because its predictions broadly conform to the Japanese historical experience during the 19th century. Other authors, notably Dixit and Nakamura, are less convinced. Dixit questions the data Jorgenson cites to confirm his hypotheses. Nakamura points out that in his formulation of the agricultural production function, Jorgenson leaves out capital as an explanatory variable even though capital played a significant part in the Japanese agricultural success during the Meiji era and after. Cf. A.K. Dixit, 'Optimal Development in the Labour Surplus Economy' in *Review of Economic Studies*, January 1968, and J.I. Nakamura, 'Growth of Japanese Agriculture 1875–1920', in W. Lockwood, ed., *The State and Economic Enterprise in Japan*, Princeton University Press, New Jersey, 1965.

18. For a discussion of the structure of the model, the specific assumptions made and the underlying growth process, see A.C. Kelly, G. Williamson and R.J. Cheetham, *Dualistic Economic Development: Theories and History*, University of Chicago Press, Chicago, 1972.

19. The Cobb–Douglas production function has the algebraic form:

$$y = A.L^a . K^b$$

where y is output, A, a, b are constant terms, L is labour and K is capital. A special property of this function is that the elasticity of substitution between capital and labour is equal to 1. The popularity of the Cobb-Douglas production function derives from both its computational simplicity and its consistency with the established body of mainstream economic theory. For a detailed discussion of its theoretical properties and examples of its application, see C.E. Ferguson, *The Neoclassical Theory of Production and Distribution*, Cambridge University Press, Cambridge, 1969.

20. The Harris–Todaro Model assumes that migration is mainly an economic phenomenon and reflects rational decisions by migrants based on the costs and benefits of migration. It portrays the migrant responding to urban–rural wage differentials in perceived rather than actual earnings, where his or her decision to migrate is based on both the urban-rural wage differential and the probability of his obtaining a job in the urban sector, minus the cost of migration. See J. Harris and M. Todaro, 'Migration, Unemployment and Development: A Two Sector Analysis', in *American Economic Review*, March 1970. For some case studies of the process of migration, consult D. Byerlee, 'Rural–Urban Migration in Africa: Theory, Policy and Research Implications', in *International Migration Review*, 1974; P. Collier, 'Migration and Unemployment: A Dynamic

General Equilibrium Analysis Applied to Tanzania' in *Oxford Economic Papers*, July 1979; and Peek and Antolinez, 'Migration and the Urban Labour Market: The Case of San Salvador', in *World Development*, April 1977. See also O. Stark, 'Migrants and Markets', Migration and Development Program Discussion Paper, No. 37, Harvard University, 1988; and J.G. Williamson, 'Migration and Urbanisation' in H.B. Chenery and T.N. Srinivasan, eds., *Handbook of Development Economics*, Vol. I., Elsevier Science Publishers, North Holland, 1988.

21. See for example, B. Renaud, *National Urbanisation Policy in Developing Countries*, 1979; N. Crook, 'On the Management of Urban Migration and Residence: An Economic Approach', in *Asian Journal of Public Administration*, 1983; and A.S. Oberai, *State Policies and Internal Migration*, St. Martin's Press, New York, 1983.

22. The rapid pace of urbanisation has also been accompanied by increasing concern for the costs of urban development. For example, urbanisation places a high financial burden on urban governments which have to meet rapidly rising demand for urban services; some have argued that the financial costs associated with urbanisation are responsible to a significant degree for the increasing international debt of LDCs during the 1970s; there are equity-related concerns over the distribution of relative rural-urban development costs – since rural areas are said to subsidise urban expansion; and costs of urban growth include pollution, congestion and crime that exceed those associated with rural development. In the eyes of a number of authors, these problems constitute a prima facie case for promoting rural development over urban development. See for example, R. Rhoda, 'Rural Development and Urban Migration: Can We Keep Them Down on the Farm?', in *International Migration Review*, Vol. 17, No. 61, 1983; and the special issue on 'Reversing Anti-Rural Development', in *Development*, No. 2, 1984.

23. Little sums up the attitude of many of the early development thinkers rather well: 'It is fairly obvious from reading their works that leading development economists of the 1950s knew nothing about tropical agriculture or rural life. One cannot perhaps blame them: they had no time for rural rides; and there was no considerable body of empirical grass roots literature on which they could draw. The planning enthusiasts also gave no clues as to how agriculture could best be planned and administered...' I.M.D. Little, *Economic Development*, Basic Books, New York, 1982, p. 106.

24. D. Warriner, 'Land Reform and Economic Development', in *National Bank of Egypt, Fiftieth Anniversary Commemoration Lectures*, Cairo, 1955, reprinted in C. Eicher and L. Witt, eds., *Agriculture in Economic Development*, McGraw-Hill, New York, 1964.

25. See, for example, CIDA, *Land Tenure Conditions and Socio-Economic Development of the Agricultural Sector: Brazil*, Washington, D.C., Organisation of American States, 1966, and CIDA, *Tenencia de la Tierra y Desarrollo Socio-Economico del Sector Agricola; Peru*, Washington, D.C., Pan-American Union, 1965.

26. The latifundio–munifundo system was found to discourage the adoption

of new agricultural technologies, first, because small holders do not have the means and the knowledge to adopt new practices. Second, share-croppers working on the latifundios do not have the necessary incentives because they can be dismissed at any time by the landowner. Third, the latifundista, with a high and assured income, is under no economic compulsion to improve farming techniques. See for example, J.M. Alier, *Haciendas, Plantations and Collective Farms*, Frank Cass, London, 1977, and M. Valderrama and P. Ludmann, *La Oligarquia Terrateniente Ayer y Hoy*, Universidad Católica del Perú, Lima, 1979. On share-cropping, see for example, A. Bhaduri, 'Agricultural Backwardness under Semi-Feudalism' in *Economic Journal*, Vol. 83, March 1973, and M.G. Quibria and S. Rashid, 'The Puzzle of Sharecropping: A Survey of Theories', in *World Development*, Vol. 12, No. 2, 1984.

27. P. Dorner, *Land Reform and Economic Development*, Penguin, Harmondsworth, 1972.

28. For a definition and discussion of the origins of populism, see for example, G. Kitching, *Development and Underdevelopment in Historical Perspective*, Methuen, London, 1982.

29. M. Lipton, *Why the Poor Stay Poor: A Study of Urban Bias in World Development*, Temple Smith, London, 1977. A critique of urban bias is provided by T.J. Byres, 'Of Neopopulist Pipedreams: Daedalus in the Third World and the Myth of Urban Bias' in *Journal of Peasant Studies*, Vol. 6, No. 2, 1979.

30. R.A. Berry and W.R. Cline, *Agrarian Structure and Productivity in Developing Countries*, Johns Hopkins University Press, Baltimore, 1979. The proposition that there exists an inverse relationship between size of holding and productivity has given rise to a heated debate in the literature. See for example, C.H. Hanumantha Rao, 'Alternative Explanations of the Inverse Relationship between Farm Size and Output per Acre in India', in *Indian Economic Review*, Newseries, Vol. 1, No. 2, Oct. 1966; A.K. Sen, *Employment, Technology and Development*, London, 1975, Appendix C; and P. Roy, 'Transition in Agriculture: Empirical Indicators and Results' in *Journal of Peasant Studies*, Vol. 8, No. 2, January 1981.

31. ILO, *Poverty and Landlessness in Rural Asia*, Geneva, 1977. Despite the ILO's call for redistributive land reform in Asia, there was considerable resistence to this policy among Asian governments. A group of Asian scholars thus remarked that 'governments essentially representing landed interests have accomplished little. There have been motions without action, legislation with loopholes, and appeals to a lack of records. Vested interests cannot liquidate themselves (and) there cannot be genuine democracy in a framework of polarized landed ownership' (W. Haque, N. Metha, A. Rahman and P. Wignaraja, 'Towards a Theory of Rural Development', in *Development Dialogue*, No. 2, 1977, p. 51). The relationship between rural poverty and the concentration of land ownership is emphasized in K. Griffin, *Land Concentration and Rural Poverty*, London, MacMillan, 1976.

32. An overview of the record of redistributive land reform can be found in

FAO, *Progress in Land Reform: Sixth Report,* United Nations, New York, 1976; S. Eckstein, G. Donald, D. Horton, and T. Carroll, 'Land Reform in Latin America: Bolivia, Chile, Mexico, Peru and Venezuela' in *World Bank Staff Working Paper,* No. 275, 1978; and A.K. Ghose, ed., *Land Reform in Contemporary Developing Countries,* Croom Helm, London, 1983.

33.   See, for example, A. de Janvry, *The Agrarian Question and Reformism in Latin America,* Johns Hopkins University Press, Baltimore, 1981.

34.   See, for example, H.P. Binswanger and M.R. Rosenzweig, 'Behavioural and Material Determinants of Production Relations in Agriculture', in *Journal of Development Studies,* Vol. 22, No. 3, 1986.

35.   de Janvry (1981), *op. cit.*

36.   B.W. Bromley, 'The Role of Land Reform in Economic Development: Comment' in C.K. Eicher and J.M. Staatz, eds., *Agricultural Development in the Third World,* Johns Hopkins Univerity Press, Baltimore, 1984.

37.   B.F. Johnston and J.W. Mellor, 'The Role of Agriculture in Economic Development', in *American Economic Review,* September 1961.

38.   Many writers have emphasised that the three key elements in the drive to raise agricultural productivity in Japan and Taiwan were a) the greater use of high-yielding varieties of seed developed by agricultural research; b) the increased application of fertilisers and pesticides; and c) strong promotion by the state of a) and b) and other attempts to diffuse improved farming practices. See K. Ohkawa, *Differential Structure and Agriculture: Essays on Dualistic Growth,* Hitotsubashi University Press, Tokyo, 1972; T.H. Lee, *Intersectoral Capital Flows in the Economic Development of Taiwan,* Cornell University Press, 1971; and M. Akino and Y. Hayami, 'Agricultural Growth in Japan, 1880-1965', in *Quarterly Journal of Economics,* August 1974.

39.   S. Kuznets, *Economic Growth and Structure,* Heinemann, London, 1965. Also influential in stimulating debate on the role of agriculture in the economy was W.H. Nicholls, 'The Place of Agriculture in Economic Development' in C.K. Eicher and L.W. Witt, eds., *Agriculture in Economic Development,* McGraw-Hill, New York, 1964.

40.   T. Schultz, *Transforming Traditional Agriculture,* Yale University Press, New Haven, 1964.

41.   Details of these two studies can be found in Schultz (1964), and W.D. Hopper, 'Allocation Efficiency in Traditional Indian Agriculture', in *Journal of Farm Economics,* August 1965. The results of a much more comprehensive empirical study of Indian agriculture covering nearly 3 000 holdings spread over six agricultural regions can be found in P.A. Yotopoulos and J.B. Nugent, *Economics of Development,* Harper and Row, New York, 1976.

42.   A criticism of applying the neoclassical model to investigate traditional agriculture in poor countries is discussed in K. Shapiro, 'Efficiency Differentials in Peasant Agriculture and their Implications for Development', contributed papers read at the 16th International conference of Agricultural Economists, University of Oxford Institute of Agricultural Economics, Oxford, 1977. In addition, see P. Bardhan,

'Interlocking Factor Markets and Agrarian Development: A Review of the Issues' in *Oxford Economic Papers,* March 1980.

43. Y. Hayami and V. Ruttan, *Agricultural Development: An International Perspective,* the Johns Hopkins Press, Baltimore, 1971.

44. Hayami and Ruttan's mechanism of induced innovation in the public sector can be compared with Hick's theory of induced innovation in the private sector. While Hick's innovation-inducement mechanism rested simply on profit-maximising firms undertaking to invest in new methods of production in response to price movements in the market, Hayami and Ruttan extend this basic analysis to public-sector officials (notably research scientists in public or publically funded research institutes) who are induced to innovate in response to economic factors and resource endowments. See also J.R. Hicks, *The Theory of Wages,* MacMillan, London, 1932, p. 124-125. For an extension of Hick's induced-innovation model in the private sector, see S. Ahamad, 'On the Theory of Induced Innovation', in *Economic Journal,* Vol. 76, June 1966.

45. Public-sector research is seen to be more socially beneficial than private-sector research in sectors like agriculture where the individual privately owned firm may be too small to reap the gains from a large investment in research. In addition, private-sector research programmes may ignore socially desirable objectives such as reduced erosion and the production of cheaper but equally efficient agricultural techniques. For more on this subject, see W.F. Hueg and C.A. Gannon, eds., *Transforming Knowledge into Food in a Worldwide Context,* Miller Publishing Co., Minneapolis, 1978; and R. Chambers and J. Jiggins, 'Agricultural Research for Resource Poor Farmers: A Parsimonious Paradigm', *IDS Discussion Paper 220,* University of Sussex, Brighton, 1986.

46. A critical perspective of the model of induced innovation is provided by R. Grabowski, 'The Implications of an Induced Innovation Model', in *Economic Development and Cultural Change,* July 1979. See also K. Boyce, *Agrarian Impasse in Bengal: Institutional Constraints to Technological Change,* Oxford University Press, Oxford, 1987.

47. T. Byres, *et al., The Green Revolution in India,* Open University Press, London, 1983.

48. For a discussion of the scientific and economic features of the green revolution, see N.E. Borlang, 'Using Plants to Meet World Food Needs' in R.G. Woods, ed., *Future Dimensions of the World Food Problem,* Westview Press, Boulder, 1981. See also M.S. Swaminathan, 'The Green Revolution Can Reach the Small Farmer' in S. Aziz, ed., *Hunger, Politics and Markets,* New York University Press, 1975.

49. The view that the green revolution has had a widespread favourable impact on income distribution and employment is widespread among orthodox development economists. For a sample of their arguments, see B.F. Johnston and J. Cownie, 'The Seed Fertilizer Revolution and Labour Force Absorption', in *American Economic Review,* 1969; V.W. Ruttan, 'The Green Revolution: Seven Generalisations', in *International Development Review,* December 1977; G. Feder and G.T. O'Mara, 'Farm Size and the Diffusion of Green Revolution Technology', in *Economic*

Development and Cultural Change, Vol. 30, No. 1, October 1981; and G. Feder and S. Zilberman, 'Adoption of Agricultural, Innovations in Developing Countries: A Survey', in *Economic Development and Cultural Change,* January 1985.

50.   K. Griffin, *The Political Economy of Agrarian Change,* (2nd ed.), MacMillan, London, 1979; H.M. Cleaver, 'The Contradictions of the Green Revolution' in *American Economic Review,* May 1972; and P. Spitz, 'Silent Violence: Famine and Inequality', in *International Social Science Journal,* Vol. 30, No. 4, 1978. Criticisms are also provided by P.T. Mooney, 'The Law of the Seed: Another Development and Plant Genetic Resources' in *Development Dialogue,* 1983: 1–2; and B.H. Farmer, 'Perspectives on the Green Revolution in South Asia', in *Modern Asian Studies,* Vol. 20, No. 1, 1986.

51.   T.J. Byres (1983), *op. cit.,* or T.J. Byres, 'Class Formation and Class Action in the Indian Countryside' in *Journal of Peasant Studies,* Vol. 8, No. 4, July 1981.

52.   Thus, for example, the green-revolution technologies cannot be significantly used to help the food crisis in sub-Saharan Africa. Not only are the main staples eaten in these countries, cassava and millet, not among the grains that have been the focus of the green revolution, there is also a technical crisis in food production. To quote a recent FAO report: 'Neither the green revolution technology of Asia nor the capital-intensive methods of western agriculture have proved viable in the very different conditions prevailing in most of tropical Africa. Soils are generally more fragile and more easily eroded than in other regions. Furthermore, their quality is being widely run down by the intensification of traditional farming systems. Outside Madagascar and the Sudan, irrigation covers a barely significant proportion of the arable land, and even a relatively short drought can cause havoc to crops'. (FAO, *World Food Report,* 1984, p. 5). See also M. Lipton, 'Inter-Farm, Inter-regional and Farm- Non-farm Income Distribution: The Impact of the New Cereal Varieties' in *World Development,* March 1978.

53.   A.K. Biswas, 'Agricultural Development and the Environment', in *Mazingira,* No. 11, 1979.

54.   The details of the Bank's thrust into rural development can be obtained from World Bank, *The Assault on World Poverty,* Washington, D.C., 1975. This book consists of a collection of five important policy papers written in the early 1970s that layed out the Bank's policy intentions in rural development, agricultural credit, land reform, education and health during this period. For an overview of the strategy, see also R.S. MacNamara, 'Address to the Board of Governors', World Bank, Washington, D.C., 1975. (See also our Chapter 4.)

55.   A useful overview of the World Bank's integrated rural development strategy can be found in M. Yudelman, 'Integrated Rural Development Projects: The Bank's Experience', in *Finance and Development,* Vol. 14, No. 1, March 1977.

56.   See H. Chenery, *et al., Redistribution with Growth,* Oxford University Press, 1974.

57.   V.W. Ruttan, 'Integrated Rural Development Programmes: A Historical

Perspective', in *World Development*, Vol. 12, No. 4, 1984.

58.   J. Ouizon and H.P. Binswanger, 'Modeling the Impact of Agricultural Growth and Government Policy on Income Distribution in India', in *World Bank Economic Review*, Vol. 1, No. 1, September 1986.

59.   See for example, Haque, Metha, Rahman and Wignaraja, *op. cit.*

60.   See for example, W.F. Owen, 'The Double Developmental Squeeze on Agriculture' in *American Economic Review*, March 1966; R.M. Bird, 'Land Taxation and Economic Development: The Model of Meiji Japan' in *Journal of Development Studies*, Vol. 13, No. 2, 1977; and J.W. Mellor, 'Agricultural Development and the Intersectoral Transfer of Resources' in C.K. Eicher and J.M. Staatz, eds., (1984), *op. cit.*

61.   See J.W. Mellor, 'Agriculture on the Road to Industrialisation' in J.P. Lewis and V. Kallab, eds., *Development Strategies Reconsidered*, Overseas Development Council, Washington, D.C., 1986; I. Adelman, 'Beyond Export led Growth', in *World Development*, Vol. 12, No. 9, 1984; and B.F. Johnston and W.C. Clark, *Redesigning Rural Development: A Strategic Perspective*, 1982.

62.   Mellor (1986), *ibid.*

63.   A. de Janvry and E. Sadoulet, 'Investment Strategies to Combat Rural Poverty: A proposal for Latin America' in *World Development*, Vol. 17, No. 8, 1989.

64.   I. Goldin and G. Castro de Rezende, *Agriculture and Economic Crisis: Lessons from Brazil*, OECD Development Centre, Paris, 1990.

65.   K. Griffin, *Alternative Strategies of Economic Development*, MacMillan in association with the OECD Development Centre, London, 1989.

66.   *Ibid.*, p. 160.

67.   See particularly J.W. Mellor, C. Delgado and M.J. Blackie, eds., *Accelerating Food Production Growth in Sub-Saharan Africa*, Johns Hopkins University Press, Baltimore, 1985.

68.   SAMs extend the early planning (input-output) models' analysis of intersectoral flows in the production accounts to government, financial and personal sectors. They are useful, for example, in forcing consistency in different parts of national accounts, linking them to household survey data, and understanding the structure of the economy in relation to income distribution and savings. They generally also provide the basic starting point against which the non-linear computable general equilibrium models (CGEs) are calibrated or validated. See de Janvry and Sadoulet (1987), *op. cit.*, for an evaluation of agriculturally focused CGEs. For an introduction to SAMS see for example, F.G. Pyatt and J. Round, *Social Accounting Matrices: A basis for Planning*, The World Bank, Washington, D.C., 1985. For a concise discussion of the use of SAMs and CGEs in development economics more generally, see N. Stern, 'The Economics of Development: A Survey' in *Economic Journal*, Vol. 99, September 1989.

69.   I. Adelman and J.E. Taylor, *Changing Comparative Advantages in Food and Agriculture: A Case Study of Mexico*, OECD Development Centre, Paris, 1990.

70.   J.C. Berthelemy and C. Morrison, 'Manufactured Goods Supply and Cash Crops in Subsaharan Africa' in *World Development*, Vol. 15,

No. 10/11, 1987.

71.   The view of aid donors regarding the importance of agriculture is captured by a comprehensive study of the effectiveness of aid co-ordination: 'The importance of agriculture to the economies of many developing countries, and particularly the poorer ones, can hardly be overstated. Up to 90 per cent of the people in some cases derive much of their incomes from farming, agriculture is the main foreign exchange earner for many countries, and the sector provides many essential inputs for early stages of industrial development. The effectiveness of aid in promoting sustainable agriculture is therefore basic to the effectiveness of aid as a whole' (R. Cassen, *et al., Does Aid Work? Report of an Intergovernmental Task Force,* Clarendon Press, Oxford, 1986, page 117).

72.   This point has been discussed by many international organisations, and several favourable projections have been made on the assumption of successful green revolutions in agriculture. See for example, FAO, *Agriculture: Towards 2000,* Rome, 1981.

73.   Details of the world food balance and the problem of hunger be found, for example, in J.W. Mellor, 'Global Food Balances and Food Security', in *World Development,* Vol. 6, No. 9, 1988;   N. Alexandratos, *World Agriculture: Towards 2000,* Belhaven Press, London, 1988;   The Hunger Project, *Ending Hunger: An Idea Whose Time Has Come,* Praeger, New York, 1985;   H. Schneider, *Meeting Food Needs in a Context of Change,* OECD Development Centre, Paris, 1984;   and J.W. Mellor and B.F. Johnston, 'The World Equation: Interrelationship Among Employment and Food Consumption' in *Journal of Economic Literature,* June 1984.

3 Open-economy Development and the Neoclassical Resurgence

During the 1950s and 1960s, as we have seen, many developing countries were pursuing import-substituting strategies of industrialisation (ISI). This was true not only in Latin America, where market forces had actually given rise to ISI in the 1914–1945 period, but in many newly independent countries in Asia and Africa, whose leaders were often outspoken advocates of ISI-type development strategies. They supported ISI because they questioned the assumption implicit in much of the orthodox literature on capital accumulation and on dual economies that demand for developing-country exports is perfectly elastic. Following Nurkse (cf. Chapter 1) and especially Prebisch (cf. Chapter 5), they thus highlighted the fact that the problem of domestic capital accumulation cannot be considered separately from a country's integration into the international economy.

Mainstream neoclassical economists increasingly voiced criticism of ISI development strategies, however, from about the late the 1960s. This criticism led to greater emphasis in the orthodox literature than had been the case in the 1950s and 1960s on *open-economy* development strategies and – in response to the issue already raised by Prebisch in 1949/1950 and by Nurkse in 1952 – on the question of a country's integration into the international economy. It also marked the beginning of what can be termed the neoclassical resurgence, whose strength, particularly since the early 1980s, has made the neoclassical approach to open-economy development the dominant school of development thinking in the 1980s.

THE NEOCLASSICAL CRITIQUE OF ISI

Among the first to criticise ISI were those writers, e.g., Viner, Haberler and Bauer and Yamey, who argued that it interfered with the natural process of economic development based on comparative advantage.[1] Their view was essentially that developing countries should remain producers and exporters of primary products and should encourage growth of their agricultural sectors and plantation economies. Although this view apparently had little effect on the inward-looking industrialisation policies followed by many developing countries at the time, it did influence subsequent work by other neoclassical economists.

More important were the neoclassical criticisms of ISI published in the 1960s. Among the earliest were those that developed measures of the 'effective rate of protection' (ERP) and the 'domestic resource cost' of ISI investment projects (DRC). An early ERP study was on Pakistan, in 1965; more extensive work was done by the OECD and the World Bank in the late 1960s and early 1970s.[2] These studies concluded that the ERP of manufacturing in the 1960s was very high in some countries (notably Pakistan, India, Brazil), that it was high to moderate in some (Taiwan, the Philippines) and zero in others (e.g. Malaysia). The studies pointed to a tendency for many developing-country governments to protect capital-goods industries and for strong anti-export biases to result from policies that sought to encourage heavy industrial development. The anti-export biases notably affected light manufacturing and agriculture.

The more micro-level DRC studies showed that many ISI projects had very low and sometimes even negative rates of return.[3]

Although the attempts to measure ERP came under heavy criticism from within the neoclassical school itself by the early 1970s,[4] the ERP and DRC studies can be regarded as having laid the groundwork for more comprehensive subsequent critiques of ISI. Probably the most influential of these was the above-mentioned study by Little, Scitovsky and Scott, which analysed the level and effects of tariff protection and other direct controls on the development of manufacturing and other sectors (particularly agriculture) in six developing countries. It also explored the scope in those countries for increasing exports and greater use of the price mechanism, i.e. for transition from inward to more outward-oriented growth. To quote André Philip, then President of the OECD Development Centre, which sponsored the study:

> The conclusions of the six volumes are clear. Emphasis should be placed on the development of exports so as to earn the foreign currency required to pay for essential imports, whether of machines, materials or food, which cannot be economically produced at home. Administrative controls should be replaced by a better use of the price mechanism; and high cost internal production should be replaced by a reorganised agriculture and industry, capable of gradually becoming competitive and assuming their place on the world market.[5]

Another influential study was that by Corden, published in 1971, which narrowed the case for economy-wide protection to the specific case of infant-industry protection. The infant-industry argument, first put forward by List in the 1840s, justified tariff protection to foster newly created industries through internal economies of scale. Corden went further than List by arguing that infant-industry protection can only be economically justified if it is temporary, and if additional distortions exist in the factor markets of the developing countries. He also noted that even then protection is not an optimal or 'first best' solution, the more efficient approach being one of using tax policies or subsidies to correct the factor-market distortions at their source.[6]

Addressing the infant-industry issue, some more recent studies have argued for protection to be geared for the promotion of export industries.[7] We return to this issue in our discussion of the 'new' trade theory below.

The policy recommendations put forward by the orthodox critics of ISI clearly reflect the general neoclassical view which stresses the importance of relying on the price mechanism in competitive markets, rather than administrative controls or planning, to achieve efficiency and maximum growth. Before reviewing the subsequent literature and debates that emerged from this view, it is therefore important to review briefly the foundations of the neoclassical view itself.

THEORETICAL FOUNDATIONS OF THE NEOCLASSICAL APPROACH

The cornerstone of the neoclassical approach to development is the classical and neoclassical theory of international trade and the concept of 'comparative advantage'. The notion of comparative advantage (or comparative cost) was first elaborated by Ricardo in the 19th century within the framework of the labour theory of value. Trade in Ricardo's model arises because of different relative labour productivities for different goods across countries, with each country tending to specialise in the production and export of goods in which it has comparatively higher labour productivity.

In the early decades of this century, Heckscher and Ohlin developed the neoclassical version of trade theory and comparative advantage.[8] The Heckscher–Ohlin model comprises two factors of production – labour and capital – and is built on a number of key assumptions: production functions differ among goods but are the same in all

countries for each good;   different goods have different facto
intensities;   there are no barriers to trade;   there is no internation
factor mobility; all factor and goods markets are perfectly competitiv
and all production functions are homogenous of the first degree.[9] Th
model's main conclusion, from a developmental perspective, is that a
countries gain from free trade and world output increases.   E
specialising in production according to its comparative advantage ar
trading, each trading country can enlarge its consumption capaci
without technical change or an increase in resources.   Th
Heckscher–Ohlin model further predicts (a) that a country will tend
export goods whose production uses relatively intensively the factor
which the country has a relative abundance, and (b) that relativ
factor-prices will tend to equalise among trading countries.[10] With
countries, the theory predicts that the gains to owners of abundal
resources, which are used more intensively in exports, will rise relativ
to those to owners of scarce resources; thus, in Third World countri
with an abundance of labour, it implies that, relative to a no-trac
situation, free trade results in a higher share of national income goi
to labour.

The Heckscher–Ohlin theory laid the foundations for the moder
neoclassical open-economy model of development.   Its factor-pric
equalisation prediction suggests that labour-abundant countries w
benefit from increased real wages and reduced capital costs throug
trade, as well as a higher share of total income going to labour.
suggests that less developed countries can develop by concentrating c
production of labour-intensive goods and land-intensive primal
products and exchanging them for more capital-intensive imports.

One of the first empirical tests of the Heckscher–Ohlin model wa
undertaken by Leontief, using an input–output matrix for the U
economy in 1947. His finding – the well-known Leontief paradox
was that the United States exports labour-intensive and impor
capital-intensive goods.[11] In defence of the Heckscher–Ohlin mode
some writers questioned the appropriateness of Leontief's data (e.
arguing that 1947 was an atypical year) and his measurement
capital.[12] Others argued that because of strong consumer preference
in the United States for capital-intensive goods, demand condition
overrode   supply   conditions   that   were   consistent   with   th
Heckscher–Ohlin model.[13] Still others argued that in fact the U
economy is natural-resources abundant, and its trade patterns refle
a comparative advantage in natural-resource-intensive products.
Others suggested the possibility of factor-intensity reversals, which le

to the empirical work using a new form of production function that assumed constant elasticity of substitution.[15]   Finally, there was Leontief's own explanation, namely that US labour was of superior quality and higher productivity than foreign labour; and it is on this human-capital type of explanation that recent research has tended to concentrate. But, despite the many attempts to explain the paradox, it still remains an area of dispute.[16]

Another important criticism of the Heckscher–Ohlin model as applied to development was that published in 1964 by Myint, who questioned the assumption of perfect competition in developing countries.[17] He pointed out that this assumption implies that market institutions are fully developed and that different sectors and markets are connected in the manner of a general equilibrium market system, while a key characteristic of underdevelopment is precisely the dualistic structure of the economy. Whereas the Heckscher–Ohlin model assumes the same production functions for producers of the same good, with the main difference between producers of different goods being differences in their production functions, this assumption seems particularly inappropriate for capturing differences between production by large-scale units using up-to-date technology in the modern sector, and that by numerous small-scale producers in the traditional sector. The latter use less up-to-date technology and are handicapped by the incomplete development of market institutions, by higher risks and costs of organising credit supplies (financial dualism), and by higher transport and transaction costs.[18]

The neoclassical approach to development theory also implies a relatively costless reallocation of factors from industries without comparative advantage to industries with comparative advantage upon liberalisation of trade. In 1963, Balogh, for example, questioned this assumption of perfect substitutability of factors between industries and of static once-and-for-all adaptation of the productive structure to the opening of trade.[19] He pointed out that the stronger trading country might take advantage of the new trade possibilities to expand its industries, leading to an 'underselling' of important industries in the weaker country. The result would be a net contraction and irremediable destruction of capital in the latter.

A closely related point is the neoclassical assumption of no unemployment or underemployment. The process just described does, of course, cause unemployment. But Balogh further observed that the static view of the trade effects as a once-and-for-all adjustment excludes a very important possible dynamic aspect as well: the recurrent displacement of the industry and exports of the weaker trading partner largely as a result of capital accumulation and technical progress by the stronger partner. The unemployment generated by this process can thus become structural in character. Moreover, trade liberalisation can shift income away from profits and savings in favour of rents accruing to landowners, thus further limiting domestic investment – already adversely affected by the 'underselling' phenomenon mentioned above – and further reducing the capacity of poor countries to compete industrially with the rich countries, while exacerbating the distribution of income within the poorer countries as well. The thrust of Balogh's pioneering theoretical analysis was further supported by the results from many empirical studies showing that the static gains from trade were likely to be very small.[20]

Finally, a number of authors argued during the 1950s and 1960s that the free working of market forces internationally is unfavourable to poor countries. Myrdal, for example, directed his attack against the factor-price-equalisation theorem.[21] His contention was that the Heckscher–Ohlin-type 'spread effects' (which allow the flow of benefits from rich to poor countries) can be outweighed by 'backwash effects' that cause increasing inequalities between rich and poor countries. But the most influential work was undoubtedly that by Prebisch and Singer, both published in 1950, on the net barter terms of trade between primary-exporting countries and exporters of manufactured goods. Their work, which we discuss more fully in Chapter 5, argued that the structure of international trade leads to declining terms of trade for poor countries relative to rich countries, and that such deterioration leads to continuing under-development.

This 'export pessimism' encouraged many developing countries to pursue relatively inward-oriented strategies to overcome the perceived secular deterioration in their terms of trade, and strengthened the emphasis many writers and policy-makers placed on industrialisation as the key to development. Moreover, it tended to be reinforced by subsequent studies, including by neoclassical economists, that pointed to the serious problems for developing countries of *instability* of export earnings (due to wide fluctuations in prices and volumes of export products) which make investment planning difficult and put a brake on growth.[22] But it attracted much criticism from orthodox writers, some of which we shall discuss below in our review of empirical work done by neoclassical writers.

ADAPTATIONS OF THE NEOCLASSICAL MODEL: GROWTH THEORY AND COST-BENEFIT ANALYSIS

The weight of the questioning of the direct applicability of the Heckscher–Ohlin model to development problems was at least partly responsible for some important adaptations of the basic neoclassical approach. One was an attempt to 'marry' Heckscher–Ohlin trade theory with neoclassical growth theory. Major contributions in this regard were another 1971 publication by Corden, which built on a lecture given by Hicks in 1953, and by Johnson, also inspired by that lecture.[23] Whereas neoclassical economists in the early postwar period had largely focused on the static gains from trade, the contribution of Hicks, Corden and the others was to draw attention to the dynamic growth-transmitting benefits to be derived from trade. In this respect, their work represents an important strengthening of the theoretical framework of the open-economy model because they attempted to counter the empirical observation that the static gains from trade were negligible.

Corden's analysis, which took into account productivity growth and increases in supplies of factors of production, identified five possible effects on growth of introducing trade: (a) the 'impact effect', i.e. the static gain, which results in a rise in current income; (b) the 'capital accumulation effect': some of the increased current income is invested, and a permanent rise in income results from the increase in capital accumulation; (c) the 'substitution effect': insofar as investment goods are import intensive, trade leads to a fall in the relative price of investment goods and the resulting substitution of investment for consumption increases growth; (d) the 'income distribution effect' which benefits the factor of production used intensively in exports: if exports are capital intensive, the savings propensity should rise and with it the rate of capital accumulation; and (e) the 'factor weight effect': if output growth is a weighted average of increases in the supplies of capital and labour, and if exports use intensively the faster-growing factor, then increased exports have a multiplier effect on growth and income. Corden pointed out that all five effects may not take place in a country that opens to trade, since they depend on local conditions of supply.

This type of analysis catalysed further work on more dynamic approaches to neoclassical trade theory, notably the work on 'stages' of comparative advantage.[24] This work argues that the resource and factor endowments of countries change over time, with the result that their comparative advantages and patterns of specialisation shift. The typical sequence or pattern, as labour surpluses are absorbed and real wages rise, is for comparative advantage to shift from simple labour-intensive goods to more skill-intensive goods, then to more physical-capital-intensive goods, more high-technology products and finally to knowledge- and human-capital-intensive goods. The argument is that as one group of developing countries moves up the chain another group can take its place at the lower level. The real significance of this work, however, as we shall see again below, is that it challenges the view that developing-country exports will run into a demand constraint in the markets of the developed countries.

It is also noteworthy that the Corden-type analysis, by remaining within the strict neoclassical framework, essentially ignored the Balogh-type analysis, which took more of a political-economy approach to analysing the implications of trade. Nor did it consider the terms-of-trade analyses, as put forward by Prebisch and Singer. Rimmer and Choucri, among others, therefore criticised Corden's approach for providing only partial and unrealistic views of the influence of trade on growth in developing countries.[25]

Project appraisal

Developments in the methodology of project appraisal and micro-level planning that took place in the early 1970s can be interpreted as another extension of the neoclassical open-economy framework. In developing countries – where insufficient development of market institutions often combines with externalities, uncertainty and risk to render markets seriously deficient as resource allocators – a major problem facing policy-makers is how to allocate scarce investment resources. In pragmatic response to the deficiencies of the market, and in implicit or explicit recognition that in developing countries social costs and benefits may seriously diverge from private costs and benefits, governments and donor agencies alike increasingly turned during the 1970s to extensive use of social cost-benefit techniques of appraisal of investment projects.

The path-breaking study in this area of applied welfare economics was the Little and Mirrlees *Manual of Industrial Project Analysis*, published in 1968 by the OECD Development Centre. It was followed in 1972 by the UNIDO *Guidelines for Project Evaluation*, and in 1974 by a revised version of the OECD Little and Mirrlees manual.[26]

Two crucial links between the project appraisal techniques and the neoclassical approach to development can be identified. First, is the net-present-value criterion for investment decisions. This criterion is based on the neoclassical assumptions that economic agents possess complete information; that markets are fully functional; that there are no externalities or interdependencies among projects; and that there are no distortions in the economy.

Second, Little and Mirrlees recommended the use of world prices as shadow prices for traded goods. For a small country, this meant that C.I.F. prices should be used for imports and F.O.B. prices for exports. By contrast, for a large country, the marginal import cost is used for imports and the marginal export revenue for exports. The justification for using world prices as shadow prices for traded goods is that they represent a set of opportunities open to a country and the actual terms on which it can trade. Underlying this is the idea that many developing countries are far from their optimum trade potential (as a result of following an import-substituting policy which requires the imposition of tariffs during the infancy period of a new industry). Little and Mirrlees' argument is that a welfare gain could be obtained if the country switched towards free trade policies. Hence, by constructing a system of shadow prices for appraising projects incorporating a pro-trade bias, they are implicitly also mapping out a case for free trade and supply-side adjustment along neoclassical lines.[27] This extension of neoclassical thought in a 'pragmatic' direction was in part to counter early criticism from reformist, dependency and Marxist thinkers – some of whom we review below – that neoclassical economics had limited relevance for developing countries because it naively approached, or even neglected, many important problems within these countries.

The 'cost-benefit' approach

The development of project-appraisal techniques in turn gave rise to what has been called the cost-benefit approach to development economics. This approach was spelled out in a 1983 paper by one of its leading proponents, Harberger, who recommends the comprehensive use of social cost-benefit analysis throughout the economy of a developing country.[28] Thus, what originated as a technique of appraising individual micro-level projects was transformed into an approach to country-wide planning covering both the public and private sectors. This type of project-centred 'planning' may in fact require more resources and manpower to implement than the present system of macro-economic planning in use in many developing countries. An even more serious problem, moreover, is that while the technique may be useful in evaluating intra-sectoral resource allocation, it is of little use in examining inter-sectoral investment decisions.

Despite many criticisms of social cost-benefit analysis – that it biases project choice against 'soft' sectors such as health and education, that it does not adequately deal with poverty elimination, and that it is badly applied or not applied at all[29] – it forms the micro-economic component in government decision-making within the overall neoclassical approach. At the macro-level the Heckscher–Ohlin model and the neoclassical theories of trade and growth are relied upon to justify policies of free trade. Particularly important in this regard have been the numerous empirical studies of the conditions for export-led growth to which we turn shortly.

Before leaving our discussion of the theoretical foundations of the neoclassical approach, however, it is important to note that the numerous criticisms levelled at this approach, both from within the orthodox literature and from heterodox writers, have stimulated considerable reaction from defenders of the neoclassical approach. Some defenders have argued that whereas neoclassical economics has become more precise in its use of mathematics and application of econometrics, 'development economics ... has relied upon large doses of casual empiricism, fairly unrigorous theorising and an eclectic approach to related social sciences'.[30] More recently and more importantly, others, notably Lal in his 1983 book on *The Poverty of Development Economics*, have argued that the policies suggested by 'development economics' are theoretically wrong and practically unsound: countries following these policies (mainly government intervention, such as central planning and redistribution-with-growth strategies) have had bad economic records compared to those (mainly South Korea and Taiwan) which, he argues, followed the neoclassical path. He thus concludes that 'the demise of development economics is likely to be conducive to the health of both the economics and the economies of developing countries'.[31] He includes on his list of non-neoclassical economists (who one may thus infer are on his list of development economists) such authors as Hirschman, Chenery and Nurkse. He also of course condemns the likes of Balogh, Myrdal, Singer, Streeten and Stewart.

Lal further argues that market failure does not by itself justify government intervention because government failure and inefficiency make things worse. In addition to his faith in private enterprise, the clear policy prescription running through his text is that 'of getting the prices right', i.e., relying on the price mechanism to promote an efficient allocation of resources. Underlying Lal's position is the view that neoclassical concepts and methods should be unambiguously applied to policy problems of poor countries.

Lal's position has in turn provoked considerable response, notably from Stewart in 1984.[32] She reiterates the argument that the theoretical welfare foundations of the neoclassical policy prescriptions advocated by Lal and others are weak. Her view can be sketched as follows: Neoclassical economics and its policy prescription that an unimpaired price system leads to optimum resource allocation are concerned with studying static equilibrium situations. In the first place, in a static context, concerns of externalities, income distribution, indivisibilities and economies of scale all pose serious problems for the neoclassical framework. Moreover, in practice, economies are in a state of continuous disequilibrium, and it is *dynamic aspects* (factors affecting growth) that are of concern to all countries. After discussing a list of special problems of applying the neoclassical framework to developing countries, she concludes: 'Taking all these together, there is no theoretical basis for concluding that an undistorted price system will lead to a higher level of welfare than one containing various government interventions'.[33]

Also, in response to Lal's wish for the incorporation of development analysis into the mainstream of orthodox economics, Toye, for example, has argued that development economics has to be established 'as one interdependent element in the multi-disciplinary undertaking which we call development studies'. Further, he says, the core of development studies is 'an intellectual commitment to find the causes of the persistence of inequality and poverty on a world-wide scale'.[34]

EMPIRICAL STUDIES

The neoclassical view of development can thus be summarised as follows. Many developing countries, influenced by the 'export pessimism' of the 1950s and 1960s and by the supposed merits of ISI, adopted inward-looking strategies aimed at developing a modern industrial sector through protectionism, government planning and other direct incentives whose combined effect was a strong anti-export bias. But the 'easy' phase of ISI (namely the production of consumer goods) ended in the 1960s, and many countries faced serious problems, including inefficient industries, foreign-exchange shortages and a bias against agriculture. A few countries – notably South Korea, Taiwan –

wisely switched to outward-looking strategies, while others stubbornly and unwisely stuck to inward-looking ISI. The former group have shown themselves to be markedly more successful in terms of growth, employment, income distribution, balance of payments and structural change.

Beyond the above-mentioned criticisms of ISI that grew out of measures of ERP and DRC, a second strand of criticism was directed at the 'export pessimism' thesis, notably the work by Prebisch and Singer. Numerous authors found fault during the 1960s and 1970s with the argument that there is a secular decline in the terms of international trade for primary commodities. Detailed and comprehensive re-investigations of this issue carried out more recently do, however, point to a long-term deterioration prior to the Second World War (although Prebisch's figures appear to have overstated the decline) followed by a sharp rise around the War and then a deteriorating trend since the 1950s, excluding petroleum.[35]

Another important debate on which neoclassical empirical analysis has focused is the role of trade as engine or handmaiden of growth. An early participant in this debate was Nurkse, who argued that during the 19th century trade served as an engine of growth for countries like the United States, Australia and Argentina (which responded to the great increase in European demands for foodstuffs and raw materials) but who was pessimistic about the possibilities for trade to do the same for developing countries after the War; indeed, his work contributed to the 'export pessimism' of the 1950s and 1960s. Nurkse's thesis was tested empirically by Kravis, in a 1970 article on 'Trade as a Handmaiden of Growth', whose main conclusions were three: First, export success is not dependent on world demand as such. Second, countries that have been successful exporters have been more successful at diversifying their exports (notably by employing pro-trade policies that help build up and diversify local supply capabilities). And third, countries that had carried out the supply-oriented reforms were those that had high growth rates. He thus concluded that trade is not an engine but a handmaiden of growth.[36]

More recent empirical studies focusing on the relationship between exports and growth include those of Michaely and Balassa, published in 1977 and 1978 respectively. Michaely, who looked at the correlation between the marginal export-output ratio and per capita GDP growth during the period 1950–1973 for 41 developing countries, found a strong correlation for 23 countries with per capita incomes above $300, and a very weak correlation for the poorest countries.[37] Balassa, who calculated the correlation coefficient between GDP growth (net of exports) and export growth for 11 developing countries, found a significant correlation for the late 1960s and early 1970s.[38] Both studies thus pointed to positive dynamic effects of exports on growth, as suggested by the theoretical literature discussed earlier, and supported the case for outward-oriented economic policies.

But it is also noteworthy that whereas Balassa found both the ratio of exports to GDP and the changes in the ratio to be statistically significant, Michaely found the latter but not the former. Moreover, Heller and Porter obtained statistically significant results using the same 41 countries studied by Michaely, but when they ran the test again after omitting the seven strongest cases they did not obtain a significant correlation between growth of exports and non-exported GNP.[39] Their work pointed to the dependence of results of such empirical tests on the choice of countries and time period. Kirkpatrick and Nixon, arguing from outside the neoclassical paradigm, further discuss the statistical problems associated with this approach; but, they conclude, 'the more fundamental objection to this form of study is that it provides no insight into the characteristics and pattern of growth – its employment effects, the distribution of gains between foreign and domestic interests, the type of output produced and the techniques of production used'.[40]

A third group of empirical studies has focused on the problems of transition to open regimes and on the performance of countries with such regimes. The most influential study has probably been that co-directed by Krueger and Bhagwati with the support of the US National Bureau of Economic Research, published in 1978.[41] The study looked at 22 experiences of trade liberalisation by ten countries over the 1952–1972 period, all involving combinations of freer exchange rates and reduced tariffs. It considered the effects of devaluation and trade liberalisation, and compared exchange-control regimes and their effects across countries.

Among the most influential findings of this study, one was a refutation of the ill effects of devaluation. Many had argued that devaluation is normally followed by recession, and that devaluation is often inflationary as well. Krueger and Bhagwati argue that post-devaluation recession is often caused by other policies, notably those designed to curb inflation or to limit imports, and that inflation often results from expansionary monetary policies. They also found that quantitative trade restrictions (e.g., quotas) are more protective than many governments realise or intend, and that under such regimes devaluation and complementary policies can decrease but not reverse the pro-import substitution (or anti-export) bias. Major improvement in export performance are obtained, they argue, by sustained liberalisation (defined as a shift from quantitative restrictions to price intervention) followed by devaluation. They also call for a variety o incentives to exporters (to encourage them to export) and a strong and clearly demonstrated government commitment to an outward-oriented strategy.

Subsequent research by Balassa, conducted during 1981-1982 for the World Bank, complements the Krueger–Bhagwati study.[42] Balassa's work looks at the effects of export-incentive systems – protection and fiscal and credit preferences – in six semi-industrial developing countries for 1960–1973, and estimates their effects on such performance indicators as growth, resource allocation and trade. He then makes a series of policy prescriptions for developing countries attempting to industrialise and export. Recommended trade policies include optima export taxes (for goods with less than infinitely elastic foreign demand) and equality of incentives (e.g., export subsidies) to all manufacturing enterprises. Credit and labour policies are to reduce distortions while compensating for the underdeveloped state of these markets by, for example, eliminating credit rationing, increasing real interest rates, subsidising use of unskilled labour and using more rational pricing systems for public utilities. Balassa argues that these measures increase growth, improve resource allocation and create employment.[43]

Numerous empirical studies, finally, have focused on the economic performances of South Korea, Taiwan, Singapore and Hong Kong. Writing in 1979 on the experiences of these countries, Little sums up well the position put forward by many of these studies: 'The major lesson is that labour-intensive export-oriented policies, which amounted to almost free-trade conditions for exporters, were the prime cause of an extremely rapid and labour-intensive industrialisation which revolutionised in a decade the lives of more than 50 million people, including the poorest among them'.[44] Important contributions by Ranis and Balassa, both published in 1981, echoed Little's view that the growth of the East Asian 'super-exporters' could be attributed to policies of free trade and to the removal of anti-export biases facing exporters.[45] Collectively, these neoclassical writers have thus conveyed the strong policy message that if other developing countries were to liberalise their economies to trade, they could replicate the success of the 'first generation' East Asian newly industrialising economies (NIEs).

Other orthodox writers have been more eclectic, or more critical of the neoclassical interpretation of the experiences of South Korea and

Taiwan, however. Adelman, for example, has argued that Korea's achievement of 'growth with equity' is attributable not only to the country's labour-intensive export policies but also to significant land reform, on the one hand, and to policies favouring widespread education and human-resources development on the other.[46] The latter point has also been emphasized by more recent studies showing that the rapid industrial take-off and export success of the East Asian NIEs was fuelled by heavy investments in human skills and technological capital aimed at creating (a) a literate workforce responsive to intensive on- and off-the-job training, (b) a pool of highly skilled middle-level technical manpower able to absorb and build on imported technologies, and (c) adequately staffed R&D departments in firms and government-funded institutes closely related to industry.[47]

Some writers have also stressed the importance of massive flows of US aid to Korea from the 1940s to the mid-1960s and the expansive international environment of the 1960s.[48] Still others point to Korea's geographical and historical proximity to Japan and the latter's major redeployment of some labour-intensive industries (e.g., textiles) to Korea for export to North America during a crucial period of Korea's development.

Some critics, furthermore, charge the neoclassical view with misinterpreting both the importance of ISI and the role of the State in these countries' export-oriented industrialisation. It is argued, for example, that ISI in Korea and Taiwan continued into the 1960s and 1970s even though the new thrust of policy was on export-led growth, and that export promotion was a means of exploiting industrial potential built up during the previous ISI stage.[49]

As regards the role of the State, furthermore, a major 1980 study on Korea by Jones and Sakong found that the 'Korean miracle' is more the result of a close interaction between the State and private enterprise than of the working of the free market. Korean culture and history, they argue, were responsible for providing a substantial class of entrepreneurs, and it was via the actions of the State that this entrepreneurial creativity was released. The State directly participated in the process of industrialisation by ownership of public enterprises and, more importantly, played an invaluable role by stimulating, guiding (e.g. through credit rationing) and controlling private firms.[50] This view of the importance of the visible hand of the State as opposed to the invisible hand of the market has been reiterated by other studies including a 1981 paper by Datta-Chaudhuri, a 1982 article by Streeten, several studies published in 1984 and 1985 by the Institute of Development Studies at Sussex University, and Amsden's major recent study of Korea.[51] The

thrust of these studies is to highlight the special features behind th
impressive performance of the four East Asian NIEs, and ultimately t
question the transferability of their development experience to othe
developing countries.

A number of recent studies have also faulted the Krueger–Bhagwati–
Balassa approach, finally, for paying too little attention to the question o
the timing and sequencing of policies to liberalise trade. A series o
studies edited by Choksi and Papageorgiou, for example, looked at 3
episodes of trade liberalisation in 19 countries and found that the mor
inward-oriented are the initial policies of a country that attempts t
liberalise, the greater will be the costs of liberalisation in terms o
unemployment and adverse changes in income distribution. It conclude
that particular attention should be given to such questions as the speed o
reform (one-shot or gradual removal of protection), its sequencing, an
the role of complementary policies (e.g., anti-inflationary measures
exchange-rate policy and direct export incentives, income-maintenanc
programmes). It also pointed out that a poorly designed liberalisatio
programme which results in high social costs relative to the economi
returns in the short run faces the danger of abandonment.[52]

Other useful contributions to the debate on the timing and sequencing
of liberalisation policies include those by Edwards, Mussa, Bruno
Dornbusch, Fischer and Sachs.[53]   Nevertheless, while there i
considerable agreement on the goal of trade liberalisation, there is littl
consensus on how to achieve it. While many authors focus on the
economic aspects of the transition from a closed to an open economy, a
recurring theme is that of the social and political constraints which are
sometimes deeply rooted in history, ethnic divisions, etc. The mair
conclusion, put forward by Choksi and Papageorgiou as well, seems to
be that policies for the transition to an open economy must be designec
on a country-specific basis with careful attention to how alternative
approaches to liberalisation are likely to affect such groups as smal
peasants, landless labourers, fixed-wage earners, civil servants
industrialists, etc. There is no simple answer to the question of how bes
to make the transition from a closed to an open economy.

THE POLICY IMPACT OF THE NEOCLASSICAL RESURGENCE

One of the most far-reaching effects of the neoclassical resurgence
during the 1980s has been its influence in the conditionality of 'structura

adjustment' lending by the World Bank. The Bank's programme of Structural Adjustment Loans (SAL) began in 1979 and was reportedly designed to fill a gap in the international capital market by providing long-term loans to support structural change in poor countries. SAL are conditional both on the borrower agreeing to an IMF standby facility, which carries the IMF conditionality of proceeding with a 'stabilisation' programme, and the borrower agreeing to introduce supply-side measures, particularly to increase exports. Although the precise nature of the stabilisation policies and supply-side measures varies from country to country, their conceptual framework is clearly that of the neoclassical outward-oriented approach.

The strong influence of neoclassical thinking is thus found, for example, in World Bank reports of the 1980s on sub-saharan Africa. These reports typically call for a 'joint programme of action' embodying four major themes: (a) using pricing policy more widely in place of administrative controls to allocate resources, (b) reducing the burden on governments by greater use of community efforts and the private sector, so that governments can undertake their central responsibilities more efficiently, (c) privatising state enterprise and giving more responsibility to managers of para-statals to operate their enterprises in a business-like manner, and (d) avoiding discrimination against exporting.[54]

The influence of neoclassical policy prescriptions is also of course clearly visible in the conditions attached to IMF loans to developing countries. Traditionally these conditions have concerned short-term macro-economic adjustment focusing on monetary and fiscal policies that restrict demand, with the efficacy of the competitive market and the price system relied on to achieve stable and balanced economic growth in the long run.[55] IMF conditionality has often been widened in recent years, however, to include such supply-side objectives as the elimination of internal price distortions, the removal of controls on interest rates and capital markets, and the deregulation of the exchange rate and liberalisation of trade.[56]

In addition to this strong indirect influence, through the World Bank and the IMF, the direct influence of the neoclassical resurgence on policy orientation in developing countries has also been quite widespread – undoubtedly enhanced by the slowdown of world growth since 1973.[57] and the debt crisis faced by many developing countries since 1982. While the number of countries where one can see this influence is large – from Kenya and the Ivory Coast in Africa to Sri Lanka and India in Asia, for example – it is the relatively extreme international monetarist experiences of the southern-cone countries of

South America (Chile, Argentina and Uruguay), pursued under military dictatorships during the latter half of the 1970s and the early 1980s, which have received the most international attention.

The effectiveness of the IMF's stabilisation policies and the World Bank's SAL programme, as well as the experiences of the southern-cone countries, have also come in for criticism within the orthodox literature. The basic argument of the critics – including Killik, Dornbush, Taylor and Fishlow – is that 'stabilisation' and 'structural adjustment' programmes frequently aggravate the problems they are supposed to solve, or cause serious undesirable side effects. Dornbush, for example, has pointed out that attempts to solve balance-of-payments deficits and to control inflation in Latin America with devaluations and restrictive monetary policies have had perverse effects, resulting in high real interest rates and overvalued exchange rates that aggravated macro-economic imbalances.[58]   Along similar lines, Fishlow has identified three major limitations of international monetarism as practised in Latin America: short-term application of what are, at best, long-term equilibrium conditions; inadequate attention to distinct components of the balance of payments; and focus on macro-economic equilibria rather than on economic development.[59]

Not surprisingly, less orthodox economists have been even more virulent in their critique. According to Foxley, for example, the monetarist stabilisation experiments of Argentina, Chile and Uruguay were accompanied by a radical transformation of society with exorbitant social costs: unemployment reached high levels and has stayed there, wages have lagged behind prices, and income distribution has deteriorated.[60] These problems, he argues, were caused both by the inadequacies of the stabilisation policies and by the pressures from radical conservatives for structural and institutional changes as well as for macro-economic adjustment policies. With policy consistency made difficult as a result of the urge to proceed on all fronts – the adjustment process turns out to be longer than anticipated and produces the painful social costs cited above – government recourse to extensive foreign borrowing became necessary both to keep the economic programmes afloat and to help finance military expenditures, including for local repression.

Similar arguments emerged at the World Bank's 1985 London Symposium on its role and recovery in the developing world.[61] Several participants expressed reservations about the Bank's promotion of privatisation and economic liberalisation in developing countries. Toye, for example, argued for slow liberalisation in a context of slow world growth and growing protectionism; he also warned against liberalisation for purely ideological reasons. Others pointed out that although the Asian NIEs may have liberalised economically, they have combined state intervention with repressive policies towards the political opposition and trade-union movements.

The 'new export pessimism'

Finally, in addition to the criticism of the IMF's stabilisation policies, the World Bank's SAL programme and international monetarism, there has also emerged what can loosely be described as a new export pessimism. In the 1960s and early 1970s, during the period of world economic prosperity and rapid expansion of trade, neoclassical economists charged the old export pessimists (notably Prebisch, Singer, Nurkse and Myrdal) with having made an error of judgement. World trade was accelerating and both the developed and developing countries achieved annual GDP growth rates averaging about 5 per cent during the period 1950–1973. But, somewhat ironically, the tide of postwar prosperity has turned since the mid-1970s, with GDP growth in the OECD region slowing to an annual average of about 2.4 per cent during 1973–1987. And of course, slower secular growth rates cast a shadow of doubt on the future export prospects of developing countries, both in primary products and manufactured goods. These prospects have been further adversely affected by rising protectionist pressures in the OECD region, particularly since the early 1980s.

Thus, already in 1980, in his Nobel lecture on 'The Slowing Down of the Engine of Growth', Lewis warned of the problems of slower world growth for developing countries. Noting the considerable capacity of more advanced developing countries to produce capital equipment, his response was to call for expanded south–south trade.[62] Various UN agencies, notably UNIDO and UNCTAD, have given considerable attention in the 1980s to the prospects for greater trade among developing countries as well.[63]

Other authors, William Cline for example, have argued that it is wrong to assume that what has worked for a few NIEs could work for many developing countries if they all pursue export-oriented industrialisation strategies simultaneously.[64] At the same time, studies of likely trends in US trade policy, by the Overseas Development Council for example, have emphasized that protectionism could get worse.[65] The net result, notwithstanding the findings of Krueger–Bhag-wati–Balassa and the critics of the 'new export pessimists',[66] has been to call into question the appropriateness of advocating development strategies that are highly dependent on the achievement of high rates of export growth.

Louis Emmerij, among others, has also drawn attention to the correlation between the movement in the West towards a neo-conservative political philosophy that stresses supply-side economics and the rolling-back of the welfare-state at home, and towards bilateralism in international relations that is marked by growing protectionism and 'managed' trade. As regards the developed countries' relations with developing countries, this bilateralism is more clearly marked by national self-interest, as conceived by the neo-conservative philosophy, and by diminished flows of aid (and a more political orientation of aid) and by growing protectionism as well.[67] Indeed, the growth of bilateralism and 'neo-mercantilism' has raised skepticism among developing as well as developed countries about the ability of multilateral negotiations under GATT to achieve trade liberalisation, at a time when developing countries are particularly concerned about future access to export markets in the OECD region. This concern is only exacerbated by talk of 'fortress Europe' after 1992, and especially by the continuing inability of the United States to reduce its huge fiscal and trade deficits.

THE 'NEW' TRADE THEORY AND STRATEGIC TRADE POLICY

It is in this context, moreover, that the very foundation of the neoclassical approach to development – the view that international trade is driven by comparative advantage, which is determined by relative factor endowments, and that free trade is optimal for all countries – has been brought into question by advances in trade theory since the early 1980s. The 'new' trade theory relaxes the neoclassical assumptions of perfect competition and of constant or diminishing returns to scale, and looks at the implications for trade policy of international oligopolies and increasing returns to scale. The basic message is that, under certain circumstances, a government can raise national income by 'targeting' industries and intervening in international competition on behalf of domestic firms. Such targeting – e.g. through subsidies, import protection or even export taxes, depending on specific circumstances – can tilt the terms of international oligopolistic rivalry so as to shift monopolistic rents or the benefits of positive externalities (e.g. moving rapidly down the 'learning curve') from foreign to domestic firms. Strategic government trade and industrial policies can, under certain circumstances, play a role analogous to strategic moves by firms, such as investment in excess capacity or R&D, as shown by standard models of oligopolistic rivalry.[68]

The origins of strategic trade theory can be traced to the much stronger growth of intra-industry trade than of inter-industry trade in Europe after the formation of the Common Market, and especially to the speed and success of Japan's transformation from a lagging to a leading industrial power and exporter. But it is widely recognised that the shift of the US political mood in the early to mid-1980s towards greater protectionism was what allowed the new trade theory to attract such widespread attention. Not only did the new theory recognise the importance of international policy rivalry as such, it shed valuable light on the role in international competition of such factors as entrepreneurial initiative and 'first mover' advantages,[69] investment in human capital, R&D, economies of scale and learning by doing, especially in the so-called 'leading edge', 'high growth' and 'high tech' industries. As Dixit pointed out in 1986, when summarising the apparent implications of the new theory for trade policy:

> Recent research contains support for almost all the vocal and popular views on trade policy that only a few years ago struggled against the economists' conventional wisdom of free trade. Now the mercantilist arguments for restricting imports and promoting exports are being justified... The fears that other governments could capture permanent advantage in industry after industry by giving each a small initial impetus down the learning curve now emerge as results of impeccable formal models. The claim that one's own government should be aggressive in the pursuit of such policies because other governments do the same is no longer dismissed as a non sequitur.[70]

Most relevant for our purposes is undoubtedly the strategic infant-industry argument developed by Krugman.[71] In our earlier discussion of Corden and traditional trade theory, we noted that support for infant-industry protection was limited to the case of distortions in domestic factor markets. The three main 'domestic distortions' are imperfections in the capital market that make it impossible (or too expensive) for potentially profitable new industries to get started; external benefits of learning by doing that occur when pioneering firms cannot retain the workers they train during the start-up phase; and external benefits of learning by doing that result from knowledge diffusion, which again may be particularly significant during the infancy stage of an industry. We also noted that while temporary import protection and/or export subsidies may under these circumstances have some justification, according to traditional trade theory, they are 'second best' solutions to such domestic distortions; the optimum response is through such domestic policies as loan guarantees, training assistance or subsidies for R&D. Krugman radically redirected the focus of the argument by pointing out that under conditions of international oligopoly and increasing returns to scale, a government that gives a privileged position to a domestic firm may be able to provide it with a scale advantage in production that translates into a cost advantage vis-à-vis a foreign rival, hence a greater market share, even in unprotected overseas markets. Krugman thus concluded that import protection can, under some circumstances, be an export promotion device.

It should also be noted, however, that the late 1980s have witnessed considerable dampening of the original excitement over the new trade theory. The reasons reportedly include a realisation that the apparent policy implications of models of strategic trade policy are highly sensitive to changes in the specific assumptions of these models (regarding market structure and firm behaviour for example); the difficulty of identifying real-world situations in which the specific assumptions apply; the recognition that the costs of implementing strategic trade policies can easily exceed the benefits, even if appropriate 'target' industries can be identified; and the apprehension that economic theory was becoming a supplier of intellectual ammunition for powerful forces that favour protection of particular sectors for the 'wrong' reasons (i.e. 'special interest' groups).[72]

The policy applicability of the new trade theory for many developing countries seems even more problematic. The strategic argument for infant-industry protection, for example, assumes a relatively large domestic market, which does not apply to many developing countries.[73] Of course, the importance of having a large home market in order to be able to take advantage of the potential benefits of strategic trade policy, or at least respond to the strategic policies pursued by others, may reinforce the re-emerging perception in many developing countries of the importance of regional integration in the South. This perception has certainly been strengthened in recent years by the acceleration of movements towards increased regional integration in Europe, North America and Pacific Asia, as noted already in Chapter 1. But the main policy implication would seem to be that growing protectionism and 'managed trade' in the OECD region is even more of a threat than many developing countries may have realised.

Notes and References

1. J. Viner, *International Trade and Economic Development*, Clarendon Press, Oxford, 1953; G. Haberler, 'Some Problems in the Pure Theory of International Trade' in *Economic Journal*, June 1950; and P.T. Bauer and B.S. Yamey, *Markets, Market Control and Marketing Reform*, London, 1968.

2. R. Soligo and J.S. Stern, 'Tariff Protection; Import Substitution and Investment Efficiency' in *Pakistan Development Review*, Summer, 1965; I.M.D.. Little, T. Scitovsky and M.F.G. Scott, *Industry and Trade in Some Developing Countries*, Oxford University Press for the OECD Development Centre, London, 1970; and B. Balassa, *The Structure of Protection in Developing Countries*, Johns Hopkins University Press, Baltimore, 1971.

3. An early application of the DRC measure can be found in A.O. Krueger, 'Some Economic Costs of Exchange Control: The Turkish Case' in *Journal of Political Economy*, October 1966; see also Little, Scitovsky and Scott (1970), *ibid*. A more recent study is F. Yagci, *Protection and Incentives in Turkish Manufacturing: An Evaluation of Policies and their Impact in 1981*, in World Bank Staff Working Paper No. 660, Washington D.C., 1984.

4. The critique ran as follows: First, there are competing formulations of ERP measurements, and even by employing all of them it is difficult to say for certain that when comparing two industries, resources will be attracted to the industry with the higher ERP. Second, there is no reason to measure the ERP if there are no revenue reasons for tariffs. Third, even if revenue reasons exist and one were to design an optimal tax system, since it would have to take into account all the necessary elasticities (of demand, supply and substitution) the ERP would be just a by-product; hence there would be no reason to measure it. See V.K. Ramaswami and T.N. Srinivasan in V.K. Ramaswami, ed., *Trade and Development*, Allen and Unwin, London, 1971.

5. Little, Scitovsky and Scott (1970), *op. cit.*, Preface.

6. A good account of Friedrich List's original infant industry argument and Max Corden's adaptation of it can be found in W.M. Corden, *The Theory of Protection*, Oxford University Press, London, 1971.

7. See for example, W. Wolfgang, 'The Infant-Export Industry Argument' in *Canadian Journal of Economics*, Vol. 17, 1984.

8. Much has been written on the Heckscher-Ohlin model in both standard textbooks and journals on international development. A useful exposition of the model is R.W. Jones, 'Factor Proportions and the Heckscher-Ohlin Theory' in *Review of Economic Studies*, January 1956.

For a review of later work on comparative advantage in the context of developing countries, see for example A.O. Krueger, 'Comparative Advantage and Development Policy 20 Years Later' in M. Syrquin, L. Taylor and L.E. Westphal, eds., *Economic Structure and Performance*, Academic Press, New York, 1984.

9. A production function sets out the relationship between the output of a good and the inputs necessary to produce the output. In a relatively simple case, output is expressed as a function of capital, labour and technical progress. A production function that is homogenous of the first degree (also known as linearly homogeneous) exhibits constant returns to scale. This implies that multiplying inputs by a constant, x, simply increases output by the same proportion.

10. Ohlin argued that full mobility of goods can serve as a partial substitute for factor mobility and will lead to a partial equalisation of factor prices. Samuelson took this analysis further by demonstrating that as long as there is partial specialisation between countries, factor prices will be equalised absolutely and relatively by international trade. For details of this proof of factor price equalisation, see P.A. Samuelson, 'International Factor-Price Equalisation Once Again' in *Economic Journal*, June 1949.

11. For a full account of the Leontief paradox, and some of the explanations behind it, see R.M. Stern, 'Testing Trade Theories in International Trade and Finance' in P. Kenen, ed., *International Trade and Finance: Frontiers for Research*, Cambridge University Press, Cambridge, 1975.

12. G.A. Loeb, 'Capital Shortage and Labour Surplus in the United States' in *Review of Economics and Statistics*, Vol. 36, August 1954.

13. S. Valavanis-Vail, 'Leontief's Scarce Factor Paradox' in *Journal of Political Economy*, Vol. 54, December 1954.

14. E. Hoffmeyer, 'The Leontief Paradox Critically Examined' in *The Manchester School of Economic and Social Studies*, Vol. 26, May 1958.

15. The CES production function is linearly homogeneous with a constant elasticity of substitution for the factors of production. It was first set out in K. Arrow, H.B. Chenery, B. Minhas and R. Solow, 'Capital-Labour Substitution and Economic Efficiency' in *Review of Economic Studies*, 1961.

16. Much more recently, a number of studies have attempted to empirically trace the sources of comparative advantage within a neoclassical framework. See for example, UNIDO, *International Comparative Advantage in Manufacturing: Changing Profiles of Resources and Trade*, Vienna, 1986; and E. Leamer, *Sources of International Comparative Advantage: Theory and Evidence*, MIT Press, 1984. On computable general equilibrium models, see H. Scarf and J. Shoven, eds., *Applied General Equilibrium Analysis*, Cambridge University Press, 1984; and K. Dervis, J. de Melo and S. Robinson, *General Equilibrium Models for Development Policy*, Cambridge University Press, 1982.

17. For some of the early criticism by Myint, see H. Myint, *The Economics of the Developing Countries*, Hutchinson University Library, London, 1964.

18. In his later work, Myint adapted the standard trade model to take into account the dualistic economic structure of developing countries. This analysis is set in a diagrammatic framework using neoclassical analytical

methods: H. Myint, 'The Place of Institutional Changes in International Trade Theory in the Setting of Underdeveloped Economies' in B. Ohlin *et al.*, *The International Allocation of Economic Activity*, MacMillan, London, 1979.

19. T. Balogh, *Unequal Partners*, Basil Blackwell, Oxford, 1963.

20. Much of the early empirical evidence to support the view that the static gains from trade are small emerged from the debate over trade creation or trade diversion in customs unions. See H.G. Johnson, 'The Gains from Freer Trade with Europe: An Estimate' in *The Manchester School*, September 1958; B. Balassa, 'Trade Creation and Trade Diversion in the European Common Market' in *Economic Journal*, March 1967; and E.A. Farag, 'The Latin American Free Trade Area' in *Inter-American Economic Affairs*, Vol. 17, No. 1, Summer 1963.

21. G. Myrdal, *An International Economy: Problems and Prospects*, Harper, New York, 1956; and G. Myrdal, *Rich Lands and Poor*, Harper, New York, 1957.

22. To mitigate the adverse effects of export instability on economic growth, international commodity agreements and buffer stock schemes have been proposed. For an extended discussion of the debate over export instability, see for example, P. Athukorala and F.C.H. Huynh, *Export Instability and Growth: Problems and Prospects for Developing Economies*, Croom Helm, London, 1987.

23. J.R. Hicks, 'An Inaugural Lecture' in *Oxford Economic Papers*, Vol. 5, No. 2, June 1953; W.M. Corden, 'The Effects of Trade on the Rate of Growth' in J.N. Bhagwati, *et al., Trade, Balance of Payments and Growth*, North-Holland, Amsterdam, 1971. For a more recent survey of the subject of trade and growth, see R. Findlay, 'Growth and Development in Trade Models' in R.W. Jones and P.B. Kenen, eds., *Handbook of International Economics*, North-Holland, Amsterdam, 1984.

24. See for example, B. Balassa, 'A Stages Approach to Comparative Advantage', paper presented at the Fifth World Congress of the International Economic Association, Tokyo, 1977.

25. D. Rimmer, 'The Abstraction from Politics: A Critique of Economic Theory and Design with Reference to West Africa' in *Journal of Development Studies*, Vol. 5, No. 3, 1969; and N. Choucri, 'International Political Economy: A Theoretical Perspective' in O.R. Holsti, R. Siverson and A.L. George, eds., *Change in the International System*, Westview Press, Boulder, 1980.

26. I.M.D. Little and J.A. Mirrlees, *Manual of Industrial Project Analysis*, OECD Development Centre, Paris, 1968; I.M.D. Little and J.A. Mirrlees, *Project Appraisal and Planning for Developing Countries*, Heinemann, London, 1974; and UNIDO, *Guidelines for Project Evaluation*, United Nations, New York, 1972.

27. The link between the neoclassical open-economy approach and project appraisal is made explicit by Little. 'It should by now be evident that investement planning criteria and the analysis of comparative advantage, originally two separate specialisations in economics, have come together. This is as it should be, since in an open economy, they must be the same thing. A planner cannot rationally ignore comparative advantage,

although he, or his political masters, may believe some inputs to be advantageous even when they show up very badly in the typical economist's calculus, which regards personal utilities as the only objective'. I.M.D. Little, *Economic Development*, Basic Books, New York, 1982, p. 138.

28. A.C. Harberger, 'The Cost-Benefit Approach to Development Economics' in *World Development*, Vol. 11, No. 10, 1983. Also see D. Lal, *The Poverty of Development Economics*, Institute of Economic Affairs London, 1983, Chapters 1 and 4.

29. The system of project appraisal has been severely criticised, for example by: B.J. Lecomte, *Project Aid*, OECD Development Centre, Paris, 1986; D.A. Rondinelli, *Development Projects as Policy Experiments*, Methuen London, 1983; N.H. Leff, 'The Use of Policy Science Tools in Public Sector Decision making: Social Cost Benefit Analysis in the World Bank in *Kyklos*, Vol. 38, Fasc 1, 1985; and W. Haque, N. Metha, A. Rahman P. Wignaraja, 'Micro-level Development: Design and Evaluation of Rural Development Projects' in *Development Dialogue*, Vol. 2, 1977.

30. S. Lall, 'Conflicts of Concepts: Welfare Economics and Developing Countries' in *World Development*, Vol. 4, No. 3, 1976, p. 181.

31. D. Lal (1983), *op. cit.*, p. 138.

32. F. Stewart, 'Limitations of the Neoclassical Approach to Development: A Review of Deepak Lal: 'The Poverty of Development Economics'', *SOAS/UCL Development Seminar Paper 64*, 1984, reprinted in *Journal of Development Studies*, 1985. See also T. Killick, 'Twenty-five years in Development: The Rise and Impending Decline of Market Solutions' in *Development Policy Review*, Vol. 4, No. 2, 1986. K. Griffin, 'On Misreading Development Economics' in *Third World Quarterly*, April 1984.

33. Stewart (1984), *ibid.*, p. 5.

34. J. Toye, 'Dirigisme and Development Economics' in *Cambridge Journal of Economics*, Vol. 9, No. 1, 1985, p. 13.

35. For a fuller description of the statistical debate over the terms of trade hypothesis and a comprehensive evaluation of the data, see J. Spraos, 'The Statistical Debate on the Net Barter Terms of Trade Between Primary Commodities and Manufactures' in *Economic Journal*, Vol. 90, No. 357, 1980 (this article was reprinted in J. Spraos, *Inequalising Trade?*, Oxford University Press, Oxford, 1983) and E. Grilli and M.C. Yang, 'Primary Commodity Prices, Manufactured Goods Prices, and the Terms of Trade of Developing Countries: What the Long-run Shows' in *World Bank Economic Review*, Vol. 2, No. 1, 1988. See also Overseas Development Institute, 'Commodity Prices: Investing in Decline', Briefing Paper, March 1988.

36. For the full details of this sub-debate, see I.B. Kravis, 'Trade as a Handmaiden of Growth' in *Economic Journal*, December, 1970; and J. Riedel, 'Trade as the Engine of Growth in Developing Countries, Revisited' in *Economic Journal*, Vol. 94, 1984.

37. M. Michaely, 'Exports and Growth: An Empirical Investigation' in *Journal of Development Economics*, Vol. 4, 1977.

38. Balassa's test and results can be found in B. Balassa, 'Exports and

Economic Growth' in *Journal of Development Economics*, Vol. 5, No. 2, June 1978.

39. P.S. Heller and R.C. Porter, 'Exports and Growth: An Empirical Reinvestigation' in *Journal of Development Economics*, Vol. 5, 1978.

40. The statistical problems associated with Balassa's work are: first, a positive correlation between output and exports is to be expected anyway because exports are part of output; second, the positive correlation does not necessarily prove causality since higher growth of output via a Keynesian mechanism would increase exports; third, if export performance is used as an index of commitment to export-oriented industrialisation, countries which failed in following this policy are not taken into account. See C.H. Kirkpatrick and F.I. Nixon, eds., *The Industrialisation of Less Developed Countries*, Manchester University Press, 1983, p. 38. Another useful study of the relationship between exports and economic growth is G. Feder, 'On Exports and Economic Growth' in *Journal of Development Economics*, Vol. 12, 1983.

41. The two synthesis studies of the results from the NBER Research Project on Foreign Trade Regimes and Economic Development are A.O. Krueger, *Liberalisation Attempts and Consequences*, NBER, New York, 1978, and J.N. Bhagwati, *Anatomy and Consequences of Trade Control Regimes*, NBER, New York, 1978.

42. See B. Balassa and Associates, *Development Strategies in Semi-industrial Economies*, Johns Hopkins University Press, Baltimore, 1982.

43. Many of these policy prescriptions are drawn from a number of neoclassical authors. For information on credit markets, for example, see R.I. McKinnon, *Money and Capital in Economic Development*, Brookings Institution, Washington D.C., 1973. On Trade Policy see H.G. Johnson, 'Optimal Trade Intervention in the Presence of Domestic Distortions' in R.E. Baldwin, *et al.*, *Trade Growth and Balance of Payments*, North Holland, Amsterdam, 1965.

44. I.M.D. Little, *The Experiences and Causes of Rapid Labour-intensive Development in Korea, Taiwan, Hong Kong and Singapore and the Possibilities of Emulation*, International Labour Office Working Paper, ILO, Bangkok, 1979. This was reprinted in E. Lee, ed., *Export-led Industrialisation and Development*, ILO, Geneva, 1981.

45. G. Ranis, 'Challenges and Opportunities Posed by Asia's Super Exporters: Implications for Manufacured Exports from Latin America' in W. Baer and M. Gilles, eds., *Export Diversification and the New Protectionism*, Bureau of Economic and Business Research, University of Illinois, 1981; and B. Balassa, *The Newly Industrialising Countries in the World Economy*, Pergamon, New York, 1981. See also W. Branson, ed., *Trade and Structural Change in Pacific-Asia*, University of Chicago Press, Chicago, 1987.

46. I. Adelman, 'South Korea' in H.B. Chenery, *et al.*, *Redistribution with Growth*, Oxford University Press, London, 1974.

47. As noted in Chapter 1, these studies argue that such investments in indigenous technological capability enabled the East Asian NIEs to lower production costs through better choice and management of technology, improve the quality of output, create a range of product designs and

undertake expansions of plant and equipment at lower cost. See for example, A. Amsden, *Asia's New Giant: South Korea and Late Industrialisation*, Oxford University Press, New York, 1989; H. Pack and L. Westphal, 'Industrial Strategy and Technological Change: Theory versus Reality' in *Journal of Development Economics*, Vol. 21, 1986; G. Wignaraja, 'Industrialisation and Social Development: Some Comparisons of South Asia with the East Asian NICs' in P. Wignaraja, *et al.*, Participatory Development: *Learning from South Asia*, Oxford University Press, Oxford and Karachi, 1990; and S. Lall, *Building Industrial Competitiveness: New Technologies and Capabilities in Developing Countries*, OECD Development Centre, Paris, 1990.

48. For an account of the role of international factors, particularly American aid and (limited) foreign direct investment in the Korean economic miracle, see L. Westphal, Y.W. Rhee and G. Pursell, 'Foreign Influences on Korean Industrial Development' in *Oxford Bulletin of Economics and Statistics*, Nov. 1979; and D.T. Steinberg, 'Foreign Aid and the Development of the Republic of Korea: The Effectiveness of Concessional Assistance' in *US Aid Special Study*, No. 42, October 1985.

49. H.W. Singer, 'Industrialisation: Where Do We Stand? Where Are We Going?' in *Industry and Development*, No. 12, 1984.

50. L.P. Jones and I. Sakong, *Government, Business and Entrepreneurship in Economic Developemnt: The Korean Case*, Harvard University Press, Cambridge, 1980.

51. M. Datta-Chaudhuri, 'Industrialisation and Foreign Trade: The Development Experiences of South Korea and the Philippines' in E. Lee, ed., *Export-led Industrialisation and Development*, ILO, Geneva, 1981; IDS, 'Developmental States in East Asia: Capitalist and Socialist' in *IDS Bulletin*, Vol. 15, No. 2, April 1984; D. Evans and P. Alizadeh, *Price Distortions, Efficiency and Growth*, IDS, University of Sussex, 1985; P. Streeten, 'A Cool Look at Outward Oriented Strategies for Development' in *World Economy*, Vol. 5, September 1982; A. Amsden (1989), *op. cit.*

52. A.M. Choksi and D. Papageorgiou, eds., *Economic Liberalisation in Developing Countries*, Basil Blackwell, Oxford, 1987.

53. See for example, S. Edwards, 'The Order of Countries' in *Princeton Essays in International Finance*, No. 156, Princeton University Press, Princeton, 1984; and S. Edwards, 'On the Sequencing of Structural Reforms', OECD Department of Economics and Statistics Working Paper No. 70, September 1989; M. Mussa, 'Macroeconomic Policy and Trade Liberalisation: Some Guidelines' in *World Bank Research Observer*, January 1987; M. Bruno, *et al., Inflation Stabilisation*, MIT Press, Cambridge, 1988; R. Dornbusch, 'Mexico: Stabilisation, Debt and Growth' in *Economic Policy*, No 7, October 1988; S. Fischer, 'Economic Growth and Economic Policy' in V. Corbo, *et al.*, eds., *Growth-Oriented Adjustment Programmes*, IMF-World Bank, Washington, D.C., 1987; and J. Sachs, 'Trade and Exchange-Rate Policies in Growth-Oriented Adjustment Programs' in Corbo, *et al.* (1987), *ibid.*

54. See for example, World Bank, *Towards Sustained Development in Sub-Saharan Africa: A Joint Program of Action*, Washington, D.C., 1984.

55. See for example, J. Williamson, ed., *IMF Conditionality*, Institute for International Economics, Washington, D.C., 1983. See also J. Pollak, *The Financing of Development*, OECD Development Centre, Paris, 1989.

56. See in particular, R.F. Mikesell, 'Appraising IMF Conditionality: Too Loose, Too Tight or Just Right?' in J. Williamson, ed. (1983), *ibid.*

57. Angus Maddison's recent study of long-term growth in 32 countries shows, for example, that the average annual rate of GDP growth in the OECD region fell from 4.9 per cent in 1950-1973, to 2.4 per cent in 1973-1987. The corresponding figures for all 32 countries covered in his study are 5.1 per cent and 3.4 per cent. Cf. A. Maddison, *The World Economy in the 20th Century*, OECD Development Centre, Paris, 1989.

58. R. Dornbusch, 'Stabilisation Policies in Developing Countries: What Have we Learned?' in *World Development*, Vol. 10, No. 9, 1982. See also T. Killick, ed., *The Quest for Economic Stabilisation: The IMF and the Third World*, Heinemann, London, 1984; L. Taylor 'IS/LM in the Tropics: Diagrammatics of the New Structuralist Macro Critique' in W. Cline and S. Weintraub, eds., *Economic Stabilisation in Developing Countries*, Brookings Institution, Washington D.C., 1981.

59. A. Fishlow, 'The State of Economics in Latin America' in Inter-American Development Bank, *Economic and Social Progress in Latin America. External Debt: Crisis and Adjustment*, 1985 (Spanish version).

60. A. Foxley, *Latin American Experiments in Neo-Conservative Economics*, University of California Press, Berkeley, 1983.

61. World Bank, *Recovery in the Developing World: The London Symposium on the World Bank's Role*, Washington, D.C., 1986.

62. W.A. Lewis, 'The Slowing Down of the Engine of Growth' in *American Economic Review*, September 1980. See also H.W. Singer and P. Alizadeh, 'Import Substitution Revisited in a Darkening External Environment' in *Imspannungsfeld von Wirtschaft Technik and Politik*, Gunter Olzog Verlag, Munich, 1986.

63. See for example UNCTAD, *Trade and Development Report*, New York, 1983; and UNIDO, *Industry and Development: Global Report 1985*, New York, 1985.

64. W.R. Cline, 'Can the East Asian Model of Development be Generalised?' in *World Development*, Vol. 10, No. 2, 1982. See also G. Ranis, 'Comment on Cline' in *World Development*, Vol. 13, No. 4, 1985.

65. G.H. Preeg, *'Hard Bargaining Ahead: US Trade Policy and the Developing Countries'*, Overseas Development Council, Washington D.C., 1983.

66. See for example, J. Riedel, 'Trade as the Engine of Growth in Developing Countries: Revisited' in *Economic Journal*, Vol. 94, 1984; and J. Bhagwati, 'Export-Promoting Trade Strategy: Issues and Evidence' in *World Bank Research Observer*, Vol. 3, No. 1, 1988.

67. L. Emmerij, 'The Neo-Conservatism in the West', *Third World Quarterly*, July 1982.

68. Pioneering contributions to the new trade theory include P. Krugman, 'Increasing Returns, Monopolistic Competition and International Trade' in *Journal of International Economics*, Vol. 9, No. 4, 1979; J. Brander and B. Spencer, 'Tariffs and the Extraction of Foreign Monopoly Rents and

Potential Entry' in *Canadian Journal of Economics*, No. 14, August 1981; B. Spencer and J. Brander, 'International R&D Rivalry and Industrial Strategy' in *Review of Econommic Studies*, No. 5, 1983; and J. Brander and B. Spencer, 'Export Subsidies and International market Share Rivalry' in *Journal of International Economics*, 1985. See also H. Kierzkowski, ed., *Monopolistic Competition and International Trade*, Clarendon Press, Oxford, 1984; and P. Krugman, ed., *Strategic Trade Policy and the New International Economics*, MIT Press, Cambridge, 1986.

69. 'First-mover advantages' are defined in O. Williamson, *Markets and Hierarchies*, Free Press, New York, 1975. They include information through learning by doing, occupying the best locations, hiring the most suitable internationally mobile talent, securing the first patents, setting industry standards, etc.

70. A.K. Dixit, 'Trade Policy: An Agenda for Research' in P. Krugman, ed., *Strategic Trade Policy and the New International Economics*, MIT Press, Cambridge, 1986.

71. See in particular, P. Krugman, 'Import Protection as Export Promotion: International Competition in the Presence of Oligopoly and Economies of Scale' in H. Kierzkowski, ed., *op. cit.* See also P. Krugman, 'Strategic Sectors and International Competition' in R. Stern, ed., *US Trade Policies in a Changing World Economy*, MIT Press, Cambridge, 1987.

72. K. Stegemann, 'Policy rivalry among industrial states: what can we learn from models of strategic trade theory?' in *International Organisation*, Vol. 43, No. 1, Winter 1989.

73. See however A. Dixit, 'Issues of Strategic Trade Policy for Small Countries' in *Scandinavian Journal of Economics*, No. 3, pp 349-367. See also P. Krugman, 'New Trade Theory and the Less-Developed Countries', paper prepared for 'Debt, Stabilisation and Development', a conference in memory of Carlos Diaz-Alejandro, Helsinki, 23rd–25th August, 1986.

4 Reformist Development Thinking

The progression of orthodox development thinking in the 1970s and 1980s was not limited to the neoclassical resurgence. Another important extension, which may be termed reformist development thinking, has brought considerable light to bear on three major interrelated areas: employment; agriculture and rural development; and inequality, poverty, redistribution with growth, and basic human needs.

From the 1960s onwards, and due partly to the improvement of data collection in many developing countries, a body of empirical research has focused on income distribution. In addition to Kuznets' times-series analysis of the historical experience of the developed countries (1955) which led to his U-shaped-curve hypothesis, Kravis, Kuznets and others carried out cross-sectional studies in the early 1960s which showed greater inequality of income distribution in developing than in developed countries.[1] In the early 1970s, Chenery, for example, focused on the question of inter- and intra-sectoral income distribution, and Fishlow pointed to growing inequality of income distribution in Brazil during that country's economic 'miracle' of the 1960s.[2]

Others brought attention to problems of widening dualism in developing countries, which was supposed to lessen as development proceeded but which in fact worsened. Singer, for example, argued in 1970 that international dualism in science and technology (with capital-intensive modern technology imported by developing countries) and high rates of growth of population and the labour force in developing countries combined to create a dual employment situation: a small group is employed in the modern sector at high wages not explained by differences in skills or rural-urban living costs, and an increasing share of the labour force is relegated to a marginal existence.[3]

Turnham, in a 1971 OECD Development Centre publication, brought considerable attention to the employment problem in developing countries.[4] Extrapolating from statistics for the 1950–1965 period on labour supply (based on demographic data) and the demand for labour (determined by output growth and productivity trends) in developing countries, he projected unemployment rates of between 12 and 17 per cent in 1980. At the time these prospects seemed rather shocking; but in fact they have turned out to be overly optimistic for many developing countries.

This body of empirical research on inequality, unemployment and dualism contributed to a growing impression that the 'trickle down' mechanism was not working as well as it should. Even in the presence of high economic growth, as occurred in the 1960s, there continued to be high and growing inequality, with the fruits of growth apparently remaining largely in the hands of the wealthiest groups and the masses still living under harsh conditions of poverty that, for many, were worsening. In an important speech to Britain's Overseas Development Institute in 1965, five years into the first UN Development Decade, Ward summed up the feelings of many at the time:

> Such were the aims five years ago ... Let us begin by trying to see where we are now, half way through the decade. In some ways, it has not gone too badly. But the reason is that it has gone so well for the developed countries that their success has been 'trickle down' or residual effects on the developers. Yet at the end of the five years, the gap between rich nations and poor is greater still, not because the poor nations have necessarily grown poorer, but because the rich have got richer by so much more.[5]

Nor did income distribution through taxation – the orthodox instrument for redistribution – appear feasible in most developing countries as a means to supplement the trickle-down mechanism. Bird and De Wulf, for example, in their 1973 study for the IMF, found that taxation can affect the distribution of wealth and, through factor prices, the demand for labour, but can do little to correct the distribution of income.[6] Their pessimistic conclusion reflected both the perception that the tax burden was relatively light in most developing countries, and that its incidence was apparently regressive in nature.

All this contributed to a process of rethinking of the approaches to development. A widely publicised lecture by Seers in 1969 signaled the shift from development being related mainly to economic growth to a broader concept encompassing reductions in poverty, unemployment and inequality. To quote Seers:

> The questions to ask about a country's development are therefore: What has been happening to poverty? What has been happening to unemployment? What has been happening to inequality? If all three of these have become less severe, then beyond doubt this has been a

period of development for the country concerned. If one or two of these central problems have been growing worse, and especially if all three have, it would be strange to call the result 'development', even if per capita income had soared.[7]

Myrdal, when outlining the following year his world anti-poverty programme, again stressed the objective of greater equality in proposing major reforms in agriculture, education, population and the State.[8]

The reaction against reducing economic development to the maximisation of economic growth was further reinforced by a similar sentiment in the advanced countries. This was first expressed by environmentalists and others critical of the process of industrial growth, which was argued to carry with it external diseconomies such as pollution, the destruction of the environment and the rapid depletion of the earth's scarce natural resources. The 1972 'Limits to Growth' report by the Club of Rome – which received tremendous publicity at the time – suggested that high rates of industrial growth in the West threatened rapidly to deplete the earth's limited stock of natural resources and cause social and economic catastrophes.

The result of all this has been the emergence of a body of literature, which we call reformist, that can be seen as a movement against what its protagonists see as a crucial weakness in much of the orthodox approach to development: the tendency to concentrate on growth and on closing the gap between rich and poor countries while giving too little attention to poverty, the quality of life, and to closing the gap between rich and poor within developing countries. The reformist literature stresses policies that developing countries themselves should attempt in order to eradicate the poverty and inequality that affect such large proportions of their populations. And, in contrast to the relatively non-interventionist focus on prices and markets of the neoclassical approach, the reformist approach tends to emphasize a role for the State, for example in the provision of health services and education or in supporting labour-intensive industries as a means to increase employment.

THE REFORMIST RESPONSE TO POVERTY: EMPLOYMENT, REDISTRIBUTION WITH GROWTH, AND BASIC NEEDS

The reformist response to the increasing concern with poverty in the 1970s essentially comprised three planks: employment-oriented strategies, redistribution with growth, and basic human needs strategies. In 1969, the International Labour Office (ILO) set up the World Employment Programme as a means of dealing with the employment side of poverty. Five years later, in 1974, under MacNamara, the World Bank unveiled its policies of redistribution with growth, jointly developed with the Institute of Development Studies of the University of Sussex in England. Both these key initiatives, and the efforts of a number of influential non-governmental organisations (NGOs) during the early 1970s, gave rise to the notion of basic-needs strategies for development at the ILO's World Employment Conference in 1976. During the late 1970s, the World Bank attempted to operationalise further the concept of basic needs for widespread use. The overall reformist response during the 1970s should be viewed as a major – some would say unique – period of international co-operation directed at one central issue: attacking poverty.

The Employment Focus at ILO: The World Employment Programme

The novelty of the ILO's approach was that it interpreted the problem of poverty as a problem of employment. It also pointed to perceived weaknesses of the growth approach that underpinned the earlier industrialisation literature, and the relative lack of success of the policies that had grown out of the dual-economy models as well. This point was subsequently brought out very succinctly by Emmerij:

> This conventional development model was therefore based on the assumption that growth, with emphasis on the modern sector, was in itself a solution to development because, so the assumption went, the fruits of this growth would automatically and within an acceptable period of time, spread to the less privileged sectors of the economy and to the poorer segments of the population. This assumption proved to be wrong.[9]

The net result of following the conventional development model was seen to be a waste of the abundant human resources of many developing countries which could have otherwise been employed productively, and a continuation of miserable living conditions for vast numbers of underpriviledged people. Productive employment was argued by the ILO to be the mechanism by which these concerns could be directly raised and in turn have a decisive impact on poverty – hence the stress on catalysing employment-oriented development strategies. The emphasis was thus shifted from the formulation of a development strategy based on economic growth per se, with employment resulting from this as the residual, to a strategy focusing on employment as the policy objective in its own right.

Country missions constituted an important component of the World Employment Programme, and one of particular interest for our purposes. The function of these missions was to help design employment-oriented strategies for particular developing countries. To this end, interdisciplinary teams studied the employment situation in a country and identified specific policies to promote employment. A brief sketch of the main findings of some of the early missions will highlight the rapid progression of this early current of reformist thought.

The earliest missions, to Colombia in 1970 and Sri Lanka in 1971, analysed the problem of poverty in rather conventional macro-econom-ic terms as a shortage of employment possibilities, inadequate income from work and underemployed human resources.[10] Building on the foundations laid by these earlier missions, the 1972 Kenya mission disaggregated the problem of poverty to focus primarily on the 'working poor' (i.e., those who work hard but do not earn a minimum income).[11]

The switch in the ILO's approach from emphasis on unemployment to employment and income distribution in the early 1970s was associated with increased interest in the problems of the informal sector in developing countries and of rural–urban migration.[12] The informal sector was defined by the ILO as comprising traditional labour-intensive urban activities and small-scale rural agricultural activities – charac-terised by ease of entry, reliance on indigenous resources, unregulated and competitive markets and skills acquired outside the formal school systems – and was found to be discriminated against by government policy in many developing countries.[13] Nevertheless, since it was found to make an important contribution to regular employment, often at wages above those obtainable in subsistence agriculture, the ILO recommended a more favourable government policy towards this sector (including ceasing the demolition of informal-sector housing and attempts to increase government purchases of goods and services from the informal sector). Rural–urban migration, by contrast, was thought to be less socially desirable and so the ILO favoured positive policies – such as land reforms and the diffusion of labour-augmenting technologi-cal change – towards developing the traditional agricultural sector.

The ILO's work on the problem of employment was influential because it represented a pioneering effort to tackle poverty and inequality by focusing on the problems of the educated unemployed, of the working poor and of the urban informal sector. The country reports also provided comprehensive location-specific strategies to deal with employment problems facing a given country. Further, by identifying and conceptualising a number of new ideas – such as that of the working poor and the urban informal sector – they helped provide a direction for future reformist thinkers and policy-makers.[14]

The World Bank and Redistribution with Growth

Increasing concerns with the poverty issue were also visible in the 1970s in the policy of the World Bank. Just after the War the Bank had concentrated its efforts on reconstruction projects in developed countries, followed by a phase of building up basic infrastructure (roads, railways, power facilities) in developing countries. Under President Woods in the 1960s, the Bank had diversified into sector-specific programmes, e.g. in agriculture and education. When MacNamara became President in 1968, he catalysed an internal assessment of the Bank's work of the previous 25 years. This assessment concluded that something was wrong: although developing countries had achieved high rates of growth, poverty and inequality had worsened.[15]

Prior to the 1970s, only fragmentary data existed on income distribution in developing countries. As part of its internal assessment, the World Bank compiled all available data and commissioned a series of country mimeographs on income distribution in developing countries.[16] An important distinction was made in these studies between the 'absolute poor' and the 'relative poor'.[17] The studies also shed light on problems of low average income levels and of national income distributions that were highly skewed in favour of the rich. Asia (especially India, Pakistan, Bangladesh) had the highest concentration of absolute poverty; in Latin America, inequality and relative poverty were found to be a great problem; Africa had severe problems of both relative and absolute poverty. Following this assessment the World Bank began to urge developing-country governments to conduct a direct attack on poverty by re-orientating their development policies.

In his famous 1973 Nairobi speech, MacNamara went further by stating that the Bank had decided 'to place far greater emphasis on policies and projects which will begin to attack the problems of absolute poverty (and) on assistance designed to increase the productivity of the approximately 40 per cent of the population of our developing member countries who have neither been able to contribute significantly to economic growth, nor share equitably in economic progress'.[18] He also outlined the Bank's approach for dealing with world poverty. First, there was the identification of the poor, referred to as the 'Target Group'. An important World Bank study entitled *Assault on World Poverty* estimated in 1975 that approximately 750 million people or 40 per cent of the total population of developing countries live in absolute poverty.[19] Asia accounted for over two-thirds of this figure, Africa for 19 per cent and Latin America and the Caribbean for 13 per cent. The data indicated that poverty was concentrated in the rural areas – some 600 million people (or 80 per cent of all poor) lived in poverty in the rural areas and constituted 40 per cent of the rural population. This study also identified three target groups which were particularly affected: small farmers; landless labourers and submarginal farmers; and the urban unemployed and underemployed.

From the Bank's discovery of the gravity of rural poverty, it followed that the solution was a strategy of rural development – directly attacking poverty in the countryside. This led to the initiatives discussed in Chapter 2. Half of all rural development lending ever undertaken by the Bank to 1975 occurred between 1974 and 1975, and by the end of 1975 rural development programme lending was receiving the lion's share of annual Bank lending.[20] Moreover, it seemed that rural development projects would continue to attract substantial funds in the future. Thus, in a 1975 speech MacNamara proclaimed, 'We expect to invest $7 billion more in this field (rural development) over the next five years; and we estimate that these projects will bring financial benefits to approximately 100 million individuals'.[21]

The Bank's strategy was also concerned with poverty in the cities of the developing world, however, which demonstrated that the Bank's fight on poverty was a general 'assault on world poverty' and not only a rural strategy. The strategy to reduce urban poverty aimed at increasing earning opportunities in the informal sector, at creating more jobs in the modern sector, at providing equitable access to public utilities, transport, education and health services, and at establishing realistic housing policies. Like the ILO country missions – and perhaps through their influence – the World Bank thus supported expansion of the urban informal sector.

In sum, MacNamara's speeches and numerous World Bank studies reflected important changes in the direction of Bank policy. From an approach centring on infrastructural investment and industrialisation in the 1950s and 1960s, the Bank was now shifting to tackle absolute poverty, especially but not only in rural areas. Higher priority was to be given to basic sectors (such as education, housing and agriculture) through support for new types of integrated rural development projects targeted at the poor and aimed at satisfying some of their fundamental needs. The volume of Bank lending was increased, and some of the increase was channelled to finance these new projects.

While the 1974–75 growth trend in rural-development lending was not sustained, and over the next few years there was in fact a decline in this lending, these policy initiatives and the Bank's substantial financial resources gave major impetus to reformist development thinking and practice. Not only did its lending power draw major attention to the problem of poverty and the need for individual governments to develop strategies to reduce it. Its efforts also helped 'legitimise' the funding of poverty and basic-needs projects in the eyes of the international donor community. Moreover, to back up its role in development policy, the World Bank's research programme was directed more firmly to investigating poverty. The early research, cited above, concentrated on quantifying the magnitude of the poverty problem and its geographical spread through detailed field surveys. This led to research on the impact of different types of 'policy packages' designed to reduce inequality and maintain or improve growth rates by the use of computerised simulation techniques. Research also turned to the issue of human resource development and basic needs, the synergistic effects on productivity of actions designed to meet basic needs in each of five core areas: education, health care, clean water, nutrition and shelter.

It should also be noted, however, that the World Bank's poverty strategy of redistribution with growth – as reflected in Chenery, *et al.,* *Redistribution With Growth* (1974) – was an incrementalist approach. This meant that with each increment of growth, the extra income was distributed to the poor, so as to increase gradually their share of national income. The incrementalist approach is very different in its scope and the instruments it employs from more radical basic-needs strategies, which stress the immediate redistribution of land as a precondition for moving towards eradicating rural poverty.

The Basic-Needs Strategy

The thrusts of the ILO and the World Bank into the problem of poverty were part of a wider international process of reformist rethinking following the realisation at the end of the 1960s and the early 1970s that past strategies of development had failed to redress the dire plight of the poor. Thus, in a book published in 1976, i.e. a few years before the neoclassical resurgence came on in full force, Mahbub al Haq could argue that development practitioners and theoreticians had accepted that the market mechanism was not an efficient method of resource allocation under conditions of an unequal distribution of income. He went on to stress that it was widely believed that the trickle-down mechanism inherent in the growth and industrial strategies of the 1950s did not result in an automatic spreading of the fruits to the majority of the population of the developing countries.[22]

This process of rethinking also resulted in the publication between 1974 and 1976 of a number of reports by influential NGOs. One was the Dag Hammarskjold Foundation's 1975 report entitled 'What Now: Another Development'.[23] This report not only emphasized the spreading disgruntlement with the traditional approaches to development but also advocated alternative development strategies and concepts: 'Another Development would be need-oriented, endogenous, self-reliant, ecologically sound and based on the transformation of social structures'. In delineating these characteristics, it emphasized that while human needs are both material and non-material, the basic needs of food, health, shelter and education should be satisfied on a priority basis.

The connection between development strategy and basic human needs was also a key element in the mathematical models of development options worked out by the Argentina-based Bariloche Foundation.[24] And these ideas were major themes in the 1976 'Reshaping the International Order' (RIO) Report, which spoke of 'the need for new development strategies – national and international – defined and designed not merely to meet the criterion of private or state profitability, but rather to give priority to the expression and satisfaction of fundamental human values. Society as a whole must accept the responsibility for guaranteeing a minimum level of welfare for all its citizens and aims at equality in human relations ... It follows that the problem of development must be redefined as a selective attack on the worst forms of poverty'.[25]

The climax of this series of diverse, yet sharply focused reformist pressures and initiatives was the approval by the ILO at its 1976 World Employment Conference of a proposal that national development strategies should place a high priority on both the generation of employment and the satisfaction of basic human needs. Thus basic needs had 'officially' arrived to the forefront of development policy and practice. The report of the Director General of the ILO to this conference provides a definition of basic needs: 'Basic needs, as understood in this report, include two elements. First, they include certain minimum requirements of a family for private consumption: adequate food, shelter, and clothing are obviously included, as would be certain household equipment and services. Second, they include essential services provided by and for the community at large, such as safe drinking water, sanitation, public transport, and health and education facilities'.[26] To these rather materially focused needs he added human rights, employment and participation of the people in making decisions that affect them.

In addition to suggesting that economic development should focus squarely on meeting these basic needs of the poor, the conference outlined some of the broad shifts in policies required to achieve those ends.[27] First, economic growth was to be accelerated. Second, the pattern of growth would be redefined so as to allow the poor access to productive resources. Hence, institutional change in the form of asset redistribution was emphasized. Third, the participation of the people in the decision-making process and the role of women in development were stressed as part of this process. Finally, there was support for international economic reforms in part to reinforce and strengthen programmes at the country level. The Programme of Action adopted by the Conference thus declared that, 'the satisfaction of basic needs is a national endeavour, but its success depends upon strengthening world peace and disarmament and the establishment of the New International Economic Order.' Moreover, 'the Conference recognises that the basic needs strategy is only the first phase of the redistributive global growth process'.[28]

These statements defined basic needs and outlined the broad features of the strategy required to satisfy them. At first glance, the basic-needs approach and redistribution-with-growth seemed very similar in that they were both reactions to the growth-centred approach of the 1950s and early 1960s. They were, however, really quite different approaches to inequality and poverty. Redistribution-with-growth was an income-centred approach: it sought to raise productivity and incomes sufficiently to allow all groups of poor to purchase the goods and services they require from the market. The State then provides other services which they cannot purchase. Moreover, as mentioned earlier, it is an incremental approach that takes place gradually and hence can be characterised as 'redistribution from growth'.

The basic-needs approach by contrast was seen as a direct and speedier attack on poverty. Although growth was considered important in achieving the ends of development, it was not the focus of this approach. Asset redistribution (especially land), social transformation and the channeling of particular resources to particular groups were stressed because it was believed that the incremental approach is too slow to bring about benefits to the poor. In addition, the basic-needs approach encompassed both economic and non-economic needs. The reasoning behind this was brought out clearly by Streeten in 1977: 'A basic needs approach to development starts from the objective of providing the opportunities for the full physical, mental and social development of the human personality and then derives the ways of achieving this objective.'[29] Non-material needs, including self reliance, participation, national self-determination and cultural identity, for example, were not only regarded as useful in their own terms, but as valuable conditions to meeting the material needs. Among supporters of the basic-needs approach, some have emphasized delivering basic services such as education, safe drinking water and health to the poor (the 'shopping list approach') whereas others (the 'progressives') have emphasized asset redistribution, mobilising the poor and giving them a voice in the political process.

Chinese economic development under Mao has been argued by some commentators to have played a role in the thinking about basic human needs strategies.[30] Sri Lanka and Tanzania have also been referred to as important examples of successful basic needs strategies. Sri Lanka in particular, has been cited as an example of a developing country whose level of social welfare was quite high in relation to its level of per capita income largely as a result of a fairly egalitarian society and a well developed system of social welfare.[31] By way of comparison, the redistribution-with-growth approach of the World Bank employed five case studies – Cuba, Tanzania, Sri Lanka, Taiwan and South Korea – for the period of approximately 1955 to 1973.[32] Of these five studies, three (Cuba, Tanzania and Sri Lanka) were said to be examples of redistribution as a result of deliberate government policy, while in the other two (Taiwan and South Korea) favourable trends in income distribution were attributed to the side effects of growth-stimulating strategies.

In 1977-78, the World Bank picked up the concept of basic human needs from the ILO and pushed it hard. The World Bank's support of the basic-needs approach may in part have been a reaction to doubts expressed about the Bank's redistribution-with-growth policies. Balogh, for example, argued in 1976 that, 'The evolution of Mr. Robert MacNamara's strategies for greater equality, which have been so striking, has as yet had no visible results. It is undeniable that the poorest, especially in the poorest countries, have suffered an absolute decline in their standards of living'.[33]

Balogh's logic was based mainly on the effects of adverse external factors. The 1973/74 oil-price shock was singled out as the prime factor responsible for a deterioration in the economic conditions facing poor countries as a whole and the poorest within them. The quintupling of oil prices forced many developing countries to cut back on their social spending and anti-poverty programmes in order to divert scarce financial resources to pay for increased oil import bills. This had a direct impact on the poor. In addition, the developed countries failed to harmonize their policies in regard to the financing of OPEC's high export surpluses. Instead, they chose to solve their deficits by restrictive fiscal and monetary policy. In turn, this led to a reduced capacity and willingness of the industrialised countries to aid development. Similarly, there has been an increasing politicisation of aid so that it is tied to the interests of the donor countries and not solely to the areas or sectors in need. Regarding policies to help the rural sector, Balogh argued that the stabilisation of primary-commodity prices and the green revolution benefitted the landlords and rich peasants most and did not contribute cost-effectively to the mitigation of world poverty.

The United Nations Research Institute for Social Development (UNRISD) argued that the social and political consequences of the green revolution (on which the World Bank's Rural Development strategy was based) had been overlooked.[34] UNRISD carried out a world-wide research project during the 1970s on the socio-economic impact of the introduction of the high-yielding varieties of seeds in developing countries. The conclusions from this project, similar to those reached by a number of analysts at the time, were that modernisation of agriculture as envisaged by the World Bank and other institutions increased yields but at the same time aggravated social and economic inequalities in the rural sector.[35]

Finally, Van De Laar drew attention in 1976 to the very rigid institutional constraints under which the World Bank operates that hinder its attempts to focus more fully on the poor.[36] He argued that the actual allocation of Bank resources up to 1976 was not determined by the consideration of helping the absolute poor. If it were, this would imply the Bank concentrating large amounts of its resources on a small group of countries – the poorest countries. After examining the pattern of Bank lending and the allocation of IDA credits (the very low interest loans of the Bank) he argued that much of the doubling of lending promised by MacNamara had gone to a few middle-income countries.[37]

and to large conventional sectors such as electric power, transport and iron and steel. In addition, Van de Laar suggested that political concerns and interests of large donors to IDA and the pressure applied by small countries at the United Nations were the determinants of geographical changes in the pattern of IDA credits, and not necessarily the criterion of need.

The criticisms levelled at the World Bank's redistribution-with-growth approach were an important but not the only factor in causing the Bank to focus on basic needs during the late 1970s. Streeten and Burki, two of the World Bank's key basic-needs strategists, argued in a 1978 article that, 'the ILO initiated work on strategies with an explicit focus on employment, and the World Bank supported emphasis on redistribution with growth. These approaches meant major conceptual advances in development analysis and policy but they have not gone far enough in attacking absolute poverty directly'.[38] Raising the productivity of the poor, improving their skills and increasing their production by raising their demand for goods and services were argued by Streeten and Burki to be necessary but not sufficient conditions for poverty elimination. In particular, the ILO and World Bank approaches during the early 1970s had not often achieved intended results, but led in the final analysis to a return to the initial distribution of income and power; they had underplayed the requirement for vital social services and, most important, the economic emphasis of these approaches tended to forget the ultimate end of policy, which is not only to eliminate poverty but to develop the full potential of people and to give them the means and possibilities to do so. 'The demand now is to put man and his needs at the centre of development'.[39] They saw the basic-needs strategy as a natural evolution of the earlier approaches, one that built upon the insights and experience of the past but also took it much further.

Streeten and Burki then defined the aim of a basic-needs strategy as being, 'to increase and redistribute production so as to eradicate deprivation that arises from a lack of basic goods and services'.[40] They identified as the most important operational issue the political framework required to support the implementation of a development strategy genuinely aimed at satisfying basic needs of the poor; their conclusion was that a major restructuring in political and economic power relationships within society is a precondition for the realisation of this strategy. The other key operational issues for country-level policies and the international community they identified were (a) the domestic and external resources required for meeting the basic needs of a very large and rising population in developing countries; (b) the designing of public services to focus on and benefit the poorest people; (c) the designing of social change and institutions that would facilitate both the voicing of their needs by the poor and their participation in maintaining the services they require; (d) the required signals and incentives of the system (prices vs. central planning); and (e) the trade-offs between basic needs and other objectives.

Some of the operational issues were deemed not to have any conclusive answers, and a systematic process of research and experimentation was launched in 1978–80 as the means to put flesh on the skeleton of the concept of basic needs. This research was to shed light on how to design strategies to meet basic needs and also on the operational difficulties and risks of doing so. It covered three groups of countries: countries that had not satisfied the basic needs of large segments of their populations (Bangladesh, Botswana, Nepal and Lesotho); countries that had given the satisfaction of basic needs an important place in their development programmes (Sri Lanka, Burma and Tanzania); and countries that could be expected to cooperate in experimenting with basic-needs strategies and policies because they were in the aftermath of a revolution or civil war and were recommencing their development efforts (Angola, Vietnam and Mozambique).[41] With the shift in the Bank's policy perspective in the 1980s, and the emergence of 'neo-conservatism' more broadly, as discussed in Chapter 2, however, the institutional focus of reformist development thinking shifted to UNICEF,[42] and its influence in the international development community has diminished considerably.

THE NIEO AND THE INTERNATIONAL DIMENSION OF REFORMISM

Many reformist writers have stressed that inequality, between as well as within countries, is at the root of underdevelopment, and that a reduction of global inequality would have a positive impact on overall poverty reduction.[43] The goal of many reformist thinkers has therefore been to establish an international framework (with poverty reduction a core element) for sustained and self-reliant development in poor countries. While the ILO's employment approach, the World Bank's redistribution-with-growth approach and the basic-needs strategy can all be seen as attempts to tackle poverty and inequality *within* developing countries – and many donor countries have been keen for developing countries to undertake internal reforms that include poverty reduction as well – this left open the international dimension of the poverty problem.

Spokesmen from the Third World have often argued that the postwar international economic order works against the interests of the poor countries. These arguments culminated in 1974, at the Sixth Special Session of the UN General Assembly, in the United Nations Declaration and Programme of Action on the establishment of a New International Economic Order (NIEO). The proclaimed goal of the NIEO was to amend the rules governing international economic relations so as to provide all states with more equal opportunities.

The debate over the NIEO boiled down to a question of the distribution of power among states, with the developing countries pursuing a more favourable distribution of power. Issues discussed within the NIEO framework, which have been the subject of protracted negotiations between countries of the North and South, include: greater access to the markets of the developed nations, especially for labour-intensive industrial products of the South; improved access to world capital markets and debt relief, since it is clear that the austerity programmes demanded of Third World governments as conditions for access to capital under current arrangements imply onerous loads for the poor; stabilisation of primary commodity markets, which would make it easier for the South to re-emphasize the growth of primary-sector exports; and greater volumes of foreign aid. Some demands have also been made for a transfer of resources to the developing countries in the form of expanded IMF Special Drawing Rights.

A number of authors have also proposed to institute some form of international bargaining process that would link negotiations over the NIEO with the implementation of basic-needs strategies within developing countries. Thus, for example, Streeten has argued that, 'the NIEO is a framework of rules and institutions, regulating the relations between sovereign nations, and BN (Basic Needs) is the important objective which this framework should serve. The way to make institutions serve the objective is to strike a bargain: donors will accept features of the NIEO if, and only if, developing countries commit themselves to a BN approach'.[44]

The 1977 creation of the Brandt Commission, whose report 'North–South: A Programme for Survival' was published in 1980, was another result of reformist thinking. The idea of creating an 'independent' commission on development issues was first suggested by MacNamara, and the UN Secretary General at the time (Kurt Waldheim) also showed an interest in the work of the Commission. The task of the Commission was 'to study the grave global issues arising from the economic and social disparities of the world community and to suggest ways of promoting adequate solutions to the problems involved in development and in attacking absolute poverty'.[45] It drew up a series of long-term structural reforms and short-term emergency measures. The long-term measures included a priority for the needs of the poorest, the abolition of hunger, reform of the monetary system and a new approach to development finance.   The emergency programme consisted of four major planks: (a) a large-scale transfer of resources to developing countries; (b) an international energy strategy; (c) a global food programme; (d) a start on some of the major reforms in the international economic systems.

Initially, the Brandt report provided some stimulus to a process of collective reflection on North–South relations, global interdependence and international poverty issues.   But with the increasing international tension during the late 1970s and the resulting focus on East–West relations, as well as the above-mentioned 'neo-conservatism' of the 1980s, its recommendations have not been implemented and the report itself has faded into the background.

Finally, it is interesting to note that during the 1970s and early 1980s, it was common among reformist writers to stress the importance of bringing the East-West arms race to a halt so as to release resources for development. Recently, prospects have come to look very promising in this regard. Somewhat ironically, however, the concern now has shifted to the prospect that massive increases in aid and private-sector resource flows to Eastern Europe may come at the expense of North–South flows.

EMPIRICAL STUDIES

The growing concern in the reformist literature of the 1970s led to – and was often reinforced by – a considerable volume of empirical research. These studies may be loosely classified under three headings: research on the relationship between growth and inequality; that on poverty and inequality, notably their measurement; and the development of social indicators to measure development.

Growth and Inequality

The relationship between growth and inequality has been studied from two angles: the impact of growth on equality, and the impact on growth of government policies that seek greater equality. As regards the first angle, the early research dates back of course to the work of Kuznets and his U-shaped-curve hypothesis.[46]   In 1973, Adelman and Morris published an important study of the relationship in 43 countries between the income share going to the poorest 60 per cent of a country's population and the country's overall economic record.[47] They found that the main impact of growth on income distribution has been (on average) to reduce both the absolute and the relative share of income accruing to the poorest groups. They also found little evidence of the operation of the trickle-down mechanism; rather their data suggested that the richest groups got richer at the expense of the middle-level income groups and the poor.

Two years later, Adelman published another important study in which she examined the structural context within which growth occurs and argued for a strategy of redistribution *before* growth.[48] Basing her analysis on the historical experiences of Taiwan and South Korea, she argued that as a precondition for equitable and rapid growth, assets must be redistributed, especially through extensive land reform, and massive educational and human capital formation programmes must be organised. Authoritarian governments may also be required to muster the necessary political power for at least the redistributive and take-off phases of the process.

More recent studies have also reached mixed or negative conclusions on the Kuznets hypothesis. A 1980 World Bank report, for example, while supporting the proposition that faster growth of average incomes is essential to reducing absolute poverty, especially in very poor countries, also argued that 'the Kuznets curve is not an iron law ... some countries are well above it, others below (and) all do not follow a path of the same shape'.[49] Ahluwalia's 1976 cross-sectional analysis also found only very weak confirmation of the Kuznets hypothesis, and the 1983 study by Saith is very skeptical about the validity of the Kuznets hypothesis as well.[50]

As to the growth impact of government policies that seek to promote greater equality, the World Bank's strategy of redistribution with growth clearly rested on the hypothesis that government policy can both reduce inequality and accelerate growth. In response to arguments that basic-needs strategies reduce growth, Hicks published in 1979 an econometric study that found that policies designed to promote better distribution and decrease poverty are on balance growth-stimulating rather than growth-retarding.[51] Finally, a 1981 study by Griffin and James on the transition to egalitarian development argued that, 'in the majority of poor countries a basic-need or anti-poverty-focused strategy of development requires both major structural changes and their rapid implementation'.[52] It also emphasized that success in terms of attaining basic-needs targets and economic growth rests on the speed of implementing structural reforms.

The measurement of poverty

Among the studies that have attempted to quantify poverty, one of the best known is that by Ahluwalia, Carter and Chenery, published in 1979.[53] Based on data for 36 countries, they found almost 40 per cent of the population of developing countries living in absolute poverty, defined as income levels that are insufficient to provide adequate nutrition. The bulk of the poor are in the poorest countries: in South Asia, Indonesia and sub-Saharan Africa. These countries account for two-thirds of total world population, and well over three-fourths of the population in poverty, with the incidence of poverty at 60 per cent or more in countries having the lowest levels of GNP. While the study projected a decline in absolute poverty from 644 million to 475 million people by the year 2000 – based on some rather optimistic assumptions about growth trends and redistribution – relative poverty was nevertheless projected to worsen, with the income share of the poorest 40 per cent falling from 9.8 per cent in 1975 to 6.5 per cent in 2000.

Other studies have focused on poverty in specific countries or regions, or affecting particular groups of people. South Asia, notably India, received much attention in the late 1970s, but considerable work has been done recently on Africa as well, due in part to improvement in survey techniques and data collection, and in part to the severe food crisis in that region.[54] Some of these studies have also identified poverty groups more precisely: not only do the poorest groups tend to be concentrated in agriculture and rural handicrafts, poverty has also been found to affect women disproportionately.[55]

Alternative development indicators

Increasingly widespread recognition of the limitations of per capita GNP as a measure of development, and the felt need to develop measures of the satisfaction of basic needs, have also given rise to research into alternative composite indicators of development. One of the most important early studies was undertaken by UNRISD in 1970. This study identified 16 key indicators from a sample of 73 economic, financial, political and social factors from which it constructed a composite index of development, and produced a ranking of countries somewhat different from the per capita GNP ranking.[56] Such studies have also been criticised, however, both because they implicitly assume that poor countries follow the path of rich countries, and because they seek to measure development in terms of structural change without giving sufficient emphasis to people and their welfare. These criticisms led to the development of a second group of indicators which focus on the quality of life of the inhabitants of a country. Probably the best known example of this second group is Morris' Physical Quality of Life Index (PQLI), published in 1979.[57] The PQLI statistic is based on three indicators – life expectancy at age one, infant mortality and literacy – for which the data are relatively easy to assemble. The study found a weak correlation between PQLI and GNP per capita. And, of course, the PQLI can be criticised for being a limited measure because it fails to include other aspects of the quality of life such as human rights or the degree of political freedom.

OTHER CRITICISMS OF THE REFORMIST APPROACH

The birth of reformism was, as we have noted, a reaction to what were viewed as failings of the conventional growth-centred approach to development. During the 1970s, it had widespread appeal among development practitioners and theorists alike. But there have been several critical opinions voiced about the theoretical basis of the approach and its policy implications.

From within the broad basic-needs paradigm, Singh, for example, has argued that the mainstream basic-needs theorists do not adequately emphasize the crucial role of industry in bringing about a long-term structural transformation of the economy. Reporting favourably on the Chinese experience – which he saw emphasizing heavy industry and modern technology as well as agriculture, consumer goods industries, small-scale enterprises and traditional techniques – Singh argued that in order to satisfy the basic needs of the poor on a sustainable long-term basis it is necessary to encourage a process of modern industrialisation, in which the production of capital goods occupies a central position.[58]

Other criticisms from within the basic-needs camp are adequately summarised by the extensive survey on 'the disenthronement of basic needs' written by Higgins in 1980.[59] The main thrust of his article is to examine whether the basic-needs strategy forms a clearly identifiable approach to development and if it is more efficient in solving the problems of poverty. He notes first of all that while many writers have tended to stick to the ILO's 1976 definition of basic needs, others have held that the definition of basic needs depends on social and ethical norms and can vary according to the time and place. Higgins finds this confusing, or worse, because if individual countries choose their own basic-needs levels, then the basic-needs approach may not lead to any significant changes in development strategy or shifts in the allocation of resources. He also points out that while the basic-needs approach overlaps with other approaches, notably the 'unified approach' of the United Nations and the redistribution-with-growth approach of the World Bank, key questions remain unanswered over who the target population is – is it the poorest people, or the poor communities? – and how basic needs should be quantified. Higgins himself does not see a basic-needs strategy as necessarily implying a focus on rural development and the transformation of villages at the expense of cities and the modern sector. Nor does he see it to be in conflict with the proposals for a NIEO or requiring developing countries to delink from the international system. Countries genuinely interested in basic needs, he argues, should design their own approach, within one generation, in line with its level of development, human and natural resources and political risks and opportunities. He also points out that mainstream basic-needs writers are not primarily concerned with revolution to achieve their ends but would support shifts in political power towards the poor or more sensitivity to the poor by ruling politicians; he himself is opposed to radical redistribution of assets, especially land, on the grounds that this will decrease output and not necessarily ensure that poverty will be eliminated.

Higgin's commentary provoked reactions from some prominent basic-needs spokesmen, notably Streeten and Emmerij. Streeten, considering the question of 'who determines basic needs', cites empirical evidence on poverty, nutrition and health, and responds that, 'it is hard to envisage any society in which the five core basic needs sectors – nutrition, education, health, shelter, water and sanitation – will not be all contained in the definition of basic needs, even if progress in all five sectors may not be required'.[60] Streeten also feels that some attention should be given to other popular demands – be it ownership of land for peasants or consumption goods such as televisions. Finally, answering the point that basic needs does not imply revolution, Streeten argues that supporters of radical change believe that other more gradual approaches 'attack symptoms rather than causes'. This does not mean that Streeten advocates revolution; rather, he sees the fundamental question that arises in tackling basic needs to be, 'whether our desire to change the world has not been ahead of our correct interpretation and understanding' of the roots of the problem.[61]

Emmerij pointed out that while the basic-needs approach is clearly connected with a broad redistribution-with-growth strategy, it focuses more specifically on the requirements of the poor (or low-income sections of the population). Responding to the alleged rural focus of basic needs by some writers, Emmerij emphasizes that the modern sector (which tends to be involved in the process of international trade) should not be neglected in the design and implementation of a basic-needs approach, but that its linkages with other sectors of the economy should be modified. For example, the surpluses of the modern sector could be used to generate the economic expansion of the rural and urban informal sector, resulting in greater economic integration of the country's economy. He agrees with Higgins that the basic-needs approach is 'very explicitly complementary' to the NIEO, and argues that both international redistribution and national redistribution within poor countries should (for moral and political reasons) take place simultaneously. He goes further by proposing a 'Third Development Strategy' consisting of a triptych:

> The first panel should focus on the internal problems of the developed countries; the second panel on the internal problems of the developing countries; and the third panel would sum up the international implications of where we want to go as nations.[62]

The expanding influence of the basic-needs approach during the 1970s also attracted criticism from neoclassical economists. In 1982, Little reiterated the criticism that the basic-needs approach has few distinctive features that make it separable from redistribution-with-growth or other general approaches aimed at tackling poverty.[63] Specifically he says that basic needs themselves are not defined anywhere and that governments are simply asked to provide subsidised services and food by increasing government spending and greater taxation of the rich. Finally, he argues that basic-needs merely fulfills the role of a 'slogan' for the supporters of greater equality in society.

Lal took this criticism a step further by phrasing the argument in terms of a conflict between the State and the free market. In his view, basic-needs spokesmen aim to change the ownership of the means of production and distribution of goods and services from the private to the state sector by nationalisation and other measures. 'The strategy,' he claims, 'is fundamentally paternalistic, entailing a vast increase in state control and bureaucratic discretion'.[64]   He also warns of the dangers of an 'imperfect bureaucracy' and urges the use of the price mechanism even in the presence of imperfect markets.   He concludes with a recommendation for poverty alleviation: efficient growth that increases unskilled labour demand 'by getting the prices right'.

Neoclassical critics have not limited their attack to national redistributive reform but have also considered aspects of the international redistribution of resources argued for by Third-World spokesmen and some basic-needs supporters.   Grubel, for example, highlighted two important defects with the NIEO proposals adopted by the UN General Assembly.[65]   First, pointing out that many NIEO supporters have proposed that a redistribution of resources between rich and poor countries could occur in part via the creation by the IMF of additional special drawing rights (SDRs), he argues that the creation of international liquidity through SDRs would entail considerable risk of inflationary pressures.   Confrontation between those developing countries that desire to create SDRs in quantities large enough to maximise their overall transfers, and developed countries that rush to restrict the quantity of new SDRs to non-inflationary levels could also result, and the bargaining exercises themselves would tend to give rise to uncertainties and inefficiencies in the international monetary system as well.   Second, he argues that attempts to stabilize and reduce the effects of price and supply fluctuations in primary products of developing countries, via international buffer stocks for example, should be rejected outright.   Rejecting the concept of the NIEO, he instead recommends the industrial countries to encourage the functioning of market forces and the expansion of world trade, to support international organisations like the IMF, the World Bank and the GATT, and to increase aid to 0.7 per cent or more of their GNPs.

In a more 'balanced' critique, Cline observed in his extensive empirical study of the potential impact of NIEO propositions that, 'The extent of world poverty is so massive that even if virtually *all* of the changes advocated by the developing countries could be enacted, the result would still be only a moderate increase in per capita income of the poor countries'.[66]   Even for advocates of the NIEO, this pointed to the sobering idea that redistribution of income on a global scale and more equitable growth could not be counted on even in the event of successful NIEO negotiations.

Finally, Krenin and Finger's analysis of the NIEO proposals concluded that 'they are not revolutionary enough to deserve the flashy title ('New Order') assigned to them, (and) in each case they are judged to be either economically ineffective or politically non-feasible in moving the world towards the advocated goals'.[67] They argue that most of the NIEO proposals depend on the 'economic altruism' of the Western countries, which is unlikely to be sufficient to provide the reforms the developing countries seek. Hence, for example, the desired large transfers of resources from the developed to the developing countries are unlikely to be forthcoming. Moreover, they argue, the NIEO proposals focus international attention on the external relations of the developing countries (especially on the trade and aid links with the developed countries) and divert attention from the more vital questions of internal strategies for development and growth, whereas 'for the most part, economic development is something that the developing countries must do for themselves'.[68] The process of internal transformation and structural change requires political stability, economic incentives and most of all, time; trade and aid can add to the resources available for development, but are by themselves not able to affect a fundamental change.

While neoclassical writers have pointed to defects of basic-needs, argued that NIEO is diverting attention from prices and markets, and stressed the importance of internal reforms, the broad reformist approach has been reproached by less orthodox writers for different reasons.

Some of the more radical views are presented by Hayter's 1981 review of the Brandt Commission's Report for example. She argues that while the Report represents progress within the context of orthodox development thinking because it focuses on poverty, it constitutes no more than an 'enlightened expression of establishment thinking'.[69] She sees the authors of the Report as preoccupied with the world economic crisis facing developed and developing countries, because of its severity and prolonged nature and also because of the inability of the institutional framework (notably the Bretton Woods system) to cope with the adjustment problems implied by the crisis. The extreme degree of poverty in developing countries, she feels, is perceived as a further threat to the world economic system because the persistence of poverty gives rise to social unrest, and in the end to rebellion and possibly to fundamental changes in social organisations that could result in the closure of some developing countries to profitable trade and direct foreign investment opportunities for the

West. Hence the mutual interest of the governments in the North and South in maintaining and expanding markets and investment opportunities coincides with humanitarian objectives: 'The proposals for reform are designed first and most crucially to ensure that the existing world economic system functions smoothly. Second, if possible, the reforms are to be designed in such a way that they achieve some alleviation of extreme poverty in underdeveloped countries'.[70] The main problem, however, is that the Brandt Report does not explain why poverty exists in the first place. If it attempted such an explanation, she argues, it might come to the embarrassing conclusion that poverty is caused precisely by the economic system which its proposals are supposed to protect.

In his analysis of different reformist policy proposals for Latin America – including employment creation, integrated rural development, redistribution with growth and basic needs, the NIEO and redistrubition before growth – Alain de Janvry argues that,

> the broadest criticism that can be, indeed must be, levelled at all these reformist positions is their theoretical poverty. Either they approach the problem of policy prescription in an ad hoc way or they lack an adequate theory of poverty upon which to base action on poverty. This is more blatant in some of the positions than others. The basic needs approach, for example, has absolutely no theoretical foundation; nor does it really need one, being as it is, nothing more than institutionalised charity based on evident presumptions such as 'operationality' (to use Streeten's term) vis-à-vis the more abstract goal of reducing inequality.[71]

De Janvry further argues that the clear cause of this lack of an adequate theory of poverty is that the inequitable growth that reformists deem undesirable is conceptualised in the framework of neoclassical growth theory. As a result, any condemnation of poverty can lead to only one of three positions, two of which are rejected by reformists.

One position is that if growth does not alleviate policy, this is either because it has not been rapid enough – implying that growth must be systematically accelerated, and the reforms advocated by international agencies to promote equity should be opposed[72] – or else simply because increasing inequality is normal during the early stages of growth, as suggested by the Kugnets-U-shaped-curve hypothesis. It is this 'grow-or-bust' position which the advocates of equitable growth denounce for both political and humanitarian reasons.

Another position is that market distortions, notably due to state intervention, are what prevent a reduction of inequalities through efficient factor reallocation in a system of free markets. This position is of course the heart of the monetarist approach, whose principal policy prescription is to eliminate government economic intervention so as to restore perfect competition. Again, the reformists denounce this position as insufficient because income distribution would remain highly skewed even if maximum ('Pareto optimal') efficiency were achieved.[73]

The only other position is that political and structural changes are necessary to reconcile growth and equity. Because politics and structure lie beyond the limits of neoclassical theory, which deals with efficiency questions within a given political and structural context, however, strategies for equitable growth must therefore be advanced on an ad hoc and voluntary basis.

De Janvry concludes his critique of reformism with the observation that, 'Any proposal to eliminate poverty and improve the distribution of income within and among countries needs to originate in a positive analysis of the sources of unequal development'.[74] His own analysis, regarding Latin America (cf. Chapter 6), focuses on the changing nature of the internal class structure and of international class alliances.

THE IMPACT OF REFORMIST THINKING

Since its appearance in the late 1960s, and through its heyday period of the 1970s, reformist development thinking and particularly its strategy-oriented focus have had considerable impact on international organisations, aid donors and Third World governments. The early strands of thought were discussed and refined at several large international conferences involving international civil servants, academics and Third World policy-makers. From this core of organisations and conferences it spread outwards to other international organisations and the academic community. This contrasts with the neoclassical current, which largely originated in the Western academic community and flowed outwards to international organisations, aid donors and developing countries.

Influenced by reformist pressures and encouraged by favourable public opinion, Western aid donors have tended to give increasing prominence to poverty. Not surprisingly, the more mildly formulated redistribution-with-growth strategies (which emphasize redistribution via employment and the market system) are more widely accepted by the

Western donor community than strategies stressing substantial redistribution of assets or revolutionary change. But at least three important shifts in aid policy – as found for example in the 1985 Chairman's Report of the OECD Development Assistance Committee (DAC), *Twenty-Five Years of Development Cooperation* – can be traced back to the influence of the reformist movement. First, in the latter half of the 1970s, there was a large increase in official development assistance to poverty alleviation. Second, there has been an emphasis on supporting basic-needs sectors such as health, education, the provision of safe drinking water, irrigation, agriculture and rural development. Third, among some agencies there has been a tendency to finance and promote small-scale localised projects (specifically geared to attacking poverty at the grassroots level) as opposed to sectoral assistance and large-scale projects.

In addition to these effects on government aid policy, the reformist period saw the emergence of non-governmental organisations as important actors in the donor community (both in terms of political pressure and as sources of finance). These NGO's – e.g. OXFAM and Christian Aid, to cite only two examples from the United Kingdom – have reinforced the tendency by some UN agencies, e.g. UNICEF and IFAD, to favour the adoption of small-scale poverty-specific projects.

Still, some writers are not very optimistic about the actual impact. Griffin, for example, has argued that 'the contribution of foreign aid to the alleviation of poverty in the Third World has at best been slight and at worst negative'.[75] Not only is the quantity of aid given insignificant (equal to about one-third of a per cent of donor countries' GNP) but a large proportion of aid donated since 1945 has gone to the 'less poor countries'. In addition, he doubts whether aid to poor countries has actually benefitted substantially the poorest sections of the population. Hence, although the developed-country aid agencies have supported the call for more poverty-oriented aid, the aid has not always been so forthcoming owing to the low priority given to aid by developed-country governments and also to the intense competition for funds among different government agencies in those countries.

The above-cited 1985 DAC Chairman's Report was also critical of the attitudes of developing-country governments towards anti-poverty strategies: 'Still (they were) not comprehensively applied by many governments of developing countries. While accepting the logic of supplementing the erratic, unbalanced 'trickle down' of economic growth with governmental interventions to broaden employment generation, income distribution and the delivery of social services, they found practical implementation to be very difficult and controversial. Political resistance or indifference and weak intra-governmental co-ordination such as had plagued 'integrated rural development' discouraged comprehensive action'.[76]

As to the debate between basic-needs strategies and the NIEO, many aid-donor countries have been keen to promote a reduction of world poverty and internal reform to this end within developing countries. On the other hand, many developing countries have vigorously pursued the call for reform at the international level with a redistribution of resources in favour of poor countries. As noted earlier, basic-needs theorists have hoped that a compromise solution could be reached so that aspects of both would be tackled. But competing interests and the demands resulting from each group have continued to be a source of confusion. Some important donors suspect that the developing countries are interested in redistribution between countries in order to promote industrialisation of the South rather than in promoting egalitarian policies at home. In turn some developing countries presume that the North wants to underplay international economic reform and redistribution by highlighting the failure of developing countries to implement more fully poverty-oriented strategies. The net result of the negotiations seems to have been another kind of solution to both issues: the neglect of both international and internal reforms and redistribution by the North and the South and the tendency to focus more urgently on other issues.[77]

One such issue that has played a part in downgrading the reformist movement among donors and Third World governments alike is the adverse international economic climate facing the developing countries following the oil and other commodity price shocks of the 1970s and 1980s. The effect was to cause a partial shift in attention from poverty and basic human-needs concerns (which were perceived to require expensive medium to long-term solutions) to macro-economic problems and stabilisation programmes (which were perceived to be short-term and require immediate solutions). Similarly, the industrialised countries, faced with problems of inflation, unemployment and recession, have tended to look inwards at domestic priorities rather than concern themselves excessively with global poverty. Many Western governments have also been searching for politically feasible ways to decrease public spending. So while aid to poor countries remains a small fraction of GNP, there have been few legislative initiatives to increase it, with the notable and very recent exception of Japan, whose aid flows remain concentrated in middle-income developing countries.[78]

In his final address to the Board of Governors of the World Bank in 1980, MacNamara elaborated on the deteriorating economic climate facing the developing countries. The sharp increase in oil prices (1979/1980) that doubled the cost of imports for non-oil developing countries and the prolonged recession in the advanced countries, which in turn reduced their demand for exports from the developing countries, were cited as the two major causes of the increase in the current-account deficits of developing countries. In the short run, MacNamara suggested that these could be financed by borrowing, but he noted that in the long run the resulting debt could become difficult to repay. He recommended internal adjustment for the developing countries – including export promotion and austerity measures aimed at cutting imports – but he also emphasized that, 'Development itself comprises a two fold task: to accelerate economic growth; and to eradicate absolute poverty.' He also reminded his audience that 'the pursuit of growth (and financial readjustment) without a reasonable concern for equity is ultimately socially destabilising'.[79]

Despite MacNamara's reminder of the importance of concerns for eradicating poverty and for equality – some would say because of it – his speech in a sense foretold the overshadowing of reformist thinking in the 1980s by the neoclassical resurgence. Moreover, as reported in a 1986 paper written for the World Bank by Brett, reformism has had only limited influence on development policy and even less impact on development practice since the MacNamara era at the World Bank.[80]

Nevertheless, the broad reformist approach or at least some aspects of it remain vitally important to many development writers and policy-makers. This emerged clearly, to cite only one example, in the recent OECD Development Centre 25th Anniversary Symposium, one of whose messages was that in today's context of accelerating economic globalisation, the danger that large segments of the world's population will be literally left in hunger and poverty, has never been greater in the postwar period [81].

Notes and References

1. S. Kuznets, 'Economic Growth and Income Inequality' in *American Economic Review*, Vol. 45, March 1955; S. Kuznets, 'Quantitative Aspects of the Economic Growth of Nations: Distribution of Income by Size' in *Economic Development and Cultural Change*, Vol. 11, January 1963; and I.B. Kravis, 'International Differences in the Distribution of

Reformist Development Thinking

125

Income' in *Review of Economics and Statistics*, Vol. 45, November 1960. See also H.T. Oshima, 'The International Comparison of Size Distribution of Family Incomes with Special Reference to Asia' in *Review of Economics and Statistics*, Vol. 34, August 1962; and J.G. Williamson, 'Regional Inequality and the Progress of National Development: A Description of Patterns' in *Economic Development and Cultural Change*, July 1965.

2. See H.B. Chenery, *et al., Redistribution With Growth*, Oxford University Press, London, 1974; and A. Fishlow, 'Brazilian Size Distribution of Income' in *American Economic Review*, Vol. LX, No. 3, May 1972.

3. H.W. Singer, 'Dualism Revisited: A New Approach to the Problems of the Dual Society in Developing Countries' in *Journal of Development Studies*, Vol. 17, No. 1, October 1970.

4. D. Turnham and I. Jaeger, *The Employment Problem in Less Developed Countries: A Review of Evidence*, OECD Development Centre, Paris, 1971. See also D. Morawetz, 'Employment Implications of Industrialisation in Developing Countries', *Economic Journal*, Vol. 84, September 1976; and R. Jolly, *et al., Third World Employment: Problems and Strategy*, Penguin, 1973.

5. B. Ward, 'The Decade of Development – A Study in Frustration' (A lecture delivered at the Overseas Development Institute on May 3, 1965), Overseas Development Institute, London, 1965, p. 4.

6. R. Bird and L. De Wulf, *Taxation and Income Distribution in Latin America: A Critical Review of Empirical Studies*, International Monetary Fund Staff Papers, 20, No. 3, 1973.

7. Quotation taken from a lecture by Dudley Seers entitled 'What are we trying to measure' presented at the 11th World Conference of the Society for International Development (New Delhi, November 1969). The speech has been reprinted in N. Baster, ed., *Measuring Development*, Frank Cass, London, 1972, p. 24.

8. G. Myrdal, *The Challenge of World Poverty*, Penguin, 1970, p. 49.

9. L. Emmerij, 'Basic Needs and Employment-oriented Strategies Reconsidered' in *Development and Peace*, Vol. 2, Autumn 1981, p. 152.

10. For example in Colombia, given current demographic trends, it was estimated that 'full employment' (employment of 95 per cent of the labour force) would require the creation of five million additional jobs during the period 1970-1985. The achievement of this target was argued to require a comprehensive employment strategy emphasising land reform, the promotion of agriculture, a labour intensive bias in industrial policy, more effective technology policies, and the provision of wider education opportunities, among other policy measures. ILO, *Towards Full Employment: A Programme for Colombia*, Geneva, 1970. See also ILO, *Matching Employment Opportunities and Expectations: A Programme of Action for Ceylon*, Geneva, 1971.

11. ILO, *Employment, Incomes and Equality: A Strategy for Increasing Productive Employment in Kenya*, Geneva, 1972.

12. More than a hundred studies were carried out on the behaviour of income distribution during the process of development, on the major factors affecting inequality, on the problems of poverty and the different groups

living under poverty, and on the policy measures used by governments to improve inequality. A good synthesis of the questions studied, methods employed and results obtained by the World Employment Programme on the subjects of employment and income distribution is J. Lecaillon, F. Paukert, C. Morrisson, and D. Germidis, *Income Distribution and Economic Development: An Analytical Survey*, ILO, Geneva, 1984.

13.   More recently, in a widely publicised study of the informal sector in Peru, Hernando de Soto has argued that heavy-handed government bureaucracy that discriminates against entrepreneurs is what drives them into the informal sector (H. de Soto, *The Other Path: the Invisible Revolution in the Third World*, Harper and Row, New York, 1989 (first published in Spanish in collaboration with E. Ghers, M. Ghibellini and the Instituto Libertad y Democracia, *El Otro Sendero: La Revolución Informal*, Instituto Libertad y Democracia, 1987)).

14.   For an internal assessment of the effectiveness and design of the employment missions to Colombia, Ceylon, Kenya and Iran, and of the overall ILO employment-oriented strategy, see ILO, *Strategies for Employment Promotion*, Geneva, 1973. See also G. Kitching, *Development and Underdevelopment in Historical Perspective*, Methuen, London, 1982.

15.   Some of the results of this internal assessment of the World Bank's role in development over the preceding 25 years and the record of the developing countries during that period can be found in D. Morawetz, *Twenty-five Years of Economic Development, 1950–75*, World Bank, Washington D.C., 1977. See also R.S. MacNamara, 'Annual Speech to the Board of Governors', World Bank, Washington D.C., September 1972.

16.   A complete list of these mimeographs on income distribution in developing countries can be found in H.B. Chenery, *et al.*, (1974), *op. cit.*

17.   The studies considered a person to be in absolute poverty if he or she earned less than US$ 50 a year and in relative poverty if the individual's annual income exceeded $50 but was below one-third of the national average. The source of the data is World Bank, *Rural Development*, Sector Policy Paper, Washington D.C., February 1975, pp. 19–20.

18.   R.S. MacNamara, 'Address to the Board of Governors', World Bank, Washington D.C., 1973, pp. 9–10.

19.   World Bank, *The Assault on World Poverty*, Washington, D.C., 1975. This book consists of a collection of five important policy papers written in the early 1970s and laying out the Bank's policy intentions in rural development, agricultural credit, land reform, education, and health.

20.   See World Bank, *World Development Report*, Washington D.C., 1977 and 1979.

21.   R.S. MacNamara, 'Address to the Board of Governors', World Bank, Washington D.C., 1975, p. 15.

22.   Mahbub ul Haq, *The Poverty Curtain: Choices for the Third World*, Columbia University Press, New York, 1976, pp. 61–74.

23.   Dag Hammarskjold Report, 'What Now: Another Development', *Development Dialogue*, 1/2, 1975.

24. See A. Herrera, *et al., Catastrophe or New Society? A Latin American Model*, International Development Research Centre, Ottawa, 1976.

25. J. Tinbergen, *et al., Reshaping the International Order, A Report of the Club of Rome*, E.P. Dutton, New York, 1976, p. 63.

26. *Employment, Growth and Basic Needs: A One World Problem*, Report of the Director General of the International Labour Office to the Tripartite World Conference on Employment, Income Distribution and Social Progress, and the International Division of Labour, Geneva, 1976, p. 3.

27. The broad strategy for the basic-needs approach was laid out in the programme for action adopted at the final plenary session. For the details of the conference and of the programme for action, see ILO, *Meeting Basic Needs: Strategies for Eradicating Mass Poverty and Unemployment*, Geneva, 1976.

28. ILO, *ibid.*, p. 14.

29. P. Streeten, 'The Distinctive Features of a Basic Needs Approach to Development' in *International Development Review*, Vol. 19, No. 3, 1977. This article also discusses the differences between the income-based approach to poverty and basic needs, and the trade-off between basic needs and growth.

30. Perkins, for example, pointed out that the Chinese had been remarkably successful both in redistributing income and in meeting the basic needs of most of their population. He saw the major mechanism for redistribution in Maoist China not to have been the cooperative and commune movements of the late 1950s, but the conventional land reforms of the early 1950s. He deemed the communes to have played a vital role in satisfying other basic needs, however, notably employment and health care. Cf. D. Perkins, 'Meeting Basic Needs in the People's Republic of China' in *World Development*, Vol. 6, No. 5, 1977.

31. See for example, D.M. Leipziger, *Basic Needs and Development*, Oelgeschlager, Gunn and Hain, Cambridge, 1981, Chapter 4; and P. Isenman, 'Basic Needs: The Case of Sri Lanka' in *World Development*, Vol. 8, March 1980.

32. H. Chenery, *et al.*, (1974), *op. cit.*

33. T. Balogh, 'Failures in the Strategy against Poverty' in *World Development*, Vol. 6, No. 1, 1978, p. 11.

34. For examples of UNRISD's research on the economic and social implications of the green revolution, see C. Hewitt de Alcantara, *Modernising Mexican Agriculture: Socio-Economic Implications of Technical Change, 1940–70*, UNRISD, Geneva, 1976; and I. Palmer, *The New Rice in the Philippines*, Geneva, UNRISD, 1975. For a good summary of the results from many of the case studies, consult A. Pearse, *Seeds of Plenty, Seeds of Want*, Oxford University Press, 1980.

35. One of the UNRISD studies by Griffin argues that the adoption of high-yielding varieties of wheat and rice tends to be biased in favour of landlords because the structures of markets and of land-tenure that exist in many developing countries tend to give the landlords favourable access to factor markets (especially credit) vis-a-vis the peasants. Griffin adds that because the landlord's real cost of capital and other material inputs is lower than that faced by the peasant, the landlord is more likely to

adopt the innovation than the peasant. This unequal access to factor
markets, which Griffin demonstrates in terms of different relative factor
prices faced by the landlord and the peasant, has several undesirable
consequences: it increases the degree of income inequality, results in a
lower level of agricultural production, creates surplus labour and
underemployment, reduces the prosperity of the agricultural sector to
innovate, and increases the likelihood that if any innovation does occur,
it will be the landlord who does it (K. Griffin, *The Green Revolution: An
Economic Analysis*, UNRISD, Geneva, 1972, p. 43). This was later
reprinted as: K. Griffin, *The Political Economy of Agrarian Change: An
Essay in the Green Revolution*, MacMillan, London, 1974.

36.   A. Van De Laar, 'The World Bank and the World's Poor' in *World
        Development*, Vol. 4, No. 10/11, 1976.

37.   Van De Laar (1976), *ibid.*, reports that the share of World Bank lending
        to seven middle income countries (Brazil, Colombia, Iran, Turkey,
        Korea, Zambia and Morocco) increased from 16.8 to 37.9 per cent under
        MacNamara during the period 1968–76.

38.   P. Streeten and S.J. Burki, 'Basic Needs: Some Issues' in *World
        Development*, Vol. 6, No. 3, 1978, p. 411.

39.   *ibid.*, p. 413.

40.   *ibid.*,

41.   The results of the World Bank's attempts to make basic needs into an
        operational strategy can be found in P. Streeten, *et al., First Things First:
        Meeting Basic Human Needs in the Developing Countries*, Oxford
        University Press, New York, 1981. See also P. Streeten, 'Basic Needs:
        Some Unsettled Questions' in *World Development*, Vol. 12, No. 9, 1984.

42.   See for example, G. Cornia, R. Jolly and F. Stewart, *Adjustment with a
        Human Face*, Oxford University Press, 1987.

43.   For developments in the NIEO and the North–South dialogue, consult
        P.K. Ghosh, ed., *New International Economic Order*, Greenwood Press,
        1984.   See also Centre d'Etudes Prospectives et d'Information
        Internationales (CEPII), *Economie Mondiale : La Montée des Tensions*,
        Economica, Paris, 1983.

44.   P. Streeten, *Development Perspectives*, MacMillan, London, 1981, p. 358.

45.   *North–South: The Report of the Independent Commission on International
        Development Issues Under the Chairmanship of Willy Brandt*, Pan Books,
        London, 1980, p. 296.

46.   See Kuznets, S. (1955), *op. cit.*

47.   I. Adelman and C.T. Morris, *Economic Growth and Social Equality in
        Developing Countries*, Stanford University Press, 1973.

48.   I. Adelman, 'Growth, Income Distribution, and Equity-Oriented
        Development Strategies' in *World Development*, Vol. 3, No. 1 and 2, 1975.

49.   The World Bank's *World Development Report*, 1980, p. 41.

50.   A. Saith, 'Development and Distribution: A Critique of the
        Cross-Country U Hypothesis' in *Journal of Development Economics*, Vol.
        13, 1983; and M.S. Ahluwalia, 'Inequality, Poverty and Development' in
        Journal of Development Economics, Vol. 3, 1976.

51.   N. Hicks, 'Growth v. Basic Needs: Is There a Trade Off?' in *World
        Development*, 1979.

52. K. Griffin and J. James, *The Transition to Egalitarian Development: Economic Policies for Structural Change in the Third World*, MacMillan, London, 1981.

53. M.S. Ahluwalia, N.G. Carter and H.B. Chenery, 'Growth and Poverty in Developing Countries' in *Journal of Development Economics*, September 1979. Other useful empirical studies that provide a global view of the poverty problem include: I. Adelman, and C.T. Morris (1973), *op. cit.*, and G.S. Fields, *Poverty, Inequality and Development*, Cambridge University Press, 1980.

54. For detailed pictures of the pattern of poverty by region and country the interested reader is referred to the following:
    On South Asia: M.S. Ahluwalia, 'Rural Poverty and Agricultural Growth in India' in *Journal of Development Studies*, April 1978; K. Griffin, 'Growth and Impoverishment in the Rural Areas of India' in *World Development*, April/May 1979; R.H. Cassen, *India: Population, Economy and Society*, MacMillan, London, 1978; and G.B. Rodgers, 'A Conceptualisation of Poverty in Rural India' in *World Development*, Vol. 4, No. 4, April 1976.
    On Southeast Asia: P. Hasan, 'Growth and Equity in East Asia' in *Finance and Development*, Vol. 15 No. 2, June 1978; and J. Fei, G. Ranis, S.W.Y. Kuo, *Equity with Growth: The Taiwan Case*, Oxford University Press, London, 1979.
    On Latin America: J. Bergsman, 'Income Distribution and Poverty in Mexico' in *World Bank Staff Working Paper No. 395*, Washington D.C., World Bank, 1980; and O. Aitimer, 'The Extent of Poverty in Latin America', *World Bank Staff Working Paper No. 522*, World Bank, Washington D.C., 1982.
    On Africa: D. Ghai and S. Radwan, eds., *Agrarian Policies and Rural Poverty in Africa*, ILO, Geneva, 1983; C. Coquery-Vidrovitch, *Afrique Noire : Permanences et Ruptures*, Payot, Paris, 1985; and J. Lecaillon and C. Morrisson, *Politiques Economiques et Performances Agricoles : le cas du Burkina Faso, 1960–83*, OECD Development Centre, Paris, 1985.

55. For more details of this subject, see for example, E. Boserup, *Woman's Role in Economic Development*, St. Martin's Press, New York, 1980; M. Buvinic and L. McGreevey, eds., *Women and Poverty in the Third World*, Johns Hopkins University Press, Baltimore, 1983; and W. Weekes-Vagliani, *The Integration of Women in Development Projects*, OECD Development Centre, Paris, 1985.

56. UNRISD, *Contents and Measurements of Socio-economic Development*, Geneva 1979. For a good survey of composite indicators, see N. Hicks and P. Streeten, 'Indicators of Development: The Search for a Basic Needs Yard Stick', *World Development*, June 1979.

57. M.D. Morris, *Measuring the Condition of the World's Poor: The Physical Quality of Life Index*, Pergamon, New York, 1979. See also D.A. Larson and W.T. Wilford, 'The Physical Quality of Life Index: A Useful Social Indicator?' in *World Development*, Vol. 7, No. 6, 1979.

58. Singh also stresses that pursuit of the basic-needs approach does not conflict with developing-country aspirations for faster industrialisation. In fact, he argues, to meet basic needs in poor countries it is necessary to

industrialise. Thus, basic needs and industrialisation go hand in hand. See A. Singh, 'The Basic Needs Approach to Development vs the New International Economic Order: The Significance of Third World Industrialisation' in *World Development*, Vol. 7, No. 6, 1979.

59. B. Higgins, 'The Disenthronement of Basic Needs? Twenty Questions' in *Regional Development Dialogue*, Vol. 1, No. 1, 1980.

60. P. Streeten, 'A Comment' in *Regional Development Dialogue*, Vol. 1, No. 1, 1980.

61. *ibid.*, p. 119.

62. L. Emmerij, 'A Comment' in *Regional Development Dialogue*, Vol. 1, No. 1, 1980, p. 122.

63. I.M.D. Little, *Economic Development*, Basic Books, New York, 1982, Chapter 11.

64. D. Lal, *The Poverty of Development Economics*, The Institute of Economic Affairs, London, 1983, p. 100.

65. H.G. Grubel, 'The Case Against the New International Economic Order' in *Weltwirtschaftliches Archive* Band 113, Heft 2, 1977.

66. See W.R. Cline, ed., *Policy Alternatives for A New International Economic Order*, Praeger, New York, 1979. See also E. Jouve, ed., *Pour un nouvel order mondial*, Berger-Levrault, Paris, 1985.

67. M.E. Krenin and J.M. Finger, 'A Critical Survey of the New International Economic Order' in *Journal of World Trade Law*, Vol. 10, No. 6, Nov/Dec 1976, p. 508.

68. *ibid.*, p. 509.

69. T. Hayter, *The Creation of World Poverty: An Alternative View to the Brandt Report*, Pluto Press, London, 1981. See also A.G. Frank, 'North–South and East–West: Keynesian Paradoxes in the Brandt Report' in *Third World Quarterly*, Vol. 2, No. 4, October 1980; and G. Williams, *The Brandt Report: A Critical Indroduction*, Third World First, London, 1980.

70. *ibid.*,

71. A. de Janvry, *The Agrarian Question and Reformism in Latin America*, Johns Hopkins University Press, Baltimore, 1981, p. 258.

72. See for example, W. Galenson, 'Economic Growth, Poverty, and the International Agencies' in *Journal of Policy Modeling*, Vol. 1, No. 2, 1979.

73. See for example, K. Griffin, *Alternative Strategies for Economic Development, op. cit.* See also I. Adelman, M. Hopkins, S. Robinson, G. Rodgers and R. Wery, 'A Comparison of Two Models for Income Distribution Planning' in *Journal of Policy Modeling*, Vol. 1, No. 1, 1979, which found on the basis of comprehensive econometric modeling that 'only a massive, wide-ranging, balanced, and continued attack on poverty and maldistribution of income has much chance of succeeding... fundamental changes in social structure and institutions are likely to be needed' (pp. 81–82).

74. De Janvry (1981), *op. cit.*, p. 259.

75. K. Griffin, *International Inequality and National Poverty*, Holmes and Meier, New York, 1978.

76. Chairman's Report, *Twenty-Five Years of Development Cooperation*, OECD Development Assistance Committee, Paris, 1985, p. 19.

77. The subject of international interests, both common North–South dialogue has been explored by R. Larsen and R. Jolly, eds., *Rich Country Interests and Third World Development*, St. Martin, London, 1982.

78. See for example, T. Ozawa, *Recycling Japan's Surpluses for Developing Countries*, OECD Development Centre, 1989.

79. R.S. MacNamara, 'Address to the Board of Governors', World Bank, Washington D.C., 1980, p. 45, is the source for both quotations.

80. E.A. Brett, 'Reaching the Poorest: Does the World Bank Still Believe in Redistribution with Growth' in World Bank, *Recovery in the Developing World*, Washington D.C., 1986.

81. L. Emmerij, ed., *One World or Several*, papers and proceedings of the OECD Development Centre's 25th Anniversary Symposium, OECD Development Centre, Paris, 1989.

PART II
Heterodox Development Thinking

Heterodox Development Thinking

Our distinction between orthodox and heterodox development thinking is admittedly subjective. It basically derives from a distinction between writers and policy-makers who portray the world economy as comprising a 'centre' of advanced capitalist countries and a 'periphery' of underdeveloped countries (writers whom we classify as heterodox) and those who do not readily accept the centre-periphery paradigm. By implication, our heterodox writers tend to go further than do our orthodox writers in their questioning and critique of the functioning of capitalism within countries as well as at the global level.

There are, however, broad differences within each group, not only in method but in politics as well. Some writers we have classified as orthodox may be as critical of the established order, or more so, than others we have classified as heterodox. Likewise, within our heterodox group, some writers clearly seek to make capitalism work, while others seek to move beyond it. And, at the other end of the spectrum, for a few economists – e.g., Deepak Lal (cf. Chapter 3) – the whole of development economics is heterodox.

Our discussion of heterodox development thinking comprises two chapters. Chapter 5 traces the evolution of 'structuralist' thinking, from the emergence of the centre–periphery paradigm in Latin America in the late 1940s and 1950s, through the divorce between 'developmentalism' (as its radical critics referred to it) and the newly emerging school of 'dependency' thinking in the mid-1960s, to the Marxist critique of dependency thinking in the 1970s and the emergence of 'neo-structuralism' in the 1980s. Chapter 5 also briefly looks at the policy influence of structuralism and dependency thinking in developing countries outside Latin America.

Chapter 6 reviews the major reversals that have taken place in Marxist thinking as regards the impact of the development of capitalism on the periphery. While the classical Marxist–Leninist view was that capitalism, and capitalist imperialism, has a progressive impact on underdeveloped countries, this view was reversed during the 1920s. The dominant view among Marxist and neo-Marxist ('radical structuralist') writers in the 1950s and 1960s tended to be that capitalism and imperialism is a major cause of underdevelopment in the periphery.

135

This 'stagnationist' view was in turn strongly criticised and essentially reversed during the 1970s, however.

Chapter 6 also reviews the rich literature on class structure and agrarian political economy (the 'modes of production' controversy). It concludes with a brief discussion of the implications of the processes of concentration and centralisation of capital for economic development as we move into the 1990s.

5 Structuralism and Dependency

Just as the Great Depression of the 1930s induced major change in the prevailing winds of economic thought in the developed countries, in the form of the Keynesian Revolution, so the economic upheavals of the Depression and two World Wars gave impulse to the first major body of development thought produced in the developing countries. And just as Keynesianism came to exert its full weight only in the postwar period, so this body of thought, known as Latin American Structuralism, emerged in the late 1940s and 1950s.

The leading figures, many of whom were strongly influenced by the Keynesian Revolution, were Raul Prebisch and a group of social scientists working at the U.N. Economic Commission for Latin America (ECLA). Like Keynes, and in contrast to Marx, the structuralists did not see capitalism as having to struggle against an inherent tendency toward self-destruction, but that active intervention by the State might be necessary to palliate some of its problems. Whereas Keynes focused on the severe but essentially conjunctural problems of unemployment in developed economies, however, the structuralists saw the problems in their own countries as structural rather than conjunctural, i.e. not as problems of unemployment per se but of underdevelopment.

STRUCTURALISM: THE EARLY PERIOD

The starting points of the structuralists, which stemmed from their efforts to conceptualise the key features of Latin America's historical growth process, were the concepts of 'outward-oriented' and 'inward-oriented' growth and the 'centre–periphery' paradigm.

The key features of outward-oriented growth, which lasted roughly until the First World War, are the leading role of raw-materials exports and, at least in the larger countries, the beginnings of industrialisation based mainly on the transformation of locally produced raw materials. The development of primary exports led to the construction of railroads and other infrastructure which were largely financed by debt in the form of bonds floated in London, Paris and New York, resulting in substantial financial flows to the region from about 1870.

The First World War further stimulated European demands for the region's primary exports, which also boosted Latin American incomes and import demands. But it curtailed the supply of exports to the region from the warring countries. Considerable 'spontaneous' impulse, i.e., stimulus from market forces, was thereby given to local manufacturing, particularly of consumer goods for which demands were strong and imports in short supply. Thus began the shift toward inward-oriented growth, in the form of import-substituting industrialisation (ISI), in Latin America.

The structuralists also saw the conjunctural impulse given to ISI by the War as having been followed and reinforced during the 1920s by a major structural phenomenon: the shift in leadership of the world economy from the United Kingdom to the United States. The latter economy's structurally lower ratio of raw-materials imports to GDP meant that the strength of its demand growth for Latin America's primary exports during upswings in the business cycle of the world economy – increasingly determined by the US business cycle – was substantially weaker than had been the case under UK leadership.

Then the crisis of the 1930s reduced both the prices and volume of Latin America's raw-materials exports. The drop in income from exports and the accumulated debt combined to create severe foreign-exchange shortages in the region. Many governments reacted by seeking to promote exports and curtail imports through exchange-rate policies, tariffs and outright prohibition of some imports. Other policies that sought to sustain incomes and employment tended to fuel consumer demands for goods whose import was restricted. The net result was to give further 'spontaneous' impulse to ISI and inward-oriented growth – 'spontaneous' because government policies did not seek to promote ISI but simply to deal with the foreign-exchange crisis.[1]

The Second World War renewed foreign demands for the region's primary exports. But the difficulties of wartime shipping and especially the supply-side constraints on exports to Latin America continued to favour inward-oriented growth and ISI.

Substantial industrial capacities – and groups of local industrialists – serving local consumer-goods markets were thus built up in Latin America over a period of three decades or more, notably in the larger countries. But at the end of the Second World War there was also a heightened sense of vulnerability to cyclical and structural changes emanating from the leading capitalist countries, and growing doubts about the sustainability of spontaneous industrialisation in the region.

It was in that context that Prebisch and ECLA put forward the 'centre–periphery' paradigm of development and underdevelopment.

The Centre–Periphery Paradigm

According to the centre–periphery concept, the world economy comprises two poles, the centre and the periphery, whose production structures are markedly different. Production structures in the periphery are seen as *heterogeneous*, in the sense that sectors characterised by backward production techniques and low productivity (e.g. subsistence agriculture) co-exist with sectors that use modern techniques and have high productivity levels.[2] Production structures in the periphery are also seen as *specialised*, both in the sense that exports are limited to a few primary products and in the sense that there is little horizontal diversification, vertical integration or inter-sectoral complementarity of local production. Specialisation is also seen as reflected in the considerable extent to which local demand growth, particularly for manufactures, is met with imports.[3]

Production structures in the centre, by contrast, are seen as essentially *homogeneous*, in the sense that modern production techniques are used virtually throughout the economy. And they are seen as *diversified* in the sense that production covers a relatively broad range of capital, intermediate and consumer goods.

These differences in production structures are in turn seen as the basis of different functions fulfilled by each pole in the 'traditional' division of labour in the world economy, reflected in the pattern of international trade in which primary products are traded for manufactured products. The periphery, which exports primary products and imports manufactures, comprises countries where the penetration of modern capitalist production techniques lagged behind not only because they got off to a late start but, more fundamentally, because technical progress 'usually only penetrated where it was needed to produce foodstuffs and raw materials at low cost to the great industrial centres'.[4]

The heterogeneous and specialised structures of production in the periphery are seen as having taken shape most markedly during the period of outward-oriented growth. But with the spontaneous shift to inward-oriented growth and ISI, heterogeneity and specialisation do not disappear. They tend to reproduce themselves and appear in new forms. Three secular tendencies that characterise spontaneous ISI are seen to result from heterogeneity and specialisation: chronic

Unemployment

Structural unemployment is seen to have two main causes, reflecting above all the heterogeneous character of production structures. One is the large share of the total labour force located in the backward sector, which, together with high demographic growth rates, make it difficult for growth in primary exports to absorb the surplus labour from the backward sector. The other is the employment effects of modern production techniques, which are generally developed in and for conditions prevailing in the centre. High capital-labour ratios tend to limit the employment-creating effects of new investment in the modern sector, and when the latter competes with production in the backward sector it tends to reduce total employment levels. Also, minimum efficient scales of production that exceed local market size are often the cause of severe under-utilisation of installed capacities. The latter implies a highly inefficient use of savings, which only exacerbates the already significant problem of capital scarcity in the periphery. It also exacerbates structural disequilibria in the sense that while there are excess capacities in some branches of industry, capital is lacking in others and, notoriously, for investment in basic infrastructure.

Scarcity of land and archaic land tenancy and ownership structures in agriculture – notably the minifundio–latifundio complex in Latin America – are also seen as a major structural cause of unemployment [5].

External deficit

The recurring external deficits are seen as a reflection above all of the specialisation of production structures in the periphery. The major cause is seen to be a disparity between the income-elasticities of demand in each pole of the system for imports from the other – analogous to Engel's Law. The elasticity of demand in the periphery for manufactured imports tends to be greater than unity, whereas the income-elasticity of demand in the centres for primary imports from the periphery tends to be lower. Technical advances in the centre that substitute synthetic inputs for imported raw materials are seen to amplify the problem.

On the financial side of the picture, foreign capital – portfolio and direct investment – is seen as useful, both as a source of foreign exchange and as a complement to internal savings. But the contribution of foreign investment is seen as necessarily limited or transitory, lest growing service obligations absorb an excessive proportion of export earnings.

Terms of trade with the centre

The secular trend towards deteriorating terms of trade is seen to reflect both the heterogeneous and the specialised character of production in the periphery. Its main cause is seen to be the above-mentioned disparity of income-elasticities of import demands, compounded both by the limited number of primary products exported by most countries in the periphery, and by a degree of monopolistic power perceived to be higher on the side of firms and trade unions in the centre involved in industrial exports to the periphery than on the side of suppliers in the periphery that export primary products to the centre. Periodical currency devaluations, induced by the recurring trade deficits, increase the internal prices of both exports and imports in the periphery and thereby stimulate local production both of primary exports and of import-substituting manufactures. The structural tendencies of growing under-utilisation of capacity and inefficiency of investment exert downward pressures on productivity and therefore on income levels in the industrial sector. In primary exports, there is no structural tendency for labour productivity to decline, but output growth tends to increase supplies on world markets faster than demand growth and exerts downward pressure on the international prices of primary-exports. The abundance of labour (structural unemployment) is seen to be what ultimately allows wages in both sectors in the periphery to absorb the relative income losses – with part of the fruits of technical progress in the primary sector thereby exported to the centre.[6]

The secular dynamics of the centre-periphery system as presented by Prebisch and ECLA in the late 1940s and early 1950s may thus be summarised in four points[7]:

– The periphery, because of its heterogeneous and specialised production structures, is unable to produce and disseminate technical progress on a par with the centre. One result is that labour productivity increases less rapidly in the periphery's primary-export sector than in the centre's manufacturing sector. Another is that average income growth is slower in the periphery than in the centre.

– The generation of surplus labour by the large low-productivity sector (i.e. heterogeneity) keeps downward pressure on wages in the periphery, relative to the centre. This also contributes to a tendency for the international terms of trade faced by the periphery to deteriorate.

– The slower growth of labour productivity and the tendency for the terms of trade to decline, together, mean that average real incomes in the periphery grow more slowly than in the centre. And this income growth-rate differential in turn contributes to the perpetuation, or reproduction, of heterogeneity and underdevelopment in the periphery.

– There is thus an inherent trend towards unequal rates of development between the centre and the periphery. This trend involves growing disparities between the two poles, both in terms of the rate of penetration and diffusion of technical progress ('structural heterogeneity') and of horizontal diversification, inter-sectoral complementarity and vertical integration ('specialisation') of production. It also involves a growing inequality of average income levels between the centre and the periphery.

Development and underdevelopment are thus seen as related processes occurring within a single, dynamic economic system. Development is generated in some areas – the centres are defined as those countries whose economies were first penetrated by capitalist production techniques – and underdevelopment is generated in others. Modern underdevelopment is therefore seen as the result of a process of structural change in the peripheral economies that occurs in conjunction with – is conditioned by, but is not caused unilaterally by – their relations with the centre.[8]

Industrial Programming and Import Protection

The basic policy position taken by ECLA and the structuralists was to favour development through industrialisation. In this they took a position that would be shared by many orthodox writers during the 1950s, as discussed in Chapter 1.[9] But in addition to rejecting outward-oriented growth strategies based on the 'traditional' international division of labour – which, in any case, they saw as having been superseded in the leading Latin American economies by the spontaneous emergence of ISI – they also came to reject a continuation of spontaneous ISI. Neither a laissez-faire strategy based solely on comparative advantage nor one of spontaneous, purely marked-led industrialisation was viewed as a viable route to development. Neither was thought likely to overcome the structural problems of heterogeneity and specialisation. Neither would overcome the secular tendencies toward inter-sectoral disequilibria (where severe excess capacities coincide with acute underinvestment, in production and in infrastructure) and toward deteriorating terms of international trade. Breaking with the neoclassical tradition rather emphatically, the structuralists saw deliberate, policy-supported industrialisation as the necessary route.

The principal policy instrument proposed by ECLA was investment planning and coordination, which was referred to as 'industrial programming' to distinguish it clearly from socialist planning. State intervention through investment planning was seen by the structuralists (very much in the spirit of the Keynesian Revolution) not as a substitute for but as a necessary complement to private initiative. Its purpose was seen as threefold: to help bring investment requirements projected at the sectoral and economy-wide levels into approximate harmony; to help harmonise projected investment requirements with projected resource availability (internal and foreign savings); and to avoid serious long-term balance-of-payments disequilibria.[10] And the criteria proposed for allocating investment between the primary-export and ISI sectors were quite neoclassical in inspiration: investment should not go into the primary-export sector beyond the point where its marginal revenue product equaled the marginal social return on investment in production for the internal market – with international relative prices seen as an imperfect but adequate measure of marginal social returns.[11] The principle of equalising marginal returns on investment was also recommended for allocating new investments among branches in import-substituting industry.

Much more controversial were the positions taken on trade and protection. Whereas the Heckscher–Ohlin–Samuelson model (cf. Chapter 3) emphasized the economic benefits to all countries participating in trade, the centre-periphery paradigm pointed to a distribution of gains from free trade that was biased against the periphery. ECLA saw trade contributing to a long-term transfer of income from the periphery to the centre, because of the secular trend towards deteriorating terms of trade explained above, such that the fruits of technical progress tended to concentrate in the industrial centres. This view, often referred to as the 'Prebisch thesis' or the 'Prebisch–Singer thesis',[12] led ECLA to take a stance in favour of import protection in the periphery.

The arguments in favour of protection were essentially two. The static argument was that industrialisation in the periphery required some protection because of lower industrial productivity levels there relative to those in the centre. This led ECLA to recommend tariffs that would protect only products targeted for import substitution in a given planning period. It opposed the use of exchange-rate policies for protection, which were seen as inefficient and difficult to administer, and opposed undiscriminating protection of industry as a whole, which could easily lead to sub-optimal investment in the primary-export sector. It also argued that tariff levels should be kept to the minimum required to compensate for the disparity between marginal labour-productivity levels in the centre and the periphery.[13]

The dynamic argument for protection derived from the view that whenever the periphery grew faster than the centre, the disparity in income-elasticities of import demands between the two poles would accentuate the tendency towards recurring trade deficits in the periphery. Protection, it was argued, could counteract this tendency. ECLA also noted that whereas protection in the centre against imports from the periphery was detrimental to total trade – because it limited the periphery's export income and therefore its capacity to import as well – the type of protection recommended for the periphery served mainly to stabilise the growth of world trade by keeping imports by the periphery in each period more in line with its long-term import capacity. The only long-term 'cost' to the centre of such protection would be that of adjusting the composition of its exports to the periphery's changing import requirements as industrialisation proceeded.

The Orthodox Critique

Criticism of the centre–periphery paradigm from orthodox writers focused heavily on the deteriorating-terms-of-trade hypothesis. These criticisms can be roughly divided into four categories. The most important is undoubtedly the criticism that the empirical data used by Prebisch did not actually sustain his hypothesis. Prebisch's original empirical study used UK trade data for the period 1870-1940, based on FOB export prices and CIF import prices, and found a secular improvement of UK industrial export prices relative to UK primary-import prices.[14] Some authors argued that major reductions in transport costs over the period could explain Prebisch's results without implying a deterioration for primary exporters.[15] Others argued that if the data series had been extended back even further Prebisch's results would not have held up.[16] Still others argued that Great Britain was not representative of the group of industrialised trading partners of the less developed countries.[17] Some authors have even argued – using data for the postwar period into the 1970s – that the *reverse* is true, i.e., that the terms of trade for the centre are deteriorating. More recent empirical studies tend, however, to support the Prebisch–Singer hypothesis for the 70 years leading up to the Second World War, and over the past three decades.[18]

A second type of reaction was that the real problem for the periphery is not any secular trend – which cannot be clearly identified empirically anyway – but the strong short-term fluctuations, which have important negative repercussions on long-term investment planning and even relatively short-term business decisions.[19]

A third type of criticism was that even if there is a secular trend for the terms of trade for primary exporters to decline, the negative income effect may be more than counterbalanced by increases in factor productivity, so that the net welfare effect of trade for primary exporters is positive in the long run.[20] This criticism somewhat misrepresents or misinterprets the basic ECLA argument, however. The 'Prebisch–Singer thesis' was not that trade led to increasing absolute poverty in the periphery; nor did it imply that autarky would be preferable to trade. Rather, it pointed to a bias against the periphery in the sharing of gains from trade and, more fundamentally, to a widening income differential between the periphery and the centre that results from trade under the 'traditional' division of labour.

The fourth type of criticism, finally, was one which argued that ECLA rejected agriculture-led development in favour of ISI on the mistaken grounds that technical progress was necessarily greater in industry than in agriculture. The historical experiences of such countries as Australia, New Zealand and Denmark were cited as evidence to the contrary.[21] While this view was debated among orthodox writers – as we discussed in Chapter 1 – as well as between some orthodox writers and the structuralists, in the latter case the debate sometimes spilled over into accusations that the structuralist view 'blamed' the industrialised countries for underdevelopment in the periphery. Given the extent to which this misconception of the structuralist position eventually spread, it is useful to clarify that the deteriorating terms of trade were seen by the structuralists to result from the functioning of the centre–periphery as a whole, i.e. from the structural characteristics of the system as a whole, and from those of the periphery itself. Only later, with the emergence of 'dependency' thinking and the work on 'unequal exchange' – including that of many writers who were inspired by the original centre–periphery concept but criticized structuralism from the left – would the view that underdevelopment in the periphery was caused by the centre gain some currency in the heterodox literature.

Other ECLA Policy Proposals

Regional integration

While the deteriorating-terms-of-trade hypothesis and the arguments for trade protection attracted the most attention from orthodox writers, ECLA made other major contributions to development policy in the 1950s. One of the most important was its support of regional integration, and especially of regional industrial integration, which it saw as a means to alleviate the contradiction between the scale requirements for efficient production and small national markets – a contradiction that seriously aggravated the internal-savings and foreign-exchange constraints as well because of the severity of under-utilisation of industrial capacities. It was even hoped that regional industrial integration, by reducing structural inefficiencies and thus increasing productivity levels, would make industrial exports to the centre feasible. ECLA played the leading role in the creation of the Central American Common Market in the 1950s. It also played a very active part in the establishment of the Latin American Free Trade Association and, a decade later, in the Cartagena Agreement to create an Andean Common Market.

International finance

In the realm of international finance, ECLA viewed foreign direct investment favourably but, regarding debt financing, recommended that borrowing countries rely more heavily on public and especially multilateral sources of funds. This was simply because the terms were seen to be more favourable from those sources than from private sources, and because those sources were more likely to provide loans for the type of infrastructural investments so much in need in the periphery. Beyond this, proposals were made for international financing arrangements to help compensate for the wide fluctuations in commodity prices, and also for the fluctuations of foreign-exchange reserves in the periphery.[22]

Domestic policies

Outside the realm of international economic relations, changed tax structures and land reform were both put forward as means to overcome the structural problems in agriculture. Fiscal policies were also proposed to help increase economy-wide savings rates. Credit policies, including direct state involvement, were proposed to channel medium-and long-term domestic and foreign savings into productive investments and infrastructure. And active state involvement in facilitating technological progress throughout the economy was encouraged.

The State

Finally, regarding the general issue of state intervention, it is not without significance, as Rodriguez would note years later, that at no time did the State itself constitute a subject of analysis for ECLA. It was implicitly seen as an economic agent charged with, and capable of, correcting distortions in the evolution and functioning of the economic system in the periphery. If not outside that system, the State was seen as capable of relatively independent, deliberate action vis-à-vis the system.[23] While this attitude was virtually imposed by ECLA's institutional status, if not by the Keynesian influences on the ideology of its leading figures, the fact remains noteworthy. It can also be argued that both the shift in ECLA's own thinking and the emergence of 'dependency' thinking in the 1960s were in part a reaction to this shortcoming.

THE STRUCTURALIST–MONETARIST DEBATE ON INFLATION

While the controversy over the terms-of-trade hypothesis remains famous still today, many orthodox economists first became acquainted with the full dimensions of structuralism through the rather heated debate that took place in the late 1950s and early 1960s over the issue of inflation in Latin America.[24] The origins of the debate were the relatively high (by pre-war standards) and sustained levels of inflation – in Chile since the early 1950s and in Argentina, Brazil and Mexico (among others) after the Korean War – and the stabilisation policies recommended by the IMF and backed by domestic orthodox opinion. These policy recommendations reflected the IMF's view that irresponsible or at least inefficient management of short-term policies were the cause of inflation. The policies most criticised by the IMF included expansion of the money supply to finance deficit spending, insufficient currency devaluations and the use of trade restrictions and price controls to deal with the trade deficits that resulted from overvalued currencies – policies which the IMF saw as seriously undermining the allocative efficiency of the price system as a whole. The IMF recommended stabilisation policies that sought to deflate and liberalise the economy by: reducing or eliminating the fiscal deficit (reduced public expenditures and increased prices on public services), limiting expansion of credit and the money supply, significantly devaluing the currency, lowering or eliminating tariff and non-tariff trade restrictions, eliminating price controls (that existed mainly for basic necessities) and reducing and/or postponing wage adjustments.

In writings published mostly outside ECLA, the structuralists strongly criticised these stabilisation policies first of all on the grounds that they were not working in practice. They saw very limited success in curbing inflation coming at high costs in terms of reduced investment and growth, increased unemployment and lower incomes that particularly affected the poorer strata of the population. Nor were fiscal deficits significantly reduced, in part because lower growth reduced tax receipts. Nor, finally, did trade liberalisation and exchange-rate devaluation succeed as hoped, because the price-elasticity of supply of primary exports proved to be low over the relevant time period and/or world prices were unfavourable, and the price-elasticity of import demands also proved to be low.

The structuralist diagnosis differed significantly from that of the IMF, particularly in that it saw inflation not simply as a short-run monetary phenomenon but also as a result of long-term disequilibria in the 'real' economy. It distinguished between structural causes and diffusion mechanisms, with the latter seen as subordinate to the former. Among the structural causes, the secular tendency toward trade deficits was important because recurring currency devaluations stimulated inflation. During periods of dynamic export growth rapid increases of imports could cool inflationary pressures. But when deficits appeared, either growth had to be severely constrained, or else imports had to be restricted in combination with policies to sustain growth. The latter approach was often chosen over the former because of political pressures that resulted from the structural concentration of power, reflected for example in the concentration of land ownership in agriculture, monopolistic structures in industry, the importance of state enterprise in the productive sectors, etc. But restricting imports while stimulating growth tended to inflate prices rather than accelerate growth because of structural rigidities in supply, most notably in the production of food supplies. And the cyclical recurrence of trade deficits, hence of currency devaluations, tended to fan the inflationary process.

The structuralists also identified a number of factors that contributed to the spread and in some cases the amplification of the effects of these underlying causes of inflation. One such diffusion mechanism was the relatively large share of family incomes spent by wage earners on food, which tended to quicken or amplify the spiral of food-wage price increases whenever food prices started to rise. Another important factor was the fiscal system: tax structures, largely inherited from the period of outward-oriented growth, were characterised by rigidity, regressivity and vulnerability to trade fluctuations because of their excessive reliance on trade-related taxes; revenues tended to become increasingly downward inflexible because of the growth and transformation of government responsibilities under ISI, and also because of the power structures mentioned earlier. Another factor was the weakly regulated banking sector, which could easily increase the money supply in response to demands for credit from clients, notably including large landowners, monopolistic industrial interests and state enterprises. Monopolistic supply structures were also important because cost increases could more easily and quickly be passed along to customers.

The structuralists thus saw the IMF stabilisation policies as acting on the diffusion mechanisms but not on the underlying structural causes of inflation. Worse, by constraining or reversing growth momentum, the 'stabilisation' policies tended to block the very mechanisms for overcoming the structural disequilibria both in international trade and in inter-sectoral linkages.

In focusing their critique of monetarist stabilisation policies on the structural causes of inflation, the structuralists did not feel compelled to offer counter-proposals to those of the IMF for short-term anti-inflationary measures. ECLA did advise on the need for fiscal reform, and pointed to a lack of fiscal discipline as causing monetary disequilibria in Latin America. But a number of writers also suggested that significant inflation might be the price to pay for maintaining growth and overcoming structural disequilibria – a view not dissimilar to the 'unbalanced growth' hypothesis put forward by Hirschman during this same period (cf. Chapter 1). Indeed, the main impact of the structuralist arguments on the inflation issue seems to have been greater official tolerance of inflation in Latin America than in other regions, and greater reliance on price controls and other practices aimed at the symptoms more than the underlying internal disequilibria when inflation threatened other objectives. They also undoubtedly influenced the evolution of ECLA's thinking in the 1960s on the long-term problems of ISI.

ECLA AND THE STAGNATIONIST VIEWS OF THE 1960s

By the end of the 1950s, ECLA's policy emphasis on industrialisation was accepted by the majority of Latin American governments. But in contrast to the relative optimism of the structuralist views of the early to mid-1950s, which saw deliberate, policy-supported ISI as a means to counteract heterogeneity and specialisation and thus to overcome underdevelopment, the early 1960s ushered in a period of relative pessimism.

This change in perspective stemmed from a number of problems that were increasingly visible in Latin America. They included the slowing of growth, which turned negative in 1961–1963 and was most evident in countries where ISI was most enrooted; growing unemployment, underemployment and social marginalisation; empirical studies showing highly skewed and worsening income distributions; growing current-account deficits; rapidly increasing foreign debt; and sustained inflationary processes that were increasingly accompanied by social tensions and political instability. Attempts to adjust the structuralist policies were not very successful, even with the financial support of the newly created Inter-American Development Bank and the Kennedy Administration's Alliance for Progress. Moreover, the reformist and re-distributive aspects awakened substantial conservative criticism, which called for more orthodoxy and less state involvement. In the name of private freedoms and anti-communism, military governments replaced civilian leaders in Brazil and Argentina in the mid-1960s, promising to bring an end to inflation and a return to healthy economic growth.

The structuralists' more pessimistic view of the early 1960s saw both a *foreign-exchange bottleneck* and *internal obstacles* to be undermining the dynamism and ultimate viability of ISI.

The foreign-exchange bottleneck

The structuralist analysis of the foreign-exchange bottleneck began with the observation that ISI has a dual effect on imports and therefore on the foreign-exchange constraint: by substituting local production for imports of some goods, it reduces imports and alleviates the constraint; but the installation and operation of the import-substituting industries themselves requires new imports, notably of capital and intermediate goods, thereby re-introducing the constraint. The key question is whether the structural tendency towards trade deficits under ISI tends to be alleviated or exacerbated as ISI advances from the 'easy' stage of substituting relatively simple consumer goods for which markets already exist, into the more 'difficult' stages of substituting increasingly complex consumer and especially intermediate and capital goods whose markets are created by the very advancement of ISI.

The lag between the time when imports are required to begin development of local production of a new good, and the time when local output can significantly reduce imports of that good, was found to be a crucial problem. This lag contributes to the trend towards trade deficits in a static sense, of course. But more importantly, empirical studies undertaken in the early 1960s found that external deficits tend to become more pronounced, not diminish, as ISI advances into greater horizontal diversification and vertical integration of industries.[25] As local production moves into more complex capital and intermediate goods, inefficiencies of investment and production tend to worsen. Narrow domestic markets (exacerbated by highly skewed income distributions) and indivisibilities of scale mean increasing under-utilisation of plant and equipment (which are increasingly sophisticated and therefore increasingly expensive to acquire as well), while the external economies to be derived from existing infrastructure tend to diminish, and shortages of skilled technical and managerial personnel further undermine efficiency.

The studies also found that the long-term trend of increasing vulnerability to the foreign-exchange constraint is not, in practice, a linear but a cyclical process, characterised by successive increases in both the trade deficit and foreign debt, with the service payments required by the latter eventually adding to the problem. The advancement of ISI into more complex products was seen, schematically, to lead first to an increasing rigidity of import composition (as the share of industrial inputs in total imports rises and that of consumer goods falls, the share of 'indispensable' imports, i.e. those that cannot be compressed without reducing industrial growth and employment, rises accordingly); then it leads to a debt spiral, and finally to a decomposition of the ISI process and/or a curtailment of ISI-based growth to the (slow) rate of growth of exports.

Internal obstacles

In addition to this more pessimistic view of the foreign-exchange bottleneck, the structuralists took a more pessimistic view in the early 1960s of the internal obstacles to development. The latter reflected new analyses of the evolution of social structures and the distribution of income, and their interaction with changes in the structures of agriculture and industrial production under ISI.

In the agricultural sector, pre-capitalist social values (e.g. the prestige of controlling vast estates of land and peasants) and structures of production and land ownership and tenancy, whose origins went back to the colonial period, were seen to have been partially transformed by the increase of market-oriented production during the period of outward-oriented growth. This transformation tended to accentuate the polarisation between wealthy landowners, whose incomes and consumption patterns benefited from export-derived rents, and the vast peasantry. Concentration of land ownership tended to increase as a result, and the introduction of more efficient techniques of production in latifundios was often accompanied by pressures to force excess labour off the land. In minifundios, the peasants' precarious rights of tenancy and very low incomes impeded investment and productivity growth. These characteristics of the agricultural sector were found to remain largely unchanged under ISI, or were exacerbated by unfavourable terms of trade between agriculture and industry.

Regarding the industrial sector, the analysis of the 1960s pointed to the doubly negative role of the highly skewed distribution of national income. On one hand, it limited the growth of demand for mass-consumption products. On the other hand, it sustained consumer demands by the upper-income strata for numerous sophisticated goods similar to those produced in developed economies, but whose markets of course remained very limited in scale. High levels of protection, low wages and monopolistic supply structures all contributed to sustaining profits in industry, and thus to a continuation of the ISI process, despite the severe and increasing inefficiencies of production as ISI advanced.

The combined result of these internal problems, as seen by the structuralists in the early 1960s, was that as ISI advanced towards the more 'difficult' phases, surplus labour continued to grow, wages lagged behind productivity growth (where it occurred) and the concentration of wealth and income tended to increase rather than diminish. Increasing inequality of income not only limited and biased internal market demands for manufactures (thus conditioning the composition of imports as well); it also reinforced the trends towards monopolistic supply structures, excessive trade protection and inefficient management. All of which led to inefficiencies of investment and production far beyond those that could be explained by limited market size per se. The savings and foreign-exchange constraints were further exacerbated as well. The result, in short, was to undermine the dynamics and viability of the ISI process.[26]

The more pessimistic 'stagnationist' views of the early 1960s, and especially the economic, social and political phenomena that largely inspired them, led to important changes in development thinking in Latin America. ECLA's own policy stance shifted in important respects. But, in addition to the conservative criticism and installation of military governments mentioned earlier, there was also increasing criticism of ECLA from the left – including accusations of vagueness, prolixity and eclecticism on crucial issues.[27] This eventually led to a schism between the more radical 'dependency' school and the 'developmentalist' approach of ECLA, as it was referred to by the dependency writers (to whom we return below).

ECLA's Policy Shifts in the 1960s

Within ECLA, one of the most noteworthy changes was a new emphasis on the need for 'non-traditional' and especially manufactured exports, particularly to the developed countries but also within the periphery. The proposal that the developed countries should extend trade preferences to countries in the periphery, which had been advanced during the 1950s particularly with respect to primary products, was energetically renewed, with the emphasis now on manufactured products. The earlier proposal for international financial arrangements to help alleviate the effects of price fluctuations was also refined and re-emphasized. And a new proposal was put forward, that developed countries help alleviate the effects of the declining terms of trade (which had seriously deteriorated after the end of the Korean War) by providing compensatory financing.

There can be no doubt that ECLA's views on international economic relations got widely diffused and began to have considerable impact in the Third World as a whole during this period. Thus, for example, ECLA made major contributions to the first and second U.N. Conferences on Trade and Development (UNCTAD) in 1964 and 1968, and the influence of some of its ideas would clearly be visible in subsequent calls for a New International Economic Order (cf. Chapter 4).[28]

As to the internal obstacles, the changes in ECLA's policy recommendations were particularly visible in the areas of agriculture and social policy. Whereas in the 1950s, tax policies and land reform were seen as possible options for addressing the structural problems of the agricultural sector, in the 1960s agrarian reform was seen as indispensable. This change in emphasis reflected not only a better understanding of the sector but also of its effects on the economy as a whole. The agrarian-reform proposals emphasized the need not only to transform the structures of land ownership and tenancy but also to stimulate production through technical assistance, credit supports and appropriate price policies.[29] It is also noteworthy that the Alliance for Progress similarly emphasized the importance of agrarian reform, as did a joint study involving the U.N. Food and Agricultural Organisation.[30]

Much more emphasis was given to social policies than had been the case in the 1950s. These included more active state support for health and education services, training and employment programmes, and housing.[31] Wage policies were also encouraged to take explicit account of social and distributional objectives.

Considerable debate emerged concerning the role of the State in development. Calls were made for rationalising both public administration (at all levels) and the fiscal system, the latter on both the expenditure side and the tax policy and administration side. The State was also seen to have a central role to play in increasing domestic savings, including public savings, and in promoting or even directly undertaking productive enterprise in strategic areas.

It was also during the early 1960s that a number of Latin American governments began to respond to ECLA's proposals for global and sectoral programming, and ECLA played a central role in helping to elaborate those plans. Planning techniques were refined, and attempts were made to more explicitly address the major social problems through those techniques.[32] But widespread difficulties with the actual implementation of plans and the worsening of social conditions also gave rise to growing criticism, including self-criticism by ECLA, of these planning techniques. This criticism focused especially on their lack of political and social viability.[33] Whereas outside ECLA it extended to the theoretical and analytical bases on which the planning techniques were developed, within ECLA the tendency was not to rethink the analytical bases but simply to try to extend the planning techniques so as to incorporate the dynamics of the social and political forces. (It was partly in this regard that ECLA came to be accused of eclectic, vague 'developmentalism', despite its somewhat more aggressive stances on the need for agrarian reform, compensatory financing and state intervention in general.)

Equally important, however, was the rapid growth of foreign direct investment in import-substituting industries in Latin America.

Multinational corporations were increasingly dominating production in branches of industry that used more advanced technologies and, even more important, whose local demand-growth was most dynamic. ECLA did not ignore the importance of this phenomenon, but it did not integrate it into its theoretical analysis or suggest any clearly defined policies to deal with it. This was another issue on which ECLA came to be accused of vagueness and eclecticism, and was one which would attract considerable attention from the dependency writers.

Indeed, following Rodriguez, it is also interesting to note the change (during the 1960s) in the relationship between ECLA's positions and the populist ideologies in Latin America.[34] During the 1950s, and the two preceding decades, populist ideologies had sustained political alliances in several countries among 'modernising' groups (comprising national industrial and some financial capitalists, urban middle classes notably including civil servants, and organised and unorganised wage labourers) in opposition to the 'oligarchy' (latifundistas and commercial and financial capitalists tied to primary exports). The populist ideologies generally supported strong state intervention, including public ownership of 'strategic' sectors, while minimising the importance of contradictions between such state intervention and the interests of local capitalists. This reflected the populist ideologies' view of local capital as weak vis-à-vis foreign capital and therefore as needing the support of the State, and especially their view of the State as incarnating the national interest.

While ECLA's analysis was somewhat more general (in part because of its regional rather than national focus) and less extreme than the populist ideologies, there was an important degree of convergence between them in the 1950s. ECLA essentially postulated the need and possibility for harmonising relations among industrial, financial, agrarian and even foreign capitalists under the leadership of national industrial capitalists, and for the gradual economic absorption and social integration of the lower strata of the population. In other words, the assumption underlying the socio-political project implicit in ECLA's analysis and recommendations was that the State possessed sufficient strength and autonomy to carry out three key functions: promote the interests of national industrial capitalists; reconcile those interests with those of other capitalist groups; and minimise and moderate the conflicts that arose with other socio-economic groups.

This convergence between ECLA's positions and the populist ideologies did not continue beyond the early 1960s, essentially for two reasons. One was the growing importance and visibility of multinational corporations in key sectors of industry which, combined with ECLA's failure to offer a clearly defined view on the issue and growing disappointment with the capacity of domestic industrial elites to lead an 'autonomous and progressive' development project, tended to undermine the image of ECLA's position as nationalistic and progressive. ECLA was also increasingly criticised from the left for failing to rethink the assumptions, especially on the character of the State, underlying the socio-political project implicit in its analyses and policy recommendations.

The second reason was that ECLA's shift to greater pessimism largely coincided with the rupture of the populist political alliances in Latin America – as reflected in the military takeovers cited earlier. Unfounded as they may have been, the socio-political assumptions underlying ECLA's analyses and policy recommendations must have derived a sense of historical realism from the populist political alliances during the 1950s. This was much less the case after the rupture of those alliances in the 1960s.

THE DEPENDENCY SCHOOL

The early 1960s witnessed considerable political and intellectual unrest in Latin America, as noted earlier. In addition to the growing perceptions that ISI was not producing the results originally hoped for, that income distribution was worsening and that social marginalisation was increasingly acute, this unrest was fed by the Cuban Revolution and its aftermath of Guevarist guerilla movements, the sending of US marines to the Dominican Republic and the 1964 military coup in Brazil. If the somewhat eclectic 'developmentalist' proposals in the official ECLA literature of the 1960s were one result, another was the emergence in the mid-1960s of a series of more radical interpretations which came to be known as the 'dependency' school. Indeed, the emergence of the dependency school may be seen not only as a reaction to ECLA's perceived limitations, and as a more radical response to orthodox development thinking of the type advanced in Rostow's recently published *Stages of Economic Growth* as well as the more neoclassical and monetarist-inspired approach of the IMF. It may also be seen as a critique of the strategies of the communist parties in Latin America which sought to promote 'bourgeois revolutions' because of their perception of the economies in the region as essentially pre-capitalist.[35] A common feature of most of the dependency writers was their explicit attention to the social nature and effects of *capitalist* development in the periphery.

Following Palma and others, it is useful to distinguish three main currents within the broad dependency approach in Latin America.[36] One emanated from within ECLA and focused on the obstacles, particularly market constrictions, that confront capitalist development in the periphery. This approach, found principally in the writings of Celso Furtado and Osvaldo Sunkel, may be seen as attempting to reformulate and overcome the limits of ECLA's analysis by better illuminating the internal and external obstacles to 'national development' in Latin America. A second current launched by André Gunder Frank and continued by Theotonio dos Santos and Ruy Mauro Marini, among others, basically negated the possibility of capitalist development in Latin America. Its main argument was that capitalism leads to the 'development of underdevelopment' and that a socialist revolution is a *sine qua non* of development in the periphery. A third current, found notably in the writings of Fernando Henrique Cardoso (who reportedly coined the term 'dependence' in a 1965 paper[37]) and Enzo Faletto, accepted the possibility of capitalist development – and was thus closer to traditional Marxist thinking – and concentrated its analysis on 'concrete situations of dependency' in Latin America, highlighting the subservient forms such development takes in the periphery.

Furtado and Sunkel

Furtado, a Brazilian economist, was one of the most influential of the more radical ECLA writers, who then left ECLA to become Director of Planning in the poorest region of his country and subsequently Minister of State until the 1964 coup. Although quite optimistic after Brazil's rapid industrial growth during the 1950s, he became a leading proponent of the stagnationist thesis of the 1960s.[38] One of his arguments, which would be picked up and refined by Samir Amin (see below), is that whereas a mutually reinforcing relationship between workers' consumption expenditures and investment is the basis of both sustained growth and industrial democracy in the advanced capitalist economies, this interdependent relationship does not exist in the periphery because mass-consumption demands do not constitute significant market outlets for local manufacturers as they do in the centre. Reminiscent of Duesenberry's 'demonstration effects' (cf. Chapter 1), Furtado also observed that the high- and middle-income groups – who constitute the principal market outlets for ISI in Latin

America – tend to equate development and progress with the attainment of consumption standards in the advanced capitalist countries, and therefore to mimic those consumption patterns and modes. The imported technologies required to produce those goods embody a bias toward capital-intensive production, and industrial growth comes to be characterised by a growing capital coefficient which increases the concentration of income, limits the spread of technical progress to other parts of the economy, and leads to the marginalisation of large numbers of the population. Those consumption patterns, he concluded, and the rigid social structures (erected under colonialism) that lie behind them, condition the entire process of ISI and constitute 'the central mechanism of dependence'.

In Brazil, Furtado saw convergent interests between foreign investors and the domestic 'oligarchy'[39] in keeping large parts of the population marginalised – since wage-workers' and other mass-consumption demands were not important as market outlets, the dommenant groups' interest was simply to keep wages very low. He also saw the control exerted by multinational corporations over the supply of technology, equipment and inputs required by local manufacturers to severely limit national economic autonomy. And he saw the multinationals benefitting from local government subsidies (e.g. as investment incentives) and guarantees to back their overseas borrowing. He concluded that ECLA's strategy of ISI had not reduced but actually increased foreign dependence, since imported luxury consumption goods had been replaced by more necessary imported intermediate and capital goods and technology, and dependence on primary exports had actually increased as well, because they alone could pay for the necessary imports.

Following his move to Paris in 1964, Furtado expanded his analysis to cover all of Latin America, emphasizing the need for increased public commitment to structural reforms especially so that modern technology could disseminate to all sectors of production, thereby improving income distribution and reducing marginalisation. He also called for increased self-reliance, notably involving some degree of technological autonomy, and new forms of cooperation within the region including greater intra-regional trade. In criticising Prebisch's development model, which he saw as sharing some of the defects of Rostow's stage theory of growth, Furtado also took issue with the traditional Marxist view that the future of backward countries was reflected in the industrialised countries. He saw underdevelopment as an historically autonomous process – not a stage through which all economies necessarily pass – with the particularities of countries in the periphery reflecting in various ways the expansion of advanced capitalist countries seeking access to natural resources and cheap labour.

The Chilean Osvaldo Sunkel also contributed his critique from within ECLA until he took a chair at the University of Chile in 1966. In a lecture that year, published in English in 1969, he identified four main 'mechanisms of dependence': i) the stagnation of traditional agriculture due to the preservation of traditional agrarian structures, which undermined trade balances both because of growing food imports and slow growth of exports; ii) the continued high commodity concentration of exports; iii) an ISI process that increased dependence on foreign technology and foreign capital, including high levels of foreign ownership and an increasing foreign-exchange cost of industrialisation; and iv) growing budget deficits caused by the expansion of a public sector whose tax receipts could not keep up because of their excessive reliance on export taxes, which induced a steady accumulation of foreign debt. Already at that time Sunkel argued, 'It is this aspect – the overbearing and implacable necessity to obtain foreign financing – which finally sums up the situation of dependence'.[40]

While Sunkel saw the countries of Latin America as highly dependent on their foreign economic relations, like Furtado he argued that economic policy should be re-oriented towards national economic development in order to overcome the constraints of the centre–periphery relationship. He particularly emphasized the importance of implementing policies to increase agricultural productivity, including agrarian reform. He also called for: expansion and diversification of traditional exports and greater local control of the multinational firms in this sector via government regulations, joint ventures or nationalisation; new 'co-production' arrangements between the host country and multinational firms in import-substituting industries to facilitate the development of local technology, managerial skills and manufactured exports; industrial policies oriented toward the creation of large, specialised units capable of securing economies of scale and of financing research and development; and greater Latin American regional integration aimed at developing technological capabilities, large-scale production in sectors with high and increasing productivity and generating surpluses of resources for investment.

Sunkel also rejected what he saw as the false alternatives of socialist revolution – which he considered highly improbable in the immediate future of Latin America because of external and internal geographic, military, political and economic circumstances – and a continuation of 'developmentalist' policies and external dependence. He argued for a strategy involving the masses in a development process more in line with the culture, traditions, institutions and history of Latin America.

Whereas ECLA, perhaps understandably, tended to tread softly on the politically more sensitive domestic affairs of its member countries, Sunkel and Furtado thus emphasized the importance of internal factors while recognising the significance of external factors: 'The possibilities of carrying out a national development policy basically depend on the domestic situation'.[41]

But Sunkel, like Furtado, also saw multinational corporations as playing a central role in dependency and underdevelopment. Pointing to simultaneous tendencies in the world economy toward transnational integration and toward national dis-integration, he defined the 'centre' of the world economy as 'transnational capitalism' comprising the 'modern' sectors of underdeveloped countries as well as most of the economic space of the advanced capitalist countries; he defined the 'periphery' as comprising some parts of the industrialised countries as well as the much larger part of the underdeveloped countries that remain stagnant and marginalised. In opposition to the orthodox trade theories' focus on transactions between countries, Sunkel's analysis thus cut across national boundaries, with polarisation seen to occur within as well as between countries. The central institution in his model of transnational integration and national disintegration was the transnational corporation, to which Sunkel devoted considerable attention in the 1970s.[42]

Finally, whereas orthodox economists tend to equate growth and development, Furtado and Sunkel brought out an important distinction between the two: economic development cannot be considered to occur when growth is accompanied by worsening income distribution, by a failure to increase social welfare and to create employment opportunities roughly on a par with demographic growth, and by diminishing national control over economic, political, social and cultural life.

Furtado and Sunkel thus went beyond ECLA not only in their focus on politically sensitive internal factors and their critique of the role played by foreign direct investment, but especially in their perception of development and underdevelopment as historically inter-active, simultaneous and mutually conditioning processes. (As Furtado put it, 'Underdevelopment should be understood as an aspect of the industrial revolution...'.[43]) But like other moderate dependency writers, they tended to look to modernising elites inspired by national collective interests for the necessary initiative, and to believe that variations of existing economic strategies – notably ISI supplemented by increased exports and greater regional integration – could lead to enhanced autonomy for the Latin American economies.

Frank and the Development-of-Underdevelopment Current

The most radical current of dependency thinking had its roots in Paul Baran's 1957 *The Political Economy of Growth*, which was the first major postwar study of a Marxist orientation to focus on the problems of underdeveloped countries, as we shall explain in Chapter 6. But unlike Marx, Baran saw economic development in the periphery as inimical to the dominant interests in the advanced capitalist countries. The gist of his argument was that those interests formed alliances with pre-capitalist local elites who would also be adversely affected by the transformations of capitalist development, in order to maintain pre-capitalist modes of extracting economic surpluses. Those surpluses were largely appropriated by foreign capital or squandered on luxury consumption by local elites. Baran concluded that the only way out of stagnation in underdeveloped countries was through political revolution.

Andre Gunder Frank, in his *Capitalism and Underdevelopment in Latin America: Historical Studies of Chile and Brazil* published in 1967, attempted to trace underdevelopment in the periphery to the global expansion of capitalism – starting with the period of mercantile expansion that began in Latin America with the Spanish Conquest in the 16th century. Such incorporation into the world economy, according to Frank, transformed the colonies into capitalist economies because production began to be for the market, and for profit.[44] Emphasizing the monopoly structure of capitalism at all levels – international, national and local – he saw in this transformation the establishment of a hierarchical chain of exploitative 'metropolis–satellite' relations in which each metropolis appropriated part or all of the economic surplus generated in the satellites under its control, and individual satellites acted as local metropoli with respect to satellites below them in the hierarchy.[45] He argued that foreign investment and aid as well as trade served as channels for the extraction of surpluses, that regional integration would only serve to enhance this process of extraction, and that industrialisation – import substituting or otherwise – would not break the cycle of surplus extraction and underdevelopment unless the existing structures of metropolis–satellite relations, internal and international, were overthrown.

Thus, according to Frank, it was the incorporation into the world capitalist system and the appropriation of economic surpluses that led to development in some areas ('for the few') and to underdevelopment in others ('for the many').   Moreover, since there were no feudal, semi-feudal or other pre-capitalist modes of production in Latin America, there was no basis to support a 'bourgeois revolution'.   Frank concluded that there could be no alternative to the 'development of underdevelopment' for satellites within the capitalist system, and that the only political solution was socialist revolution, which he saw as necessary and possible *now*.

While Frank's simplified scheme was not fully accepted by many dependency writers, outside Latin America the dependency school has been more or less identified with Frank.   This is probably partly because he served as a link between the Latin American debate and the outside world by publishing most of his work in English.   But it is also probably due to his polemical tone in explicitly, sometimes vehemently criticising specific orthodox writers, notably including many at the heavily neoclassical and monetarist-oriented 'Chicago School' and its prestigious journal *Economic Development and Cultural Change* to which Frank himself had previously been a contributor.   Frank's polemics also stood in stark contrast to the relative 'lethargy' of the communist parties in Latin America.   And, indeed, it was from the left that Frank was most strongly criticised – for focusing on relations of exchange rather than of production in his interpretation of capitalism in Latin America, as we explain below.   But there was wide consensus that an important contribution of Frank's work was its rejection of the 'dual economy' models (cf. Chapter 2) by showing in his historical analysis of Brazil and Chile that the 'traditional' and 'modern' sectors had both been closely linked to the world economy since early in their colonial history. Frank's work also inspired a great deal of research by others, whether to support or to criticise his views, both in and outside Latin America.

Frank's central thesis on the 'development of underdevelopment' was also pursued during this period, though critically, by the Brazilian sociologist Theotonio dos Santos.   It is dos Santos' formal definition of dependence published in 1970 in the *American Economic Review* which, though criticised from the left as static and unhistorical, is probably the best known and most widely cited.[46]

Whereas Frank emphasized the similarities and continuity of dependency relations under capitalism, much of dos Santos' work focused on the differences and discontinuities among different types of dependency relations and the internal structures they helped bring about. He identified three main types of dependence, corresponding to three different periods: colonial; financial–industrial (which in Latin America prevailed during the latter half of the 19th century); and technological–industrial, which emerged in the postwar period based on investments by multinational corporations in the most dynamic import-substituting industries. Under this 'new dependency', profit repatriation is high, so that capital outflows exceed inflows, and deficits are also important in certain services that are largely under foreign control as well (e.g. freight transport, technical services). The net result is a severe balance-of-payments constraint on imports needed for industrialisation. Dos Santos concluded that financial inflows in the form of loans and aid to cover the balance-of-payments deficit and to finance investment serve mainly 'to fill up the holes that they themselves created'.[47]

Critical of Frank's view of underdevelopment as the result of external exploitation, dos Santos argued that it resulted from certain *internal* structures which were in turn *conditioned* by international relations of dependency. But in his empirical work dos Santos, like Frank, saw inter-regional contradictions and transfers of surplus as playing the central role in underdevelopment, and his view of the alternatives facing Latin America was similarly polarised: military regimes that would open the door to fascism versus revolutionary regimes that would lay the foundation for socialism.

A third well known dependency writer whose central thesis was the development of underdevelopment was Ruy Mauro Marini.[48] His work can be summarised in the first instance as an application to the situation in Latin America of Rosa Luxemburg's 1913 analysis of imperialism (cf. Chapter 6). Starting from the view that the periphery tends to be dominated by foreign capital producing primary exports and that local market demands (notably workers' demands) are insignificant to profit realisation for the dominant firms, he argued that capitalism in the periphery is characterised by the 'super-exploitation' of workers. He saw such 'super-exploitation' made possible by the subsistence goods supplied to workers by the pre-capitalist sectors, enabling wage levels to be kept very low. Since increases in labour productivity do not require increases in local market demand (notably workers' purchasing power) to help absorb the increased output in the capitalist sector of the periphery, they therefore serve to increase the surpluses that can be transferred to the central economies. In this way not only owners of capital but also, Marini argued, *workers* in the central economies benefit from the super-exploitation of workers in the periphery employed by multinational firms.

In pointing to the exploitation of workers in the periphery by workers in the centre, albeit indirectly, Marini clearly subordinated class conflict to inter-regional conflict. Moreover, whereas Rosa Luxemburg had seen firms in the centre moving into the periphery in search of market outlets as leading eventually to the incorporation of peripheral production into capitalist production, Marini saw them impeding internal accumulation and the growth of the domestic market. He concluded that 'super-exploitation' and the surplus transfer it gives rise to are the principal cause of stagnation and underdevelopment in the periphery.[49]

Thus, whereas ECLA and the structuralists never imputed to the centre direct responsibility for backwardness in the periphery, Frank, dos Santos and Marini explicitly argued that the metropolis–satellite relationship is the basis for the exploitation of the latter by the former. In addition, their work drew attention to an issue which had been obviated by the official ECLA literature but which was given considerable attention, as we shall see, within the postwar Marxist literature. This issue was the role of *clientele social classes* (in particular the 'national bourgeoisie') in the periphery, who were seen to carry out certain functions on behalf of foreign interests and in return to enjoy a privileged and increasingly hegemonic position within their own society. Their position was seen as based on economic, political and/or military support from abroad, and their ranks to include the state bureaucracy and other sectors of the 'middle classes' – e.g. technical, managerial, professional and intellectual elites – whose interests and privileged positions are derived directly or indirectly from their ties to foreign interests. The alliances and conflicts of clientele classes with other domestic classes within the periphery were seen to be shaped to a considerable extent by each group's previous and present alliances with particular foreign interests.

For some development-of-underdevelopment theorists the notion of dependency did not refer simply to external domination 'à la Frank' (in essence unilaterally imposed and unilaterally producing 'internal consequences'). Nor did it necessarily refer to some form of colonialism, in which the colony is directly and overtly administered by the coloniser. Rather, the internal dynamics of dependency were often seen to be as much a function of penetration as of domination, and in many ways more subtle and difficult to break.

But the broad consensus was that the various efforts to build 'bourgeois nationalist' or 'national capitalist' or, more recently 'state capitalist' solutions must in the end fail because the social classes on whom such solutions are based (one or more factions of the local bourgeoisie) are themselves limited by their role in the international system. They may advocate an 'independent' or 'non-alligned' foreign policy, and may even go so far as to successfully expropriate foreign holdings in some sectors (as was done in Mexico under Cardenas, for example, or more recently in Peru under Velasco). But so long as they follow the capitalist road, they will continue to depend on foreign investment, and will thus eventually have to make their compromises with and cater to foreign interests. Regardless of their intentions to implement far-reaching domestic reforms, furthermore, they are limited in practice by the legacy of dependency as institutionalised both within their own class interests and alliances, and in the existing industrial base. (The latter was seen to be characterised by technological dependency, by increasing foreign control over the most dynamic and strategic industrial sectors – through direct ownership, control of marketing, patents and licenses, etc. – and hence by an outflow of capital which is greater than the inflow derived from aid and direct foreign investment, by the absence of a domestic capital goods industry and hence by dependence on capital imports, by the use of highly capital intensive production techniques and hence by growing unemployment and marginalisation, etc.) To break out of dependency meant, according to this current of dependency writers, to break out of the capitalist order whose expression in the periphery is underdevelopment.

Cardoso and Faletto

In contrast to Furtado and Sunkel, who in attempting to reformulate ECLA's analyses focused on the obstacles to capitalist development in Latin America (particularly market constrictions), and in opposition to the 'development of underdevelopment' writers who did not accept the possibility of capitalist development in those countries, a third current did not see dependency and development as necessarily incompatible. This current is closely identified with the writings of Fernando Henrique Cardoso, a Brazilian sociologist (and now an active politician), and the Chilean historian Enzo Faletto, particularly their 1967 study *Dependency and Development in Latin America* (first published in English in 1977).

Closer to the classical Marxist analysis of capitalist development, with its emphasis on the dialectics of class conflict, and especially to Lenin's analysis of imperialism (cf. Chapter 6), this group constituted a critical current within the broad dependency school. Like the other currents, it saw the Latin American economies as part of a world capitalist system whose dynamics are determined largely in the centre and limit the options open to the peripheral economies. But this current rejected the stagnationist view as overly simplistic and mechanical (some also correctly perceived the downturn of the late 1950s and early 1960s as a cycle phenomenon) and, more importantly, negated the possibility of creating a generalised theory of dependency. Considering the Marxist–Leninist theory of imperialism adequate in its portrayal of the *general* laws of motion of the capitalist system, this current focused instead on the diversity of *concrete forms* adopted by capitalism in peripheral economies.

Cardoso and Faletto gave particular attention to how different local classes in dependent countries allied or clashed with different foreign interests, organised different forms of state, sustained different ideologies, tried to implement various policies or defined alternative strategies to cope with imperialist challenges in diverse moments of history. They felt that only in this way could one understand, for example, why the single process of mercantile expansion in the world capitalist system had produced slave labour, systems based on the exploitation of indigenous populations, and incipient forms of wage labour in different Latin American societies. Their studies of how general (external) and specific (internal) determinants interacted in particular and concrete situations extended the dependency analysis of the internal determinants of development in each economy. (Some of the best empirical research by non-Latin American dependency writers – e.g. Peter Evans' 1979 study *Dependent Development. The Alliance of Multinational, State, and Local Capital in Brazil* – is also closest to this current.)

Cardoso and Faletto saw 'external domination' re-appearing as an internal phenomenon through the practices of local groups and classes who share its interests and values; other internal groups and forces oppose this domination, and the specific dynamics of a society are generated in the concrete development of these contradictions. They did not see one part of the world capitalist system as 'developing' and the other as 'underdeveloping', or see imperialism and dependency as two sides of the same coin with the underdeveloped or dependent part reduced to a passive role determined by the other.[50]

While Cardoso and Faletto did not seek to supersede the Marxist–Leninist framework of analysis of the general laws of motion of capitalism, they did perceive changes since Lenin's time which they felt called for a reappraisal of the emergent structures in world capitalism. Particularly important in this regard, they, like the other dependency writers, saw the multinational corporation as having come to play a central role. But they more correctly perceived that multinational corporations were increasingly investing in manufacturing for local markets, and that the struggle for industrialisation, which was widely seen as an anti-imperialist struggle (by other dependency writers as well as by Lenin, in his analysis of Russia in 1920) was increasingly becoming the *goal* of foreign capital. Dependency and industrialisation thus ceased to be contradictory, and for at least some parts of the periphery, a path of 'dependent development' was conceivable.

Cardoso and Faletto nevertheless concluded that such development would merely redefine the links of dependency (so as to sharpen the choices facing Latin America) and would largely benefit the higher income groups, causing greater disparities in income distribution. And, beyond a certain point, they saw severe political limits to such a development path and further industrialisation requiring a 'profound political–structural change' of either 'opening the market to foreign capital or making a radical political move towards socialism'.[51] They further argued that because capitalism will not bring about prosperity for the masses, the important question is how to achieve socialism (they did not, however, analyse what socialism would mean or how a radical political change toward socialism might be brought about). They thus went considerably beyond those dependency theorists who treated domestic policies as simply the result of external forces: since domestic oppressed groups can challenge dominant interests, they looked into concrete cases of 'how the internal and external processes of political domination related to one another and external factors are interwoven with internal ones', and they tried 'to determine the links between social groups that in their behaviour actually tie together the economic and political spheres'.[52]

The Critique of Dependency

As others have pointed out, it would be misleading to speak of a real debate between orthodox economists and the dependency school.[53] Neoclassical economists generally did not consider the dependency school 'scientific'. The earliest and most forceful criticisms came from Marxists. The 'development of underdevelopment' writers, and Frank in particular, were singled out for criticism.

168   *The Postwar Evolution of Development Thinking*

Marxist Critique

Probably the most noted of the early Marxist critics was Ernesto Laclau, an Argentinian whose 1971 article 'Feudalism and Capitalism in Latin America' questioned Frank's conception of capitalism and his view that capitalism had pervaded Latin America since the Spanish Conquest. Whereas for Frank the transition under colonialism to production of goods for the market implied a transition to capitalist production, for Marxists the fundamental characteristic of capitalism is the proletarian- isation of labour (the 'freeing' of labour from control of its physical means of production: cf. Chapter 6) which must then sell its labour power to capitalists.[54] Laclau went on to argue that pre-capitalist and capitalist modes of production could co-exist – although he agreed with Frank in rejecting the 'dual economy' models (cf. Chapter 2) because he saw the interaction between pre-capitalist and capitalist modes of production as crucial to understanding the functioning of the economy as a whole. (A rich debate among Marxists ensued on the 'articulation of modes of production', which we examine in Chapter 6.) Thus, whereas for Frank the transfer of surplus from the periphery to the centre was the *cause* of underdevelopment, for Laclau it was an *expression* of the class structure and the nature of social relations associated with material production in the periphery.

Even Cardoso, who broadly supported the thesis that capitalist development was taking place in Latin America and felt that the Marxist–Leninist framework of analysis of imperialism was adequate to understand the general laws of motion of capitalism, came in for some criticism by more orthodox Marxists. This was because Cardoso based his analysis of 'concrete situations of dependence' on a concept of class that comprised structural and institutional factors, ethnic groups, races and religions, which he argued to be more useful for analysing the functioning of peripheral societies. Pointing out that Marx defined class in terms of a group's relationship to the means of production, Myer flawed Cardoso for his concept of class.[55]

While Cardoso was criticised for overextending the definition of class, Frank and the development-of-underdevelopment current were criticised for displacing class relations from the centre of their analysis. Brenner, for example, argued that they saw 'the actions of money or trade or merchant capitalists as being behind the original emergence of capitalism' rather than recognising it as the result of class conflict in which the peasants struggled to free themselves from the control of feudal landlords while the landlords obtained ownership of the land.[56]

The dependency theorists thus fail to take account of the way in which class structure, class interests and class conflicts determine the course of development or underdevelopment.

Frank's conclusion, and that of other radical dependency writers, that the only way to escape the development of underdevelopment is to break with capitalism in favour of the post-capitalist mode of production (socialism) is thus seen as the logical outcome of their failing to recognise the existence (or co-existence) in Latin America of pre-capitalist modes of production. In Marxist eyes, this 'theory of revolution', since it neglects class conflicts, is more of a 'nationalist ideology': 'Socialism has become then, something which is 'chosen' for its superiority over capitalism... The arguments centre on why it is necessary, not whether it is immediately possible'.[57] Moreover, the logical consequence of Frank's 'theory' would be autarky rather than socialism.[58]

These theoretical criticisms were complemented by Warren, on the basis of empirical work published in 1973 and in his 1980 book *Imperialism: Pioneer of Capitalism*.[59] Warren's main arguements are: that considerable capitalist development has already taken place in the Third World, particularly since the Second World War; that potential obstacles to this development are more to be found among the internal contradictions in underdeveloped countries than in external factors (imperialism); that the imperialist countries' policies and overall impact on the Third World tend overall to facilitate industrialisation and to loosen the ties of dependency; and, therefore, that the prospects for successful capitalist development are relatively good in many underdeveloped countries, and will result in some shift of power within the capitalist world. In making this frontal attack on the thesis that imperialism stands in the way of capitalist development in the periphery, Warren emphasizes the importance of political independence as a direct cause of more rapid Third World industrialisation since the War. He also points to 'East–West rivalries and inter-imperialist rivalries, which have been the major external influence [and] have linked with internal forces, especially the rise of new ruling groups and the increase in popular, often petty bourgeois mobilisation'.[60] Warren thus also sees imperialism as contributing to development by breaking down the traditional and more static societies, and paving the way for industrial society.

Non-Marxist Critique

In contrast to the strong and sustained Marxist criticism of the dependency school during the 1970s, there were few reactions by non-Marxists, many of whom considered the experience of the East-Asian 'NICs' to be ample evidence of the fallacy of dependency thinking. A notable exception was Sanjaya Lall's 1975 attempt to evaluate dependency theory on its own terms.[61] He argued that for the term 'dependence' to be useful in a theory of underdevelopment it should satisfy two criteria: a) it must lay down certain characteristics of an economy which are not found in a non-dependent economy; and b) these characteristics must be shown to adversely effect the course and pattern of development of dependent countries. He then identified a number of economic and social features claimed by dependency writers to characterise dependent economies – the dominance of foreign capital is a good example – and found that, 'Canada and Belgium are more 'dependent' on foreign investments than are, for example, India or Pakistan, and yet the former two cannot be categorised as 'dependent countries'. (...) Both dominance and dependence exist, but they are as commonplace in the Centre as in the Periphery'.[62]

Regarding his second criterion, Lall found no causal connection between the static characteristics of dependence and underdevelopment, and thus no basis for a theory of Latin American underdevelopment.[63] He concluded that, 'When reading the literature, you often get the impression that 'dependence' is defined by circular reasoning: less developed countries are poor because they are dependent, and they show all the characteristics of dependence.'

DEPENDENCY THINKING OUTSIDE LATIN AMERICA

Unequal Exchange

Although there was little debate between neoclassical economists and dependency theory as such, an important aspect of dependency thinking is the theory of unequal exchange. As noted earlier, a key component of the original centre–periphery paradigm was the 'Prebisch–Singer' thesis that there is a secular tendency for the terms of international trade to deteriorate against the periphery, which meant that a major part of the fruits of progress are transferred to the centre through trade. The principal causes were thought to be a disparity between the centre and the periphery in terms of their respective income-elasticities of demands for imports from each other, and in terms of the degree of monopolistic power of both firms and labour. This view was then expanded by dependency writers in Latin America, particularly the development-of-underdevelopment current, to include the role of foreign investment and to highlight the role of surplus extraction as the main cause of stagnation and underdevelopment in the periphery.

The surplus-extraction approach to underdevelopment gained major theoretical status when Arghiri Emmanuel, a Greek economics professor in France, published his 1969 study *L'echange inégal* (published in English in 1972). Using the Ricardian labour theory of value, he went beyond the Latin American writers to show that even under conditions of 'perfect competition' (in the neoclassical sense) and perfectly free trade, there is a trend for international prices to deteriorate against the periphery. Emmanuel identified the source of unequal gains from trade as the centre–periphery wage differential.

Emmanuel opposed the Ricardian theory of comparative advantage (cf. Chapter 3) by assuming perfect international mobility of capital, and hence a trend towards equalisation of profit rates between the centre and the periphery, while assuming immobility of labour and hence the persistence of international differences in wage rates. According to this model, an international gap in wages between the centre and the periphery leads to terms of trade that favour the higher wage-cost products exported by the centre relative to the lower wage-cost products exported by the periphery. (Equally priced products have different values if they incorporate different amounts of 'socially necessary labour time', so that an exchange of equally priced products may entail an unequal exchange of values, i.e. an exchange of unequal amounts of 'socially necessary labour time'.[64]) Unequal exchange in trade thus becomes a factor of surplus extraction which in turn helps explain stagnation in the periphery – even assuming perfect competition, free trade, international equality of labour productivity, and no exploitation of labourers working under pre-capitalist modes of production in the periphery. Moreover, *labour* as well as capital in the centre benefit from unequal exchange – at the expense of labour in the periphery – with obvious negative implications for the possibility of international labour solidarity in the struggle between labour and capital.

Despite the serious empirical difficulties of showing that international prices have deteriorated against the periphery, the theoretical 'purity' of Emmanuel's model, perhaps even more than its potentially important implications for orthodox trade theory and policy, attracted considerable interest from orthodox economics (including Paul Samuelson.[65]). As in the case of the Latin American dependency school, however, the most penetrating criticism came from Marxists. Probably the single most serious objection is that wages cannot be taken as exogenous variables, i.e. taken as determined by class struggle *independently* of the objective conditions of accumulation (level of development) in peripheral economics. This is all the more crucial if unequal exchange is to be seen as an integral element of a process of accumulation on a global scale.[66] Other important objections are: i) that unequal exchange does not apply to exported goods that are produced in both the centre and the periphery, which actually constitute a majority of the goods traded internationally;[67] ii) that unequal exchange assumes equilibrium in the capital market, i.e. that capital movements have already resulted in a global equalisation of the rate of profit, an assumption that seems to contradict observed facts and that, if true, would contradict perpetuation of a wage gap between centre and periphery;[68] and iii) that international capital movements would in fact imply faster growth rates in the periphery – an interpretation of unequal development that is contrary to Emmanuel's very perception of the process of underdevelopment.[69] Further criticisms include the observation that the periphery cannot be characterised by capitalist relations of production alone, because significant low-productivity non-capitalist spheres of production remain,[70] that the rate of surplus value may be greater in the centre – where labour productivity, as well as wages, are higher – than in the periphery,[71] and that it is not clear that the postulate of the internationalisation of value holds.[72]

African Dependency Thinking

Samir Amin

Samir Amin – who in important respects straddles the Marxist and development-of-underdevelopment schools – was undoubtedly the single most important contributor to dependency thinking in Africa. It was in 1970 that his book *L'accumulation à l'echelle mondiale* was published (the English translation appeared in 1974) and also that he became head of the U.N. African Institute for Economic Development and Planning (IDEP), in Dakar. Drawing heavily from the Latin American structuralist and dependency writers,[73] Amin brought to their most elaborated forms the interpretation of backwardness as the development of underdevelopment, and the interpretation of unequal development on a world scale as a pattern of homogeneous growth in the centre and stagnation or highly uneven growth in the periphery.[74] Moreover, Amin's model, which made surplus extraction the key element in underdevelopment, incorporated unequal exchange mechanisms in which wages are not exogenous – as was the case in Emmanuel's model – but are determined by the dynamics of capital accumulation as well as by class struggle.

Amin saw the economies of the industrialised countries – in a fashion reminiscent of Furtado and not unlike the Harrod–Domar growth model – as characterised by an 'articulated' pattern of growth and accumulation in which part of the gains in labour productivity translate into wage increases. Workers' consumption capacity thus increases along with output and creates the possibility of a dynamic equilibrium both between aggregate consumption and production, and between key sectors (notably the mass-consumption and capital goods sectors). But Amin also saw an underlying tendency towards under-consumption and the emergence of an idle financial surplus that puts downward pressure on the average rate of profit. State intervention can counteract this tendency to a point, notably through the 'squandering' of part of the surplus and through 'social contracts' between organised labour and big capital. The latter empower the State to manage wage and profit demands in relation to productivity gains so as to reduce conjunctural fluctuations and contribute to making a self-sustained process of accumulation possible in the centre. (Writing in the 1960s, Amin found considerable empirical support for his model of 'articulated accumulation' in the centre.)

While Amin saw an internal solution to the maintenance of a dynamic equilibrium as possible in the centre, he also saw an external solution that functionalised the periphery in the maintenance of that dynamic equilibrium on a world scale. Because the State and the 'social contract' in the centre has not been sufficiently effective in fully overcoming the downward pressures on profit rates, the external solution has been utilised as a secondary equilibrating mechanism for the centre – with devastating consequences for the periphery.

For Amin, the periphery has had two functions in the world economy as the industrialised centre economies evolved from the age of competitive capital to the predominance of 'monopoly' capital towards the end of the last century (cf. Chapter 6). During the earlier period, the main function of the periphery was a market outlet, i.e. it allowed the centre to extend its markets into pre-capitalist areas. Moreover, because wages were still equally low worldwide, there was no unequal exchange through trade at that time. But the role of the periphery changed with the rise of monopoly capital, which created the conditions both for wages in the centre to increase with the rise in productivity, and for the export of capital on a large scale to the periphery. While reducing the role of peripheral economies as market outlets, this change reinforced their role in sustaining the rate of profit – which was tending to decline faster in the centre – through exports of capital which benefitted from lower wages in the periphery. It was then that unequal exchange appeared.

Unequal exchange and the repatriation of profits sustain the rate of profit in the short run, according to Amin's model, but aggravate the rise of a financial surplus in the centre in the next period. However, new capital exports (and a squandering of part of the surplus through state intervention) re-establish the (unstable) equilibrium on a world scale, and so on. In the periphery, unequal exchange and the outflow of profits bloc accumulation – although rapid growth can occur in specific periods and sectors.[75]

Amin thus saw the periphery fulfilling a dual function in global accumulation under 'monopoly' capitalism on the basis of cheap labour: providing cheap exports and high rates of profit on expatriated capital. (The expansion of the world market is now located mainly in the centre economies, with the consumption of luxuries by elites in the periphery playing a secondary role.)   This dual function is developed by maintaining a process of accumulation in the periphery that is 'extroverted' (outward-oriented) and 'disarticulated' (production is not sustained by local market demands). High labour productivity in the modern sector is accompanied by semi-proletarianisation of labour[76] in the non-capitalist spheres of the peripheral economies, which cheapens the cost of maintenance and reproduction of labour power in the modern sector (similar to Marini's model for Latin America). With a functional articulation between capitalist production and non-capitalist modes enhancing capital accumulation on a world scale, the periphery is thus highly dualistic or 'disarticulated': growth tends to concentrate in the capitalistic production of exportables and of what by local income standards are luxury consumer goods;   the production of mass-consumer goods tends to remain outside the capitalist sector, and to remain stagnant;   and the production of capital goods remains essentially non-existent. And it is principally in the non-capitalist sectors that the impoverished masses bear the social cost of unequal global development.

In sum, according to Amin's model, the periphery is functionally integrated into a self-reproducing world system of accumulation that blocks capitalist accumulation and development in the periphery. For such development to take place, it is necessary to 'articulate' consumption and capital-goods production in the periphery. To achieve this, he concluded, a break with the system, a 'delinking' of ties with imperialism, is necessary.

There can be little doubt that Amin's writings, like those of the Latin American structuralists and dependency school, influenced positions adopted by numerous delegates to international negotiations, e.g. at UNCTAD, and in the calls for a New International Economic Order during the 1970s (cf. Chapter 4). And, perhaps in response to those positions as much as to the actual writings of Amin, there has been some thoughtful criticism of Amin in the more orthodox literature.[77] But, again like the Latin American writers, and even though Amin's more elaborated model avoids some of the important pitfalls of the Latin American dependency school and Emmanuel's theory of unequal exchange, it is from the more classical Marxist perspective that Amin's model has primarily been criticised. We return to that critique in Chapter 6.

The Tanzanian Experience: 'African socialism', Rural Development and Basic Needs[78]

For the first six years after gaining political independence in 1961, Tanzania's leaders were guided by a strategy that favoured modern capital-intensive farms and the development of industry, which at the time was almost non-existent. As in much of Africa after independence, the strategy was largely inspired by W.A. Lewis' proposals for 'industrialisation by imitation' (see below) since imports of manufactured goods were too small to constitute a base for import-substituting industrialisation. But Tanzania's leaders soon perceived that their approach was not working and that a new strategy was necessary. Greatly influenced by Nyerere's social philosophy, the new strategy was proclaimed in the Arusha Declaration of 1967. During the 1970s the country became something of a laboratory for heterodox development thinking, and was an important centre of the theoretical debate on dependence and underdevelopment in Africa.

Tanzania's new development strategy sought to revitalise 'traditional African socialism', with capitalism seen as the main enemy. It gave priority to the development of the rural areas (well over 90 per cent of the labour force is in agriculture even today) where the population was widely dispersed with only small plots at their disposal. The idea was to increase production efficiency in agriculture and facilitate the provision of improved social services by grouping the peasants into so-called

Ujamaa villages. Another key objective was to increase self-reliance and thwart dependence on foreign countries. Strategically important firms were nationalised and foreign investment was no longer to be allowed as long as it 'favoured only the urban aristocracy'. Foreign aid was to be channelled to projects which increased domestic activity, and imports were to be controlled to eliminate goods that could be produced domestically. Increased trade with other underdeveloped countries ('South–South cooperation') was to lessen Tanzania's dependence on trade with the centre.

Development thinking and policy in Tanzania were strongly influenced during this period by a group of Tanzanian scholars at the University of Dar es Salaam, as well as by the work of Amin and a number of expatriate Western and Caribbean scholars who came to the University.[79] The standard approach, it is probably fair to say, was a rather uncritical application of the problems and methods borrowed from the Latin American dependency theorists, notably Frank.[80]

One important debate that emerged in the 1970s was over the role of industry. Clive Thomas, in particular, argued that a strategy of self reliance required not only cutting ties with capitalism (and imperialism) but also rapid industrialisation.[81] Focusing on the issue of *basic needs* – which would be widely discussed internationally among orthodox economists and institutions (cf. Chapter 4) – Thomas saw a need for 'consumption planning' to reduce the role of the market while bringing about a convergence of consumption expenditures (demand), resource use, and the basic needs of the population. This strategy, he argued, should serve not only to increase production for basic needs but also to rationalise agriculture through a spread of industrialisation techniques, thereby shifting the balance of power in favour of industry. The ensuing debate over the appropriate industrialisation strategy culminated with a greater emphasis being given to heavy industry in Tanzania's third five-year plan (1976–1981), in sharp deviation from the Arusha Declaration.

Another important debate was launched by Issa Shivji's 1970 article criticising the government's strategy on the grounds that 'without a real class analysis it is impossible to chart out a correct strategy and formulate appropriate tactics. More important still: it is impossible to make correct alliances. How can we talk about a 'Tanzanian Revolution' without even knowing the friends and the enemies of such a revolution?'[82] Shivji went on to argue that the current strategy did not lead to socialism in Tanzania. Despite the nationalisations, he perceived Tanzania to be trapped in a class society (which he referred to as the 'neo-colonial system'), mainly because the rapidly growing government bureaucracy now formed the basis of a new class stratification.

Shivji's critique of Tanzania's development strategy paved the way for subsequent critique of the dependency school. Wuyts, for example, criticised Amin's approach for focusing on the structural interaction (or 'disarticulation') between economic sectors while not explaining how the partial dissolution and partial conservation of non-capitalist modes of production ('semi-proletarianisation') actually conditions the development of productive forces.[83]

Another critique, based on empirical studies, focused on the so-called *peasant mode of production*. Goran Hyden in particular argued that the cause of African underdevelopment should not be sought in the international system, but in the rural areas where specific non-capitalist forms of organisation of production had not only managed to survive but to dominate the social formations in those countries, and to block all roads to cheaper production of the means of subsistence.[84] Whereas the dependency school based its arguments for socialism on the notion that those who control the State also control society, Hyden saw this notion as completely misleading in Tanzania, where the peasants have remained relatively independent of the State's instruments of power. Those in control of the State have therefore not been in control of society, and the State has not had at its disposal the means to increase agricultural production.

In sum, while the dependency theorists blamed Tanzania's ailments largely on imperialism, their critics (mainly Marxists) gave more attention to internal causes. This led to something of a power struggle, and the first round went to the dependency theorists, supported by the rulers of the country ('who were not interested in admitting their own mistakes'[85]). But attitudes began to change when the country experienced an economic crisis during the mid-1970s, and the expected surplus from agricultural production had not materialised. Nor did the shift to greater emphasis on heavy industry under the third five-year plan, and subsequent adjustments, prove very successful. The result has been a clear shift away from heavy reliance on the dependency perspective, which proved difficult to translate into practical, usable policies.

The Kenyan debate on the 'National Bourgeoisie'

Outside of Tanzania, the dependency debate did not have far-reaching effects on actual development strategies in Africa, and where it led to research that research was largely done by non-Africans – as with most development research on Africa. Following Blomström and Hettne, we nevertheless find it useful to look briefly at the debate that emerged during the 1970s on the 'national bourgeoisie' in Kenya because of the broader importance of the subject – as will be further clarified in Chapter 6 – even though the dependency school never gained much influence in Kenya.

The debate was launched by Colin Leys in his book *Underdevelopment in Kenya: The Political Economy of Neo-Colonialism*, in which he was pessimistic about the prospects for Kenyan capitalism because he perceived the indigenous bourgeoisie (which he referred to as an 'auxiliary bourgeoisie') to be largely defined by its alliance to foreign capital. He was supported in his view that Kenya could not adopt and develop its productive forces within the 'bourgeois mode of production' by Steven Langdon, for example.[86] But other foreign scholars in Kenya argued that the political base of Kenya's post-colonial State was founded on the interests of a local bourgeoisie whose roots went back to pre-colonial times, and that indigenous capital accumulation was substantial and growing.[87] Pointing to a growing number of joint ventures between Kenyans and foreigners, the Africanisation of management in foreign firms, and the nature of government regulations on foreign enterprise, this group argued that a relatively independent and active group of local capitalists had 'extended their control over the means of production'.[88]

In a striking reversal of position, undoubtedly influenced by this work, Leys returned to the debate critical of his own earlier dependency analysis.[89] He now saw settlers' capital as having undermined the pre-capitalist relations of production and prepared the way for the takeover by an industrial bourgeoisie. He saw the latter's use of its control over the State to promote manufacturing as indicating favourable prospects for it to play a leading role in the transition to industrial capitalism.

Other scholars mobilised considerable empirical evidence in support of Leys' earlier analysis and in reaction to his new position. Langdon argued that growing industrialisation was having very limited effects on social transformation. Raphael Kaplinsky argued that although an indigenous capitalist class had managed to carve out a slice of the benefits through its alliance with foreign capital in large scale industry, inherent contradictions made it unlikely for the pattern of accumulation to continue – with or without foreign capital.[90] Still another scholar argued that the evidence was inconclusive, not because the data were contradictory but because of the weaknesses of the theoretical positions from which the evidence was selected and interpreted.[91]

Whatever the 'correct' position in this debate, it seems fair to conclude that the early dependency view, that capitalist development in Kenya was not possible, has been modified to incorporate much of the Marxist critique and views on the importance of developing a more refined analysis of the historical process of change. We return to this in Chapter 6.

W.A. Lewis, 'Industrialisation by Invitation' and the Heritage of Small Plantation Economies: the Jamaican Experience

Whereas in Latin America the dependency debate was launched largely in reaction to the 'reformist' positions adopted by Prebisch and ECLA, and in opposition to both orthodox economists and the local communist parties, in the English-speaking Caribbean it emerged largely as a reaction to the highly influential policy prescriptions of W.A. Lewis for 'industrialisation by invitation'.[92] Like Prebisch, Lewis was a strong advocate of industrialisation (cf. Chapter 1), both because of population growth – agriculture had been unable to feed the population of the British West Indies for several decades already – and because of the exacerbation of employment problems by the increasing mechanisation of plantation agriculture. Lewis saw the market mechanism and laissez-faire as incapable of initiating industrialisation in the small Caribbean economies. He therefore argued in favour of government intervention, notably to attract foreign investment through subsidies, limited tax exemptions and the construction of industrial estates. He also saw regional integration in the form of a customs union as necessary. In contrast to Prebisch, however, he argued for the establishment of *export* industries, which would benefit from low wages, since local markets were too small to support a strategy of ISI.[93]

Governments in the West Indies pursued strategies of 'industrialisation by invitation' more or less consistently during the 1950s and 1960s. The result was limited industrialisation which did little to reduce the high levels of unemployment and misery in the rural areas and urban slums. In Jamaica, where popular traditions dating from the period of slavery emphasized collectivism and self reliance – notably in the form of the Rastafari movement, which the ruling conservative party reportedly saw as a greater political threat than communism – the economic difficulties gave rise to a socially and politically explosive situation in the late 1960s and early 1970s. This situation culminated in the parliamentary victory of Michael Manley's PNP (People's National Party) in 1972.

It was in the early 1960s that a loosely knit group of Caribbean intellectuals aiming to develop 'an indigenous view of the region', called the New World Group, had adopted the general dependency perspective while emphasizing two specifically regional problems: the small size, and the plantation heritage, of the island economies. On the issue of size, they agreed with Lewis about the necessity of regional integration. But they also argued that in a context of 'industrialisation by invitation' the region would be dominated by multinational corporations and would not produce broad-based development of the internal market for mass-consumption goods. The failure of the Caribbean Free Trade Association was seen as indicative of the problems of dependence.[94]

They saw the plantation economies of the region combining African labour and European capital with Caribbean land, as characterised by three phases: slavery (1600–1838); the emergence of marginal peasant producers alongside the plantations after the abolition of slavery (1839–1938); and further modifications since the War, notably by the development of exports oil (in Trinidad) and bauxite (Jamaica, Surinam) under the control of multinational corporations, and by limited industrialisation. But they saw the plantation economy as continuing to 'generate underdevelopment': its land requirements restrict domestic food production; its supply rigidities make it difficult for the economies to adapt to fluctuations in the world economy; the international terms of trade for its products tend to deteriorate; its weak spread and linkage effects give little impulse to the rest of the economy; and its labour requirements are reflected in low-levels of education for workers.[95] The oil and bauxite sectors were seen as enclave economies characterised by similar structural problems.

From the late 1960s, the dependency perspective, combined with economic nationalism, turned into party politics. While some of the more radical writers were absorbed into a new political current that sought to combine Marxism and Black Power, the People's National Party shifted its orientation towards the views of the New World Group. The influence exercised by dependency thinking thus reached new heights after the PNP electoral victory, and culminated when some dependency writers were absorbed into the new political power structure in Jamaica.[96] Manley himself was an intellectually oriented politician who wrote on development,[97] and between 1972 and 1980 the Prime Minister of Jamaica was 'one of the leading politicians in the Third World who had made dependency theory his ideology'.[98]

Two of the most noteworthy changes introduced by the Manley regime were in the realm of international relations: its swing towards the non-alligned movement (and fraternal relations with Cuba), and its imposition in 1974 of an excise tax on bauxite production which led to negotiations and finally in 1976/77 to government assumption of 51 per cent ownership of the Jamaican operations of the multinationals Kaiser and Reynolds. The multinationals also cut back their demand for Jamaican bauxite, however, and Manley was eventually forced to reduce the production levy, which mollified the multinationals. This and other factors – including a sharp decline in tourism – finally led Manley to accept IMF conditions, which in effect put an end to 'self reliance' and 'democratic socialism' after 1978. As Jefferson, a leading dependency writer who was deputy chairman of the Central Bank under Manley put it, 'One of our assumptions was that ownership of resources does in fact constitute control, which is not really true...' – thus pointing to one of the central findings of subsequent studies of 'new forms' of investment in developing countries.[99] Jefferson concluded, 'What we need now is a theory on how to break dependence - without breaking our neck in the process'.[100]

The conservative party returned to power following parliamentary elections in 1980, and Jamaica was given special treatment under the Reagan administration's Caribbean Basin Initiative (CBI), one of whose major goals was to promote market-led industrialisation with the support of aid and favoured access to the US market. The CBI nevertheless proved less than fully successful. Moreover, Manley was once again elected Prime Minister in 1988, though apparently intending to pursue less radical policies than was the case during the 1970s.

Dependency in Asia

One might have expected India rather than Latin America to have given birth to dependency thinking. Indeed, in Baran's analysis, which inspired Frank, the focus was on Asia. Baran saw the underdevelopment of India as the result of colonialism (which led to the extraction of surpluses and the destruction of the village economy and artisan industries), and he cited Japan as evidence that the avoidance of colonisation was the most important prerequisite for an indigenous process of capitalist development. Baran himself was influenced by the debate in India over the 'drain theory' which emerged in 1866, and was elaborated by Dadabhai Naoroji along lines strikingly similar to those that would be developed much later by Prebisch and Singer.[101] But in the postwar period the development debates in India have in fact been influenced much more by Ghandi's ideas, by the orthodox debates we discussed in Part I, and by a strong Indian Marxist tradition to which we return in Chapter 6. The dependency debate as it emerged in Latin America has had little influence on development thinking in India.[102]

In other parts of Asia, the debate on dependency along Latin American lines is even more conspicuous by its absence than in India. China has of course been important for the strategy of self-reliance embedded in Mao's ideas of development. Mao is often portrayed as a Marxist–Leninist, but his Marxism was of a very unorthodox kind. He emphasized the need to resolve three contradictions in the construction of new economic, social and political structures: city vs. countryside, industry vs. agriculture, and intellectuals vs. manual labourers. Mobilisation of the masses and decentralisation were key features of Chinese economic policies under Maoist inspiration – most markedly during the Cultural Revolution – and by the early 1970s the economic policies of Maoism were increasingly criticised. After Mao's death in 1976 and the subsequent defeat of the 'Gang of Four', the emphasis was shifted to the need for *modernisation*. Under Deng Xiaoping, self-reliance has been stressed as a reason for importing foreign technology in order to develop the productive base of the country. Mobilistion called for material as well as moral incentives. And the cultural aspect of dependency has been largely ignored, as illustrated by the fact that thousands of young intellectuals were sent abroad during the 1980s.

In East and Southeast Asia, the dependency debate has remained virtually absent. Notable exceptions to this have been a few empirical studies inspired by the dependency concept. These include, for example, the writings of H.C. Lim and Don Long on Korea, and those of Wynn on Taiwan.[103]

THE AFTERMATH OF DEPENDENCY THINKING IN LATIN AMERICA

The Chilean experience under Allende (1970–1973) – and the earlier 'populist' regimes in Latin America – showed that redistributive processes could generate major sectoral and balance-of-payments disequilibria (including capital flight and fiscal evasion, not to mention pressures from overseas) which in turn created severe instability and, in the end, led to the opposite of the desired effect.[104] Moreover, a number of empirical studies and simulation exercises undertaken in the 1970s and early 1980s concluded that at best only a small positive impact on growth could be expected from improved income distribution in Latin America.[105] The combined result was to raise serious doubts about the likelihood that even if achieved, improved income distribution would be able to sufficiently alter consumption and hence production patterns in a context of inward-oriented growth so as to alleviate the balance-of-payments constraint, as many structuralist and dependency writers had implicitly or explicitly argued. These doubts have been reinforced by the increasingly apparent success of the export-oriented industrialisation processes in East Asia.

It was the quadrupling of oil prices in 1973/74 and the onset of sustained and rapidly growing inflows of foreign capital, along with slower growth in the OECD region, however, which more than any other factor gave impulse to the movement beyond dependency thinking in Latin America. Whereas in some countries, including Brazil, there was a resurgence of import-substituting industrial growth along with increasing manufactured exports, in others, notably Chile and Argentina, international monetarism became the dominant paradigm in the 1970s.

The declared objectives of the monetarist strategies were, first, to reduce domestic inflation through predetermined downward adjustments in the exchange rate, and then to keep inflation down by maintaining a fixed exchange rate in a context of relatively free trade and capital flows which, it was announced, would facilitate stability and development. But the results were not those announced. In Argentina, a highly overvalued peso sustained by large increases in foreign debt contributed to frenetic financial speculation and industrial stagnation. In Chile, foreign debt rose to the highest level in Latin America on a per capita basis, and per capita income declined by over 11 per cent between 1981 and 1984. Brazil also briefly flirted with the monetarist approach in 1980 in an attempt to reduce inflationary expectations, but the resulting overvaluation then required a major devaluation which boosted inflation.[106]

While international monetarism eventually succumbed to the severe depression in Latin America in the early 1980s, IMF stabilisation packages have been introduced in most of the countries of the region in conjunction with the debt crisis since 1982. These packages, though necessarily more eclectic than theoretically pure, reflect the short-term monetarist focus and seek to control external disequilibria through internal credit management (cf. Chapter 3).

The result has been to give rise to 'neo-structuralist' thinking in Latin America which has picked up many of the arguments from the structuralist–monetarist debate on inflation of the late 1950s and early 1960s. But whereas the earlier structuralist approach distinguished between the structural causes and the diffusion mechanisms of inflation, and proceeded to emphasize the importance of dealing with the former (which led to a relatively high tolerance of inflation in the region), the neo-structuralist focus of the late 1980s has been above all on the diffusion mechanisms. As one author put it: 'Any alternative [to the IMF's policies] could not stand arms crossed in the face of galloping inflation with the argument that long-term structural changes were the only real solution to the problem', especially when no long-term policy is likely to succeed in a world plagued with uncertainty and where the bulk of people's energy is spent seeking ways to avoid the tax of inflation.[107] Moreover, the years of military dictatorship and repression leading up to the crisis of the 1980s have aroused awareness of the need for greater social consensus. Neo-structuralist analyses have thus sought to design economic policy packages that could generate stability while minimising the social costs and negative impact on growth generally associated with orthodox stabilisation packages. It is these analyses that have been behind the so-called heterodox shock treatment of inflation in Brazil and Argentina under the new democratic governments (the 'cruzado' and 'austral' plans), whose principal objective, largely unattained, has been to stop 'inertial' inflation and minimise distributional conflicts by freezing prices and wages.[108]

Neo-structuralism thus stands in contrast to structuralism in the considerable attention it gives to the short term. This attention has been strongly reinforced by the perception that there can be no viable long-term strategy as long as the real transfer of resources overseas associated with debt servicing remains such a heavy burden.[109] The transfer burden has severely limited domestic investment, moreover, and the need for investment and to enhance export capacities, combined with the virtual absence of voluntary foreign bank lending, have led to a new receptivity to foreign direct investment.[110] Indeed, the drop in investment-GDP ratios and the foreign-exchange constraint are seen – very much along the lines of the 'two-gap' model developed by Chenery in the early 1960s (cf. Chapter 1) – as seriously threatening possibilities for sustained growth in the longer run. Perceptions of the negative consequences of the earlier structuralist-inspired policies on public and private productive efficiency have also led to greater skepticism about direct or indirect state control over resource allocation, and to widespread discussion of a crisis of the State in Latin America. Neo-structuralism has thus, in important respects, inverted the earlier structuralist approach to ISI in Latin America.

There is also movement toward looking beyond the debt problem. While there has been little support for unilateral moratoria on debt payments or for breaking international economic relations,[111] and the need for greater exports is now widely accepted, there is also little support for continuing to sustain the real transfer burden. One reason is that the policies required to sustain the transfer contradict the need to control inflation. Another is that by limiting investment today the transfers imply a major cost in terms of tomorrow's production and export capacities and, in the end, development. A third is the likelihood that as the United States seeks to reduce its huge trade deficit, it will be increasingly difficult to find the markets necessary to sustain the required trade surpluses.

Nor has Latin America's experience with the stabilisation programmes of the IMF led even the more conservative local groups to favour more austerity. There is considerable sensitivity to the question of income distribution (which has probably become even more skewed during the 1980s) if for no other reason than because of the latent explosive instability inherent in the abundance of misery and spectacular inequality in the region. And if there is less faith in state involvement in resource allocation, the credibility of 'laissez faire' strategies is also low – probably reflecting the experience of the southern-core countries. The emphasis is rather on greater selectivity and transparency in the realm of industrial policy, on greater attention to sound macroeconomic policy, on integration into international financial markets (but only insofar as this compensates for rather than exacerbates vulnerabilities to internal and external disturbances), and on maintaining or increasing export capacities in the face of rapid technological change and the formation of regional economic groupings in Asia-Pacific, North America and Europe.

With the renewal of democracy still fragile, there is also considerable awareness in Latin America that in the final analysis, economic policies must depend as much on political considerations and their ability to build social consensus as on their strict theoretical coherence.[112]

Notes and References

1. In Argentina – where Prebisch was Under Secretary of Finance in the 1930s – as in much of Latin America, a sharp drop in the country's international terms of trade at the outset of the Depression led to a foreign-exchange crisis. In 1933, Argentina required 73 per cent more exports to achieve the same level of manufactured imports as on the eve of the Depression.

2. Given its obvious similarity to the traditional/modern-sector dichotomy of the orthodox dual-economy models (cf. Chapter 2), it is perhaps worth noting that the structuralist concept of 'heterogeneity' was put forward in the ECLA documents of 1949/50 and thus preceded the dual-economy literature by a few years. There is no evidence however that the dual economy models grew out of or were inspired by the Latin American structuralist literature (for an interesting account of Lewis' inspiration in formulating his dual-economy model, see W.A. Lewis, 'Development Economics in the 1950s' in G. Meier and D. Seers, *Pioneers in Development*, Oxford University Press for the World Bank, New York, 1984). Nor are the structuralist concept of 'heterogeneity' and the 'traditional'-'modern' dichotomy of the orthodox models identical: whereas Lewis saw the 'traditional' sector as non-capitalist (and the Ranis-Fei and other neoclassical models see it as capitalist), for the structuralists the 'backward' sector may comprise *both* capitalist and non-capitalist institutions and production structures, whose common characteristic is low levels of labour productivity reflecting technological backwardness. Nor did the structuralist literature ever portray the 'modern' and 'backward' sectors of the economy as functioning independently of one another to the same extent as did the dual-economy models. (The structuralist and dual-economy concepts are compared, for example, in A. Pinto, 'Naturaleza e implicaciones de la 'heterogeneidad estructural' de la America Latina' in *El Trimestre Economico*, No. 145, January-March 1970.)

3. See especially O. Rodriguez, 'Sobre la concepción del sistema centro-periferia' in *CEPAL Review* 1977 (first half), and O. Rodriguez, *La Teoría del Subdesarrollo de la CEPAL*, Siglo XXI, Mexico, 1980.

4. ECLA, *Economic Survey for Latin America, 1949*, 1951, p. 3.

5. 'Because of its technological backwardness, land scarcity and very low levels of productivity, the minifundio is incapable of being capitalised and of retaining the increases in its active population.... On the latifundio...the tendency is toward use of mechanised techniques that use little labour per hectare and per unit of output (which) generate less employment than other available techniques, and more technological unemployment, when they are used in activities that compete with pre-existing production. (...) The Latifundio is unfavourable to capital accumulation, both because of under-utilisation of large areas of land and because of the high consumption propensity that are linked to the high concentration of land ownership and to the social condition of the landowner' (O. Rodriguez (1980), *ibid.*, pp. 253–254).

6. The view that more rapid wage increases in the developed countries than in the periphery result in deteriorating terms of trade for the periphery is similar to the argument later put forward by A. Emmanuel in his *Unequal Exchange*, as we explain below.

7. O. Rodriguez (1980), *op.cit.*, Chapter IX.

8. Whereas much of the orthodox literature implicitly or explicitly portrays a lack of structural change as the key obstacle to self-sustaining growth (e.g. Rostow, in his second stage), the centre-periphery paradigm thus considers structural change as a key cause of underdevelopment as well as of development.

9. See also G. Meier and D. Seers, eds., *Pioneers in Development*, Oxford University Press for the World Bank, New York, 1984.

10. Industrial programming techniques were first elaborated in R. Prebisch, *Problemas teóricos y prácticos del crecimiento económico*, 1951. See also CEPAL, *Introducción a la técnica de programacón*, Santiago, 1975, and J. Mayobre, 'Global Programming as an Instrument of Economic Development Policy' in H. Ellis and H. Wallich, eds., *Economic Development for Latin America. Proceedings of a Conference held by the International Economic Association*, St. Martin's Press, New York, 1961.

11. O. Rodiguez (1980), *op. cit.*

12. Hans Singer put forward a similar argument in 'The Distribution of Gains between Investing and Borrowing Countries' in *American Economic Review*, May, 1950.

13. See in particular, R. Prebisch, 'Commercial Policy in the Under-developed Countries' in *American Economic Review*, Papers and Proceedings, May, 1959.

14. See in particular, ECLA, *The Economic Development of Latin America and its Principal Problems*, 1950. See also Prebisch, *ibid.*, and Rodriguez (1980), *op. cit.*

15. See for example P.T. Ellsworth, 'The Terms of Trade between Primary Producing and Industrial Countries' in *Inter-American Economic Affairs*, Vol. 10, 1956, and G. Haberler, 'Terms of Trade and Economic Development' in H. Ellis and H. Wallich, eds., *op. cit.*

16. T. Morgan, for example, found that by extending the series back to 1801, the results did not support Prebisch's thesis (T. Morgan, 'The Long-run Terms of Trade between Agriculture and Manufacturing' in *Economic Development and Cultural Change*, Vol. 3, No. 1, 1959).

17. For example, G. Meier, *International Trade and Development*, Harper and Row, New York, 1963, and G. Haberler, *op. cit.*

18. While Spraos found no evidence of a trend for the period 1900–1970 in his 1980 study, more recent studies have found a long-period decline during 1870–1930, followed by a sharp rise around the Second World War and then a substantial decline over the last 30 years, excluding oil (cf. J. Spraos, 'The Statistical Debate on the Net Barter Terms of Trade between Primary Commodities and Manufactures' in *Economic Journal*, Vol. 90, March 1980, and *Inequalising Trade? A Study of Traditional North–South Specialisation in the Context of Terms of Trade Concepts*, Oxford University Press, Oxford, 1983; Overseas Development Institute, 'Commodity Prices: Investing in Decline,' Briefing paper, March 1988;

and especially E. Grilli and M.C. Yang, 'Primary Commodity Prices, Manufactured Goods Prices, and the terms of Trade of Developing Countries: What the Long Run Shows' in *World Bank Economic Review*, Vol. 2, No. 1, 1988).

19. G. Haberler, *International Trade and Economic Development*, National Bank of Egypt, Cairo, 1959.

20. Haberler, *ibid.*, and Meier (1963), *op. cit.*

21. J. Viner, *International Trade and Economic Development*, Clarendon, Oxford, 1953.

22. See for example, R. Prebisch, 'La Cooperación internacional en la política de desarollo latinamericano', ECLA, Santiago, 1954.

23. O. Rodriguez (1980), *op. cit.*, pp. 181–183.

24. See for example, W. Baer and I. Kerstenetzky, eds., *Inflation and Growth in Latin America*, Richard Irwin, Homewood, 1964; and R. Prebisch, 'Five States in My Thinking on Development' and A. Fishlow, 'Comment', in G. Meier and D. Seers, *Pioneers in Development, op.cit.* See also Rodriguez (1980), *ibid.*, pp. 304–306, for a comprehensive bibliography on the structuralist–monetarist debate on inflation.

25. See especially M.C. Tavares, 'Auge y declinación del proceso de sustitución de importaciones en el Brasil', in *Boletín Economico de América Latina*, Vol. 9, No. 1, March 1964.

26. P. Vuskovic, 'Distribución del ingreso y opciones de desarrollo' in *Cuadernos de la Realidad Nacional* (Santiago), No. 5, September 1970, integrates these views. For a summary of the studies of the 1960s, see ECLA, *La distribución del ingreso en América Latina*, September 1970.

27. See for example, F.H. Cardoso, 'The Originality of a Copy: CEPAL and the Idea of Development' in *CEPAL Review*, Second half of 1977, p. 30.

28. Prebisch was Secretary-General to UNCTAD from 1964-1969. For a discussion of the influence of ECLA views at UNCTAD I and UNCTAD II, see A. Dadone and L. DiMarco, 'The Impact of Prebisch's Ideas on Modern Economic Analysis' in L. Dimarco, ed., *International Economics and Development*, Academic Press, New York, 1972. See also Prebisch's report to UNCTAD I, *A New Trade Policy for Development*, 1964.

29. R. Prebisch, *Hacia una din mica del desarrollo latinoamericano*, Fondo de Cultura Económica, Mexico, 1963.

30. CEPAL/FAO, 'Una política agrícola para accelerar el desarrollo económico de América Latina' in *Boletín Económico de América Latina*, Vol. 6, No. 2, October 1961.

31. R. Prebisch, *Transformación y desarollo, la gran tarea de América Latina*, Fondo de Cultura Económica, Mexico, 1970.

32. See for example G. Martiner, *Planificación y presupuesto por programas*, Siglo XXI, Mexico, 1967; H. Soza, *Planificación del desarrollo industrial*, Siglo XXI, Mexico, 1966; and R. Cibotti and E. Sierra, *El sector público en la planificación del desarrollo*, Siglo XXI, Mexico, 1970. See also footnote 10.

33. See for example ILPES, *Discussiones sobre planificación*, Siglo XXI, Mexico, 1966.

34. O. Rodriguez (1980), *op. cit.*, Chapter 9.

35. Most communist parties in Latin America saw the struggle for socialism as a two-stage process, requiring first a 'popular front' in which the urban proletariat was allied to the 'national bourgeoisie' in opposition to the 'imperialist–oligarchy' alliance. Once the latter had been overcome and the 'bourgeois revolution' had set the country on the path of capitalist development, the struggle for socialism would enter its second and final phase, where a dictatorship of the proletariat would eventually replace the (still-to-be-attained) dictatorship of the bourgeoisie. The theoretical debates behind this strategy are clarified in Chapter 6.

36. G. Palma, 'Dependency: A Formal Theory of Underdevelopment or a Methodology for the Analysis of Concrete Situations of Underdevelopment?' in *World Development*, Vol. 6, 1978.

37. F.H. Cardoso, 'El proceso de desarrollo en América Latina: Hipótesis para una interpretación sociológica', ILPES, Santiago, November 1965, reported by M. Blomstrom and B. Hettne, *Development Theory in Transition*, Zed, London, 1984.

38. Furtado's stagnationist thesis appeared most forcefully in *Subdesarrollo y estancamiento en América Latina*, C.E.A.L., Buenos Aires, 1966. See also C. Furtado, *Economic Growth of Brazil*, University of California Press, Berkeley, 1963; and C. Furtado, *Development and Underdevelopment*, University of California Press, Berkeley, 1965.

39. At the top of Brazil's social structure Furtado saw a ruling class composed of various interest groups, 'in many respects antagonistic to one another and therefore unable to form a plan for national development [but] holding the monopoly of power unchallenged'; lower down he saw a heterogeneous mass of urban wage workers in services, below this a class of industrial wage workers 'which hardly represents one tenth of the active polulation,' and finally the peasant masses. (Furtado, 1963, *ibid*.)

40. O. Sunkel, 'National Development Policy and External Dependency in Latin America' in *Journal of Development Studies*, Vol. 1, No. 1, 1969, p. 31.

41. *ibid*., p. 46.

42. See for example, O. Sunkel, 'Big Business and Dependency' in *Foreign Affairs*, Vol. 24, no. 1, 1972; 'Transnational Capitalism and National Disintegration in Latin America' in *Social and Economic Studies*, Vol. 22, No. 1, 1973; and 'Transnationalisation and its National Consequences' in J. Villamil, ed., *Transnational Capitalism and National Development: New Perspectives on Dependence*, Harvester Press, Sussex, 1979.

43. Furtado (1966), *op. cit.*, p. 11.

44. Others who had argued that Latin America had been capitalist since colonial times include S. Bagu, *Economias de la Sociedad Colonial*, Ateneo, Buenos Aires, 1949, and L. Vitale, 'América Latina: feudal o capitalista?' in *Estrategia*, No. 3, 1966.

45. For example landless labourers (satellites at the bottom of the hierarchy) may be exploited by small (even peasant) landowners who act as metropoli in their relations with the landless labourers. But the small landowners may in turn be satellites in their relationship with large landowners and traders, for example, so that part of the surplus they

appropriated from the labourers may be passed along to the traders or large landowners (who may also of course establish direct relations with landless labourers).   And so on, in a tree-like configuration, with economic surpluses flowing right up to the world metropoli in the advanced capitalist countries.

46.   The definition reads: 'Dependence is a conditioning situation in which the economies of one group of countries are conditioned by the development and expansion of others.   A relationship of interdependence between two or more economies or between such economies and the world trading system becomes a dependent relationship when some countries can expand through self-impulsion while others, being in a dependent position, can only expand as a reflection of the dominant countries, which may have positive or negative effects on their immediate development' (T. dos Santos, 'The Structure of Dependence' in *American Economic Review*, Vol. 60, No. 2, 1970, pp. 289-290). See Palma, *op. cit*., p. 901 for a synthesis of the critique of this definition.

47.   Dos Santos, *ibid*., p. 233.

48.   See for example R.M. Marini, 'Dialéctica de la dependencia: la economía exportadora' in *Sociedad y Desarrollo*, No. 1, 1972. See also R.M. Marini, 'Brazilian Sub-imperialism' in *Monthly Review*, No. 9, February 1972.

49.   Marini also introduced the concept of 'sub-imperialism' in his analysis of Brazil's role in the region.   In an apparent attempt to transpose Lenin's concept of imperialism, he portrayed Brazil as a dependent capitalist country that had nevertheless reached 'the stage of monopolies and finance capital.' (Marini, 'Brazilian Sub-Imperialism', *ibid*.)

50.   In the words of Cardosa and Faletto: 'We conceive the relationship between external and internal forces as forming a complex whole whose structural links are not based on mere external forms of exploitation and coercion, but are rooted in coincidences of interests between local dominant classes and international ones, and, on the other side, are challenged by local dominated groups and classes.   In some circumstances, the networks of coincident or reconciliated interests might expand to include segments of the middle class, if not even alienated parts of working classes.   In other circumstances, segments of dominant classes might seek internal alliance with middle classes, working classes and even peasants, aiming to protect themselves from foreign penetration that contradicts its interests' (F.H. Cardoso and E. Faletto, *Dependency and Development in Latin America*, University of California Press, Berkeley, 1979, pp. 10-11).

51.   Cardoso and Faletto, *ibid*., p. 155.

52.   *ibid*. pp. 15, 21.

53.   For example, M. Blomström and B. Hettne, *op. cit*.

54.   Frank was criticised by the Marxists for focusing on the 'sphere of exchange' or 'sphere of circulation' of products, rather than the 'sphere of production', i.e. on the 'social relations of production' which Marxists see as the fundamental characteristic of a mode of production (cf. Chapter 6).

55.   J. Myer, 'A Crown of Thorns: Cardoso and the Counter Revolution' in *Latin American Perspectives*, Issue IV, Vol. 2, No. 1, 1975.

56. R. Brenner, 'The Origins of Capitalist Development: A critique of Neo-Smithian Marxism' in *New Left Review*, No. 104, 1977.

57. A. Phillips, 'The Concept of 'Development'' in *Review of African Political Economy*, No. 8, 1977.

58. Brenner, *op. cit.*

59. B. Warren, 'Imperialism and Capitalist Industrialisation' in *New Left Review*, No. 81, 1973; and B. Warren, *Imperialism: Pioneer of Capitalism*, New Left Books, London, 1980.

60. Warren (1973), *ibid.*, p. 13.

61. S. Lall, 'Is Dependence a Useful Concept in Analysing Underdevelopment' in *World Development*, Vol. 3, No. 11, 1975.

62. *ibid.*, p. 802.

63. Thomas Weisskopf tested Lall's conclusions empirically and found them correct (cf. T. Weisskopf, 'Dependence as an Explanation of Underdevelopment: A critique,' M.S. University of Michigan, 1976, reported in Blomström and Hettne, *op. cit.*).

64. Marx's concept of 'socially necessary labour time', which determines the *value* of a product but does not fix its price (price is also influenced by market conditions, e.g. monopolistic supply structures, changes in demand to which supply has not fully adjusted, etc.), is often poorly understood. It can be roughly translated as the total amount of time *society* (in this case the world economy) requires to produce the total actual supply of a given product, divided by the number of units produced. It thus reflects the state of technological know-how and other 'best practice' conditions of production in society as a whole, at the time of production (the 'socially necessary' time is an average for society and will exceed best practice labour-time requirements insofar as not all production can actually take place under best-practice conditions). It includes 'live' labour, of course, but also the socially necessary labour time embodied in all required inputs, including the depreciation of capital goods, energy resources, etc.

    Because Emmanuel used Marx's concept of value in his determination of the value of traded *products*, he is often thought a Marxist. But Emmanuel did not apply what Marx himself considered to be one of his main advances over Ricardo: the 'discovery' that the value of labour power itself is determined by the amount of labour time socially necessary to produce (or reproduce) it (cf. Chapter 1 of Marx's *Capital*). Emmanuel has pointed out, in a personal conversation with one of the authors, that he in fact disagrees with Marx on this fundamental point.

65. A summary of this debate is presented by D. Evans, 'Emmanuel's Theory of Unequal Exchange: Critique, Counter Critique and Theoretical Contribution', IDS–Sussex, Discussion Paper 149, 1980.

66. See especially C. Bettelheim, 'Theoretical Comments' appendix to A. Emmanuel, *Unequal Exchange: A study of the Imperialism of Trade*, Monthly Review Press, New York, 1972 (originally published in French in 1969). See also the second paragraph of our footnote 64.

67. See for example A. de Janvry and F. Kramer, 'The Limits of Unequal Exchange' in *Review of Radical Political Economy*, Vol. 11, No. 4, 1979.

68. E. Mandel, *Late Capitalism*, (Revised edition), New Left Books, London, 1976.
69. A. de Janvry, *The Agrarian Question and Reformism in Latin America*, Johns Hopkins University Press, Baltimore, 1981, p. 15.
70. *ibid.*
71. Bettelheim (1972), *op. cit.*
72. Mandel (1976), *op. cit.*
73. Amin was reportedly greatly influenced by the French growth theorists such as F. Perroux (cf. Chapter 1) but especially by the Latin American writers. Amin wrote, 'I have probably not reminded readers sufficiently of the debt which I, as well as the entire non-apologetic economic theory of underdevelment, owe to Latin America. The initiator is Raul Prebisch, and it is to him and ECLA that we must be thankful for the main part of the critical theory to which I belong' (S. Amin, *L'accumulation à l'échelle mondiale*, Anthropos, Paris, 1970, cited in Blomström and Hettne, *op. cit.*, p. 161).
74. Our summary of Amin's work draws heavily from de Janvry (1981), *op. cit.*
75. 'The dialectic of this contradiction between the tendency to external deficit and the resorption of this deficit through structural adjustment of the periphery to the centre's needs for accumulation explains why the history of the periphery consists of a series of 'economic miracles'... followed by periods of blocked development, stagnation and even regression...' (S. Amin, *Unequal Development*, Monthly Review Press, New York, 1976, p. 259, cited in de Janvry, *ibid.*, p. 17).
76. The term 'semi-proletarian' refers to a labourer who retains direct access to one or more parcels of land that are nevertheless insufficient to provide full family subsistence.
77. See in particular, C. Diaz-Alejandro, 'Delinking North and South: Unshackled or Unhinged?' in A. Fishlow, *et al., Rich and Poor Nations in the World Economy*, McGraw-Hill, New York, 1978.
78. Our discussion of the dependency debates in Tanzania, Kenya and Jamaica draws heavily from Blomström and Hettne, *op. cit.*, pp. 98–121 and 138–162.
79. Notable works of Tanzanian scholars include I. Shivji, 'Tanzania - The Silent Class Struggle' in *Cherche*, 1970, 'Capitalism Unlimited. Public Corporations in Partnership with Multinational Corporations' in *The African Review*, Vol. 3, 1973, and *Class Struggles in Tanzania*, Heinemann Press, 1975; and J. Rweyemamu, 'International Trade and the Developing Countries' in *Journal of Modern African Studies*, Vol. III, No. 2, 1969, 'The Political Economy of Foreign Private Investment in the Underdeveloped Countries' in *The African Review*, Vol. 1, 1971, and *Underdevelopment and Industrialisation in Tanzania*, Oxford University Press, Oxford, 1973.

   Notable contributions by Western scholars include L. Cliffe and J. Saul, eds., *Socialism in Tanzania*, Vols. I and II., East Africa Publishers, 1972/1973, and G. Hyden, *Beyond Ujamaa in Tanzania*, Heinemann, 1980. Two important scholars of Caribbean origin working in Tanzania were W. Rodney and C. Thomas (cited in the following footnotes).

80. A typical example was W. Rodney, *How Europe Underdeveloped Africa*, Tanzania Publishing House, Dar es Salaam, 1972.

81. C. Thomas, *Dependence and Transformation. The Economics of the Transition to Socialism*, Monthly Review Press, New York, 1972.

82. I. Shivji (1970), *op. cit.*, p. 2, cited in Blomström and Hettne.

83. He thus criticised Amin's analysis as structuralist, not Marxist. Cf. M. Wuyts, *On the Nature of Underdevelopment: An analysis of Two Views on Underdevelopment*, ERB, University of Dar es Salaam, 1976.

84. Hyden (1980), *op. cit.*

85. Blomström and Hettne, *op. cit.*, p. 154.

86. See for example, S. Langdon, 'The State and Capitalism in Kenya' in *Review of African Political Economy*, No. 8, 1977.

87. See for example M. Cowen, 'The British State and Agrarian Accumulation in Kenya after 1945,' mimeo, CDS Swansea, 1980, and numerous other works by Cowen cited in Blomström and Hettne.

88. See especially N. Swainson, 'The Rise of a National Bourgeoisie in Kenya' in *Review of African Political Economy*, No. 8, 1977, and *The Development of Corporate Capitalism in Kenya, 1918–1977*, Heinemann, 1980.

89. C. Leys, 'Capital Accumulation, Class Formation and Dependency - The Significance of the Kenyan Case' in *Social Register*, 1978; see also his article 'Kenya: What does Dependency Explain?' in *Review of African Political Economy*, No. 16, 1980.

90. R. Kaplinsky, 'Capitalist Accumulation in the Periphery - the Kenyan Case Reexamined' in *Review of African Political Economy* No. 16, 1980.

91. B. Beckman, 'Imperialism and Capitalist Transformation: Critique of a Kenyan Debate' in *Review of African Political Economy*, No. 16, 1980.

92. See in particular, W.A. Lewis, 'Industrial Development in Puerto Rico' in *Caribbean Economic Review*, Vol. 1, Nos. 1-2, 1949, and 'Industrialisation of the British West Indies' in *Caribbean Economic Review*, Vol. 2, No. 1, 1950.

93. Lewis argued, 'If the British islands were to follow the Puerto Rican example, they would be giving much less emphasis than they do at present to local markets, local capitalists and local raw materials, and would be concentrating on trying to persuade some of those UK manufacturers who are already supplying markets in Latin America, in the USA, or in Canada, to establish factories in the British West Indies, and to supply their American markets from the islands. Local markets are so small that it is only if the islands can build up a large export of manufactures that industrialisation will be able to contribute substantially to employment' (Lewis, 1949, *ibid.*, cited in Blomström and Hettne, p. 120).

94. See in particular, G. Demas, *The Economics of Development in Small Countries with Special Reference to the Caribbean*, McGill University Press, Montreal, 1965. A later study of economic integration under dependent conditions in the Caribbean is W. Axline, *Caribbean Integration: The Politics of Regionalism*, Frances Pinter, London, 1979.

95. Cf. L. Beckford, *Persistent Poverty: Underdevelopment in Plantation Economies of the Third World*, Oxford University Press, Oxford, 1972.

96.   For example, Norman Girvan became head of planning, Owen Jefferson became deputy chairman of the Central Bank and Rex Nettleford, who had dealt primarily with questions of cultural dependence, became the Prime Minister's special adviser on cultural affairs. (Girvan's writings include *Foreign Capital and Economic Underdevelopment in Jamaica*, ISER, Kingston, 1972, and *Readings on the Political Economy of the Caribbean*, New World, Kingston, 1971, which he co-edited with Jefferson; Jefferson's other writings include *The Postwar Economic Development of Jamaica*, ISER, Kingston, 1972.)

97.   Manley's writings include *The Politics of Change: A Jamaican Testament*, André Deutsch, London, 1974, and *A Voice at the Workplace: Reflections on Colonialism and the Jamaican Worker*, A. Deutsch, London, 1975.

98.   Blomström and Hettne, *op. cit.*, p. 114.

99.   Cf. C. Oman, *New Forms of Investment in Developing Country Industries: Mining, Petrochemicals, Automobiles, Textiles, Food*, OECD Development Centre, Paris, 1989. See also C. Oman, *New Forms of International Investment in Developing Countries*, and C. Oman, ed., *New Forms of International Investment in Developing Countries: The National Perspective*, OECD Development Centre, Paris, 1984.

100.   Jefferson interview cited in Blomström and Hettne, *op. cit.*, pp. 117–118.

101.   D. Naoroji, *Poverty and Un-British Rule in India*, Government of India, Delhi, 1901. See also *The Drain Theory, Papers read at the Indian Economic Conference*, Popular Prakash, Bombay, 1970, cited in Blomström and Hettne, *op. cit.*

102.   'Indian social scientists have, on the whole, assumed a rather sceptical attitude towards Latin American dependency theory. In the words of Rajni Kothari, 'The dependency theory is very relevant but it becomes an alibi for lack of self-development. You can always put the blame on the door of the exploiters but the exploitation that takes place in your own society is not questioned" (Interview cited by Blomström and Hettne, *op. cit.*, p. 127).

103.   H.C. Lim, 'Dependent Development in the World System: The case of South Korea, 1963–1979' Ph.D. Dissertation, Department of Sociology, Harvard University, 1982; Don Long, 'Development and Repression in South Korea' in *Jomo*, 1983; S. Wynn, 'The Taiwanese 'Economic Miracle" in *Monthly Review*, Vol. 30, No. 11, 1982.

104.   For a recent analysis along similar lines, comparing the Peruvian experience under Alan Garcia with Chile under Allende, see R. Dornbusch and S. Edwards, 'Macroeconomic Populism in Latin America', NBER Working Paper No. 2986, Cambridge, May 1989.

105.   See for example, W. Cline, *Potential Effects of Income Redistributions on Economic Growth: Latin American Cases*, Praeger, New York, 1972; J. Wells, 'The diffusion of durables in Brazil and its implications for recent controversies concerning Brazilian development' in *Cambridge Journal of Economics*, No. 1, 1977; N. Lustig, *Distribución del ingreso y crecimiento en Mexico: Un análisis de las ideas estruduralistas*, El Colegio de Mexico, 1981; and R. Bonelli and P. Vieira da Cunha, 'Distribucao da renda e padroes de crescimento: un modelo dinamico da economia

brasileira' in *Pesquisa e Planejamento Economico*, Vol. III, No. 1, 1983, cited in N. Lustig, 'Del Estructuralismo al Neoestructuralismo: la busqueda de un paradigma heterodoxo' in *Colección Estudios CIEPLAN*, No. 23, 1988.

106. For a critique of both international monetarism and of IMF stabilisation policies in Latin America, see A. Fishlow, 'El Estado de la ciencia económica en América Latina' in *Progreso Economico y Social en America Latina. Deuda externa: crisis y ajuste*, Interamerican Development Bank, Washington, D.C., 1985.

107. N. Lustig, 1988, *op. cit.*, p. 47. See also S. Bitar, 'Neo-Conservatism versus neo-structuralism in Latin America' and other articles on neo-structuralism in *CEPAL Review*, No. 34, April 1988.

108. A crucial dilemma which the heterodox stabilisation programmes have tried to resolve, largely unsuccessfully, has been the need to eliminate the indexation of wages and prices for inflation (such indexation has been a major contributor to inertial inflation) while at the same time achieving distributive 'neutrality' of the de-indexation shock, i.e., of the potentially enormous and differential impact of de-indexation on the real values of individuals' incomes and assets. See in particular the special issue of *El Trimestre Económico*, Vol. LIV (September 1987) on the austral and cruzado plans. See also J. Ros, 'On Models of inertial inflation', WIDER, mimeo, July 1987; E. Bacha, 'La Inercia y el Conflicto: el Plan Cruzado y sus desafios' in *Estudios Economicos*, El Colegio de Mexico, 1987; and M. Bruno, *et al., Inflation Stabilisation: The Experience of Israel, Argentina, Brazil, Bolivia, and Mexico*, MIT Press, Cambridge, 1988.

109. For a discussion of the problems of adjustment in Latin America during the 1980s, see for example V. Corbo, *et al., Growth-Oriented Adjustment Programs*, International Monetary Fund and The World Bank, Washington, D.C., 1987, especially the paper by A. Bianchi, 'Adjustment in Latin America, 1981–1986' (pp. 179–225); for an analysis of the transfer burden, see also H. Reisen and A. Van Trotsenburg, *Developing Country Debt: The Budgetary and Transfer Problem*, OECD Development Centre, Paris, 1988.

110. See for example, C. Oman (1989), *op. cit.*, especially Chapter 1; W. Peres Núñez, *Foreign Direct Investment and Industrial Restructuring in Mexico*, OECD Development Centre, Paris, 1990; and W. Fritsch and G. Franco, *Foreign Direct Investment and Industrial Restructuring in Brazil*, OECD Development Centre, Paris, 1991.

111. For a game-theory analytic approach to this issue, see for example, R. Fernandez and J. Glazer, 'Why Haven't Debtor Countries Formed a Cartel?' NBER Working Paper No. 2980, Cambridge, May 1989.

112. See A. Fishlow (1985), *op. cit.*

6 Marxism

The first major postwar study of Marxist orientation to focus on the underdeveloped countries, as noted earlier, was Paul Baran's 1957 study *The Political Economy of Growth*. Since Baran argued that the main cause of modern underdevelopment is the transfer of economic surpluses from poor to rich countries, and was followed in this view by many dependency writers, non-Marxist economists often see the concept of international transfers of economic surplus as the main contribution of Marxism to the postwar debates on development.[1] They also often assume that Marxists largely blame the problems of poverty and underdevelopment of the Third World on the rich capitalist countries. In important respects, they are mistaken on both counts.

Marx himself wrote little about the backward areas of the world. His remarks on today's 'developing' countries were basically confined to a superficial critique of what he called the 'Asiatic mode of production' (he saw the indigenous social formations in India and China as stagnant and constituting a drag on history in those countries) and to observations on the role of colonies in the development of capitalism in Europe. Regarding the latter, he emphasized the importance of 'primitive accumulation', i.e. the plundering of wealth which, notably in Spanish America, stimulated the colonial power's demands for manufactures and thereby gave major impulse to capitalist industrialisation and accumulation in Europe, especially in Great Britain. He also pointed to the export of capitalist manufactures from Europe to the colonies, where local artisans could often be undersold, despite high transport costs and the latter's use of much cheaper labour, because of the much more primitive state of their production facilities.

While condemning the brutality and hypocrisy of colonialism, Marx regarded it as historically progressive in its destruction of pre-capitalist structures, and even necessary for the development of backward societies. He also believed that the dynamism of capitalism and its capacity for expansion would be reproduced in any society where it penetrated – as he saw happening in the United States and believed would happen in India. He saw the backward countries suffering 'not only from the development of capitalist production, but also from the incompleteness of that development' and concluded that 'the country that is more developed industrially only shows, to the less developed, the image of its own future'.[2]

It was late in the 19th century and especially in the early 20th century that Marx's analysis of the dynamics of capitalism was extended to the concept of 'imperialism', i.e. capitalist imperialism. It was then that Marxists focused on the questions of capitalist development in less developed societies and of uneven development, i.e. the joint occurrence of development and underdevelopment on a world scale.

The 'classical' writers on imperialism, notably including Lenin, continued, like Marx, to see the international expansion of capitalism as having a fundamentally progressive impact on pre-capitalist societies. They did, however, highlight the difficulties of 'late' industrialisation, the ambiguous role of foreign capital in the less developed economies, and the considerable survival capacity of pre-capitalist structures in those economies. In a qualification of Marx's analysis, some writers also pointed to limitations imposed on the development of capitalism in the less developed economies by the imperatives of the advanced countries.

Since the 1920s, Marxism has witnessed two major reversals regarding the implications of imperialism for development in pre-capitalist societies. The first occurred with Kuusinen in 1928, at the Sixth World Congress of the Comintern. Kuusinen argued that one could not see the progressive consequences of capitalism expected in the colonial and 'semi-colonial' countries, despite the increase in foreign investment in those countries. His explanation was that, 'When the dominant imperialist power needs social support in the colonies it makes an alliance first and foremost with the dominant classes of the old pre-capitalist systems, the feudal-type commercial and money-lending bourgeoisie, against the majority of the people'.[3] This reversal of the 'classical' Marxist view of the fundamentally progressive impact of capitalist expansionism on the underdeveloped economies was the direct predecessor of what can be called the 'underdevelopment school' – including Baran, the development-of-underdevelopment current of dependency thinking, the writers on unequal exchange and, in general, those who identified international transfers of economic surpluses as the main cause of modern underdevelopment.

Referred to as Marxists or neo-Marxists by many orthodox economists, and often referring to themselves as such, the underdevelopment school has in turn been heavily criticised, as we saw in Chapter 5, by more orthodox Marxists (who often refer to them as 'radical structuralists'). It is precisely this critique that gave rise, in the 1970s, to the second major reversal in Marxist thinking on uneven development and the problems of capitalist development in the Third World. It also gave rise to a number of important debates, notably on the 'modes of production', with which the non-Marxist development community is largely unfamiliar. To clarify those debates, and the sharply contrasting policy and political implications of the positions adopted by the more orthodox Marxists and the underdevelopment school, it is important to review their historical foundations, as developed by Marx and the classical Marxist writers on imperialism.

HISTORICAL FOUNDATIONS

Marx

The hallmark of Marxism is a materialistic interpretation of history that seeks to explain the evolution of social systems. According to Marx, the change of social systems is not a function of extra-social factors such as climate or geography – since these remain relatively constant during periods of major historical transformation – or of the emergence of new ideas, but is rather a direct result of the material interests that motivate people in their dealings with one another. History, then, follows certain discoverable laws of motion that produce ever-changing and new forms of social organisation.[4]

The process of production, in his framework, is central to the development of society.[5] The process of production has two aspects: the forces of production (or productive forces of labour) and the relations of production. The forces of production are the inputs of production, including technology, tools, machines, and raw materials as well as people, their experience and their knowledge, individual and collective. The relations of production are the relations established among individuals and groups in production, such as in slavery, serfdom and wage labour; they comprise property rights or ownership relations ('relations of coercion') and work relations ('relations of cooperation'). The forces of production and the relations of production together constitute the mode of production which, in the abstract, is a specific social organisation of production.

For Marx, struggle, rather than peaceful growth, is the engine of progess. Accordingly, historical change is the result of conflict between the forces and relations of production. Each social order is characterised by continuous change in the forces of production, as scientific and technological progress takes place and capital is accumulated. A certain state or level of development of forces of production requires the predominance of a certain type of relations of production. As the forces of production evolve, however, the relations of production harden due to class struggle – competition between an oppressed and a ruling class – which becomes more intense. The ruling class, which benefits as a group from the existing structure of property relations (i.e. the legal or political means by which one group maintains control over the means of production) resists change, while the oppressed class that would benefit from a modification in property relations asserts itself and tries to gain political power. Eventually, social revolution results (the entire superstructure of ideas and institutions is more or less rapidly transformed) and the society moves to a higher mode of production with a new paradigm of social relations of production that are more in harmony with the forces of production.[6]

Even after the adjustment between the forces and the relations of production, the process of change continues (i.e. the cycle of progressive conflict, revolution, disintegration and evolution followed by conflict, etc.), but at a higher level of economic and social development. In fact, Marx and Engels argued that all of history can be periodised by a series of successive modes of production: primitive communal, ancient, feudal, capitalist, socialist and communist.[7]

The capitalist mode of production was examined in detail by Marx in *Das Kapital*. Capitalism is characterised by production for the market – generalised commodity production, i.e. production of goods for their quantitative 'exchange' or sale value, as opposed to their qualitative use value – by many different units of production competing with one another. But one class of people (the capitalist class) collectively owns the means of production, and another (the proletariat), whose members have been 'freed' from the control and ownership of their means of production, has been reduced to selling its labour power to capitalists in exchange for wages. Market relations, and in particular wage relations, are thus the predominant social relations of production under capitalism.

Building on the classical labour theory of value – developed by Ricardo and others – Marx argued that under capitalism, accumulation and growth result from the appropriation and investment by capitalists of 'surplus value', i.e. the economic surplus that is the difference between the value of labour's product and the value of labour power itself.[8] Moreover, while competition among 'free' workers[9] for jobs tends to hold down the value of labour power – hence its cost for capitalists – competition among capitalists tends to stimulate downward pressure on the average rate of profit. In response to that pressure, i.e. in seeking to sustain their profits or to achieve above-normal profits, individual capitalists invest and innovate in order to increase the surplus value generated by their workers, by increasing the productivity of their labour power. The result is to increase output, which in turn increases competition among capitalists to *realise* the value embodied in production, i.e. to sell their output, and maintains downward pressure on the average rate of profit. But in the process, capitalism stimulates innovation (including new forms of work organisation often involving greater 'socialisation' of labour, as well as new products and new technologies), investment and accumulation, and rising labour productivity.

Marx also observed that under capitalism, the process of capital accumulation is characterised by a trend towards increasing *concentration* of capital, in the sense that capitalists collectively appropriate control of a growing share of society's means of production. And he observed a trend, particularly marked during economic crises, towards increasing *centralisation* of capital, in the sense that fewer capitalists take control over a given amount of capital. These trends are generated by the dynamics of competition.

Economic crises periodically decrease the rate of accumulation, and of profits as well as wages; they stimulate further centralisation; and they lead to a subsequent renewal of growth and accumulation, once profit rates have been restored by the devaluation of the existing stock of fixed capital during the crisis. Or they can lead to social revolution and the replacement of capitalism by a higher mode of production (which Marx saw as socialism). But Marx also remarked that, 'no social order ever disappears before all the productive forces for which there is room in it have been developed; and new, higher relations of production never appear before the material conditions of their existence have matured in the womb of the old society'.[10]

Although Marx focused on the development of capitalism in Europe, he saw the downward pressure on the average rate of profit generated by capitalist competition as an important stimulus to capital exports and trade with pre-capitalist societies, as well as to the plundering of wealth and slaves ('primitive accumulation') in those societies, which gave impulse to colonialism. In his later writings he nevertheless saw colonialism to be a dying system. He associated it with the presence of merchant (as opposed to industrial) capital and with the mechanisms of primitive accumulation, and therefore with early capitalism. He saw colonialism as giving way to the development of 'the world market'.

Lenin on the Development of Capitalism in Russia

Lenin's 1899 study of *The Development of Capitalism in Russia* was the first important Marxist analysis of a concrete experience with capitalist development in a 'developing' economy (and as Palma argues, can be considered the first study of 'dependent development' along the lines proposed years later by Cardoso).[11] The study emerged from Lenin's debate with the Narodniks over the necessity and possibility of capitalist development in their country, a debate similar in important respects to the one that emerged some 70 years later between the underdevelopment school and their more orthodox Marxist critics.

The Narodniks emphasized the problems of 'late entry' into the process of capitalist industrialisation, and were convinced that the Russian peasant commune – a system of common land tenure with periodical redistribution of individual allotments which prevailed under serfdom and had survived its abolition in 1861 – was essentially socialist and therefore capable of forming the basis of a future socialist order. They felt that capitalist development was not necessary for the attainment of socialism in Russia, and that capitalism was probably not even feasible for a backward country such as Russia. Noting that backwardness provided an advantage in that the technological benefits of modern capitalism could be used (in a line of reasoning not unlike that pursued more than half a century later by Gerschenkron (cf. Chapter 1)), the Narodniks concluded that it was not only possible but economically imperative to escape from the capitalist stage and move directly towards socialism. (Caught in the blind alley of terrorism, the Narodniks were nevertheless losing influence in Russia already towards the end of the century).[12]

While Lenin agreed with the Narodniks that capitalism was a brutalising system, he, like Marx, also stressed its progressiveness in increasing the productive forces of labour, and in socialising labour. Moreover, his study provided considerable empirical evidence that capitalism was developing rapidly and that Russia should already be considered essentially a capitalist country. And as to the problems of unemployment and underemployment identified by the Narodniks as obstacles to the capitalist development of Russia, Lenin chided them for confusing a basic characteristic of such development with proof that it was impossible.

For Lenin, on the other hand, an important question was why the capitalist development of Russia, though rapid in comparison with the pre-capitalist period, was slow in comparison to the development of other capitalist countries. He identified three causes. First, he saw a relatively weak bourgeoisie in Russia, which he related to the role of foreign capital in accelerating industrialisation while leaving the local bourgeoisie relatively underdeveloped. Second, the lateness of capitalist industrialisation in Russia meant that it had to compete not only with pre-capitalist artisan industries (as the early industrialisers also had to do) but with the far more efficient industries of the advanced countries as well. The third cause he identified was a remarkable capacity for survival of pre-capitalist institutions and 'producers who [quoting Marx] "suffer not only from the development of capitalist production, but also from the incompleteness of that development"'.[13] Preceding critics of the orthodox view of 'dualism' (cf. Chapter 2), Lenin also noted that 'the facts utterly refute the view widespread here in Russia that 'factory' and 'handicraft' industry are isolated from one another. On the contrary, such a division is purely artificial'.[14]

In contrast to the Narodniks, Lenin thus saw the development of capitalism in Russia as politically necessary and economically feasible.

Imperialism: the 'Classical' View

Rosa Luxemburg: Merchant Capital

Whereas Lenin's analysis of the development of capitalism in Russia focused on the concrete experience of one country, Rosa Luxemburg was the first Marxist to produce a general model of the effects of capitalist expansionism on the less developed countries. Her theory, published in *The Accumulation of Capital* in 1913, followed Marx in assuming competitive (as opposed to 'monopoly') capitalism. But she added two new assumptions: on-going capital-using technological change and constant real wages. The model pointed to increasing deficits in the production of capital goods and surpluses in consumer goods relative to effective demand, and therefore to crises of 'under-consumption' (i.e. realisation crises) in the advanced capitalist countries. To palliate these crises, Luxemburg argued, capitalism seeks new markets in the pre-capitalist regions of the world. She thus saw capitalist imperialism above all as the conquest of pre-capitalist markets – involving violence among the rival imperialist powers at home as well as in the pre-capitalist societies (as reflected in the run-up to the First World War).

Luxemburg has been criticised for underestimating the internal inducements to invest generated by technological change, and especially the importance of wage increases as capitalism developed in the advanced countries. She has also been faulted for an illogical mix of dynamic (technological change) and static (constant wage) assumptions. Her analysis nevertheless provided an insightful description of the process of destruction of pre-capitalist spheres by the penetration of capitalism. She saw the penetration of merchant capital in the colonies temporarily postponing the development of capitalism there, by competing with local industry and reinforcing pre-capitalist social relations of production. She saw it eventually spreading capitalism to the sphere of production, however, and thus promoting development of the forces of production.[15] She thus saw the capitalist mode of production tending in the long run to absorb all pre-capitalist modes on a global scale. In doing so, however, she also saw it introducing the tendency towards over-production of consumption goods relative to effective demand into the less advanced countries.

The 'under-consumptionist' crisis in the advanced capitalist countries, Luxemburg concluded, is therefore only postponed until all pre-capitalist societies have been absorbed into capitalism. For the 'developing' countries, the implication was one of catching up to the advanced countries – after a transition period of postponement characterised by the domination of merchant capital.

Lenin: Imperialism and 'Monopoly' Capitalism

Six years after publication of Lenin's analysis of the development of capitalism in Russia, the 1905 revolution awakened an awareness – in Lenin as well as in the Czar's reputedly brilliant minister Stolypin – both of the limitations of capitalist development in Russia and of the concrete possibility of its interruption. Stolypin embarked on a policy of major social, economic and political restructuring that produced an important industrial boom and, by 1917, peasant ownership of more than three-quarters of Russian farmland.[16] For Lenin (and other revolutionaries, notably including Trotsky) the events of 1905 also implied the concrete possibility of transferring the task of completing the 'democratic-bourgeois revolution' to the working class. In fact, the industrial boom that followed helped strengthen the left in general, and the Bolsheviks in particular.

Looking at the advanced countries, Lenin's view was also affected by the collapse of the Second Communist International and the capacity of capitalism to assimilate politically important segments of the working class. He ascribed that capacity largely to the increase in real wages that was accompanying growth in those countries. Moreover, he saw the wage increases contributing not only to political stability but also to an expansion of effective demand, which was of course vital for the realisation of surplus value. The result was to stimulate further Lenin to change his position on the necessity, and especially the risks, of continuing with capitalist development in Russia. It was no longer clear that the development of capitalism would necessarily and inevitably lead to socialism.

In his 1917 study on *Imperialism: The Highest Stage of Capitalism*, Lenin developed his explanation of the capacity of advanced capitalism to extend some of the benefits of its development to workers. Building on Marx's observation of the tendencies toward concentration and centralisation under competitive capitalism, Lenin argued that capitalism had attained its 'monopoly' phase. He did not share Karl Kautsky's view of 'Ultra-Imperialism', published in 1914, according to which concentration and centralisation would ultimately lead to a single world organisation, a global trust (the equivalent of absolute monopoly in the neoclassical sense of the term), and thereby lead to stability and planning under capitalism. Rather than leading to an elimination of competition, Lenin saw concentration and centralisation transforming the dynamics of competition among large capitalist interests – into something roughly analogous to the neoclassical notion of oligopoly. He saw those dynamics characterised by tendencies toward monopoly pricing and profits in the advanced countries (whence the possibility to increase wages with growth of labour productivity) but also toward reduced output, hence slower growth, and considerable potential for instability. He also saw a tendency for large financial surpluses to accumulate because of a relative lack of 'profitable' investment opportunities (reflecting restrictions on expansion imposed by cartels and trusts) and to be exported to less developed economies in search of such opportunities.

Whereas Luxemburg had assumed competitive capitalism and focused on the implications for pre-capitalist societies of merchant capital and product exports from the advanced countries, Lenin's analysis thus focused on the export of 'finance' capital – industrial and financial capital[17] – by the advanced countries under monopoly capitalism. Rather than developing an under-consumptionist theory of crisis, he argued that the necessity for exporting capital arises from the fact that in a few countries, capitalism has become 'over-ripe' in the sense that it is not generating new investment opportunities as quickly as it generates new capital. Unlike Luxemburg, he did see the possibility for the capital-goods sector to grow relatively autonomously from the consumption-goods sector, offering domestic investment opportunities; but he also saw this leading to the accumulation of masses of capital that only accentuated the downward pressure on the average rate of profit. Surplus capital then seeks investment opportunities in 'young areas [where] profits are usually high, for capital is scarce, the price of land is relatively low, wages are low, raw materials are cheap'.[18]

In contrast to Luxemburg's export of manufactures in search of new markets, Lenin thus saw imperialism in the monopoly – 'the highest' – phase of capitalism taking the form of exports of financial and industrial capital seeking to sustain or increase its rate of profit overseas. Moreover, while he saw the effect on the capital-exporting countries to be one of slowing accumulation at home, he saw it as accelerating development in the recipient countries. For Lenin, as for Marx and for Luxemburg and the other classical writers on imperialism[19], the expansionist tendencies of capitalism in the advanced countries have a progressive, if brutalising, impact on pre-capitalist societies and lay the foundations for capitalist development on a global scale.

The First Reversal of Uneven Development: the Underdevelopment School

Kuusinen: The 'Feudal–Imperialist' Alliance

It was with the adoption of Otto Kuusinen's thesis at the Sixth World Congress of the Comitern in 1928, as noted earlier, that the idea of uneven development on a global scale was transformed from a theory of accelerated growth in the less developed economies to one of stagnation. Observing that British imperialism was hindering the industrial development of India, Kuusinen argued that under capitalism, 'the development of some countries takes place at the cost of suffering and disaster for the people of other countries' and that, 'colonisation made possible the rapid development of capitalism in the West'.[20]

Kuusinen's analysis of the obstacles that imperialism creates in the process of industrialisation in less developed economies emphasized the alliance that foreign capital, in search of local support, forms with traditional elites, which he referred to as 'feudal oligarchies'. He saw this 'feudal-imperialist' alliance blocking the emergence of a 'national bourgeoisie', thereby reversing the 'classical' Marxist view of capitalist expansionism as historically progressive for the colonies and other less developed economies. This was mainly because the pre-capitalist bases of power of the traditional elites – social, political, economic – would be threatened by the transformations that would inevitably accompany the development of capitalism in general and industrialisation in particular (the 'bourgeois revolution').

The political implication of this thesis, which was the guide to many communist parties in the Third World, was that the struggle against feudalism was a necessary stage in any progressive strategy. This often implied the formation of broad alliances to promote 'national bourgeois revolutions'. In politically independent countries (notably in Latin America) the ability of the incipient national bourgeoisie to develop was also often seen to depend on its political capacity to assert itself over the 'feudal-imperialist' alliance; this included, for example, preventing the adoption of free-trade policies, which the feudal-imperialist alliance often sought to impose so as to keep the young local industrial bourgeoisie weak, as well as to favour its own primary-export-based economic interests.

THE POSTWAR DEBATES

Baran and Sweezy: the Extraction of Surplus

While Kuusinen's thesis pointed up the problem for the colonies and 'semi-colonies' of surplus extraction by imperialism, its emphasis was on the role played by the feudal-imperialist alliance in blocking the development of a national bourgeoisie. In contrast, the analyses put forward in the 1950s and 1960s by Paul Baran and Paul Sweezy, who followed Kuusinen's lead in reversing the 'classic' Marxist-Leninist view of the progressive role of capitalist expansionism, gave much greater emphasis to the role of surplus extraction. From their work also followed the development-of-underdevelopment and unequal-exchange schools of thought, as we saw in Chapter 5, whose political implications were sharply at odds with those put forward by Kuusinen.

In his 1957 study *The Political Economy of Growth*, Baran drew a distinction between actual and potential surpluses, defining the latter as potential output minus essential consumption. He argued that the potential economic surplus in all countries is large, so that there is no natural or technical obstacle to self-reliant development, but that a country's actual growth depends on the size and utilisation of its actual surplus. He argued that in underdeveloped countries much of the potential surplus is not realised (because of severe inefficiencies in production and wasteful expenditures by the traditional elites and by the State, notably to preserve internal security) and that much of the actual surplus is transferred abroad, in the form of profit repatriation by foreign investors, service payments on foreign debt, and capital flight by local elites.

Focusing on European colonialism in Asia, Baran further argued that while the surpluses extracted from the colonies accounted for only a fraction of European overseas income during the 19th and 20th centuries, they came largely into the hands of capitalists who could use them for investment purposes. He thus saw them as having contributed significantly to accumulation in Europe. He estimated that about 10 per cent of India's gross national product was transferred each year to Great Britain in the early decades of the 20th century, and that, had that amount been invested in India, 'India's economic development to date would have borne little similarity to the actual somber record'.[21]

Baran thus saw European colonialism interfering not only with development in the pre-capitalist colonies but modifying their future development path as well. For example, by breaking up self-sufficient agricultural communities and forcing shifts to production of export crops, colonialism left many countries with exports concentrated in a very limited range of primary products, and often directed to but a few foreign markets as well.

Baran's analysis thus also pointed up the importance of asymmetrical power and political relations – rather than god-given 'natural endowments' and free-market-determined 'comparative advantages' – in determining the growth path followed by many underdeveloped countries. He concluded that, 'Far from serving as an engine of economic expansion, of technological progress, and of social change, the capitalist order in these countries has represented a framework for economic stagnation, for archaic technology, and for social backwardness'.[22]

In another work of major importance, Baran joined Paul Sweezy to write *Monopoly Capital*, published in 1966. Building on the path-breaking analyses of Michael Kalecki[23] and Josef Steindl[24] as well as on Sweezy's own *Theory of Capitalist Development* (1942), Baran and Sweezy's theses on the postwar development of capitalism had a major impact on radical thinking, notably in the 1960s and 1970s. Often referred to as the *Monthly Review* School, their theses were formed at a time when the United States had recovered from a major recession, was clearly the hegemonic capitalist country, and was going through a sustained period of growth characterised by strong government intervention. A succession of hot and cold wars were absorbing large amounts of the US labour force and public spending, and the operations of US-based multinational corporations were growing rapidly in less developed countries – often with a high degree of local financing – notably in Latin America.

Baran and Sweezy's analysis of monopoly capitalism in the United States pointed to a concentration of profits in the monopolistic sector, i.e. to a distribution of surplus value among capitalists that benefitted large monopolistic and oligopolistic capital to the detriment of average profit rates in the more price competitive sector, and to a tendency for productivity gains to be retained as extra profits rather than passed along through falling prices. The defence of monopolistic positions and insufficient expansion of effective demand meant insufficient investment opportunities to absorb the accumulated economic surplus, which, in sitting idle, put downward pressure on profits as a whole.

Baran and Sweezy saw various factors brought into play to counteract that pressure, including socially wasteful consumption expenditures by capitalists, Keynesian deficit spending and especially military expenditures by the State to 'burn' part of the surplus. Like Lenin, they also saw exports of capital to be a response. But their analysis of imperialism, and its effects on the underdeveloped economies, differed from Lenin's analysis in two important respects. They rejected his view of the semi-autonomous growth of the capital-goods sector as an important source of effective demand. And, even more important, they saw the major exporters of capital to the less developed countries – the multinational corporations – to be repatriating profits, so that the underdeveloped countries were being drained of their investable surplus. The result, they argued, was to block or retard the development of the productive forces in the under-developed countries while enriching the advanced countries: 'Indeed, except possibly for brief periods of abnormally high capital exports from the advanced countries, foreign investment must be looked upon as a method of pumping surplus out of the underdeveloped areas, not as a channel through which surplus is directed into them'.[25]

Following the lead of Kuusinen, Baran and Sweezy thus inverted the law of uneven development on a world scale relative to the formulations of the classical Marxist analysis of imperialism: rather than slowing down accumulation in the advanced countries, imperialism blocked development in the less developed economies. Whereas Kuusinen's inversion was based on the 'feudal–imperialist' alliance and pointed to the need for development of a 'national bourgeoisie' in opposition to that alliance, Baran and Sweezy's approach focused on the extraction of surpluses by foreign investment. The internal dynamics of under-developed societies thus came to be seen as fundamentally determined by their insertion into the world capitalist system.[26]

The Baran-Sweezy approach was followed, as we saw in Chapter 5, by Frank and the development-of-underdevelopment school of depen-dency writers (the 'radical structuralists') who, in attempting to explain the perceived failure of import-substituting industrialisation strategies, found the national bourgeoisie inexistent or tied to the interests of imperialism. Moreover, following the position adopted by Sweezy in his debate with Maurice Dobb over the transition from feudalism to capitalism[27] according to which capitalism is defined by the predominance of production for the market and for profit-making, they tended to neglect the study of class relations and to see Latin America as capitalist throughout. Tactical alliances with the national bourgeoisie, as suggested by Kuusinen's thesis and supported in the postwar period by most communist parties in Latin America, were thus seen as impossible. And the shift to 'inward-oriented' growth and ISI merely enlarged the basis for surplus extraction.

The political consequences of this approach were considerable. With capitalism, not Kuusinen's feudal oligarchies, seen to be everywhere, and with surplus extraction seen to be blocking development of the productive forces, it was not difficult to demonstrate the need for socialism as the only objective solution to underdevelopment. In Latin America, after the galvanising success of the Cuban Revolution, this interpretation tended in fact to dominate revolutionary thinking well into the 1970s, creating the intellectual justification for guerilla activity on the left and contributing to violent reaction from the right.

As de Janvry points out, 'The misery of the workers and peasants was seen to have created the objective conditions for armed struggle. (...) The insurrectional foco, a small group of determined individuals willing to make sacrifices, was enough to create the subjective conditions for catalysing the revolutionary potential of the masses. The doctrines of Che Guevara were thus to draw a generation of idealistic young people into hopeless warfare rather than political organisation and the task of developing socialist consciousness'.[28]

The Second Reversal of Uneven Development

During the 1970s, the underdevelopment school came under severe criticism from Marxists whose views were closer to the 'classical'

positions of Marx and Lenin. Moreover, the world economy changed
considerably over the course of the decade. Sustained expansion in the
OECD region gave way to slower growth and 'stagflation'. The 'welfare
state' and social-democratic bases of political harmony (Amin's 'social
contract') became increasingly strained as the combination of slower
output and productivity growth and inflationary pressures implied
higher unemployment levels and stagnating or declining real wages in
the advanced countries. In the North-South context, increased rivalry
among OECD countries for access to both raw materials and markets
meant that the terms of trade had turned largely in favour of the less
developed countries. The outcome of the Vietnam War, the successful
revolutions in post-colonial Africa and the successes of OPEC were also
seen as signs that the capacity of the advanced countries (especially the
United States) to determine external events had seriously deteriorated.
And growth rates, which had been roughly equivalent in the OECD
region and in the underdeveloped countries as a whole during the 1950s
and 1960s, diverged in the 1970s (GDP growth rates in the Third World
increased by over 20 per cent while OECD rates fell by over 30 per cent).

It was in this context that the more orthodox Marxist critics of the
underdevelopment school brought about the second reversal of Marxist
thinking on uneven development. We have already highlighted many of
these criticisms in Chapter 5. Suffice it here, therefore, to recapitulate.
Following de Janvry,[29] the Marxist critique of the underdevelopment
school can be summarised as comprising four main points.

First, rather than defining capitalism in terms of the dominant social
relations of *production* and locating exploitation in the production
process itself, the underdevelopment school is criticised for defining
capitalism in reference to the market and locating exploitation in the
sphere of *circulation* (i.e. in relations of exchange rather than
production). The global economy, whose parts are seen to be related
both within and between countries through the market, is thus
mistakenly seen by the underdevelopment school as capitalist
throughout since the dawn of Western mercantilism in the 16th century.

For the more orthodox Marxists, including Dobb, Laclau (cf.
Chapter 5) and Robert Brenner[30] among others, capitalism is defined by
a set of social relations that imply the transformation not only of
production but also of labour power and the means of production into
commodities. Capital accumulation is thus based on the appropriation
of surplus value generated not in the sphere of circulation but of
production (though, of course, for surplus value to be realised as money
and for capital to grow, production must be sold, so there is a dialectical

unity in the spheres of production and circulation). The transition from pre-capitalist production to capitalism and the subsequent development of the forces of production occur when pre-capitalist relations of production are displaced by a predominance of wage labour relations. The concepts of social class and 'modes of production' (to which we return below) are thus essential to the analysis of uneven development.

Second, in focusing on *surplus extraction* as the prime cause of modern underdevelopment (and as a significant source of accumulation in the advanced countries as well), the underdevelopment school is criticised for over-emphasizing the *external* causes of underdevelopment. The underdevelopment school identifies three main such causes: plunder and pillage;[31] the repatriation of profits and super-profits on merchant, financial and industrial investments (the last of these often financed in large part first by local savings and then by re-invested local profits,[32]) with profits repatriated openly and/or through transfer-pricing mechanisms;[33] and unequal exchange, be it under competitive conditions (à la Emmanuel) or under monopoly capitalism (à la Amin).

Their Marxist critics do not deny the occurrence of international surplus transfers, but tend to de-emphasize them as an explanation for uneven development. For them, *internal class structures* that retard or block development of the forces of production are the main causes of modern underdevelopment.[34] And limited development of the forces of production means that the growth of labour productivity and the generation of surplus value remain limited. Some thus conclude that, 'capital created underdevelopment not because it exploited the underdeveloped world, but because it did not exploit it enough'.[35] For others, capitalism can rapidly develop the forces of production in the Third World, but in many countries that development is based on an internal class structure that tends to dissociate growth from improved living standards for large segments of the population – thereby perpetuating underdevelopment for extensive periods.[36]

Third, by focusing on the external factors, the underdevelopment school tends to see relations of exploitation between *geographical* areas, within and between countries, rather than between social classes. It also tends to see capitalism overcoming class conflict in the advanced countries (as in Amin's 'social contract') and to see workers there participating in the fruits of imperialism, i.e. benefitting from the surpluses extracted from the underdeveloped world. The over-exploited masses in the Third World are thus the main victims in the world capitalist system, and hence constitute a likely source of socialist revolutions. Calls for an international alliance between workers in the advanced and underdeveloped countries, on the other hand, lack an objective basis.

For many of their Marxist critics, in contrast, the average rate of labour exploitation is actually higher in the advanced countries than in the Third World. This is because the real wage differential between the two groups of countries is surpassed by the labour productivity differential. The objective basis for class struggle is therefore actually stronger in the advanced countries than in the Third World. But more importantly, there is a strong convergence of interests between workers in the North and in the South, i.e. 'the key feature of capitalism is antagonistic class relations on a national and a world scale, and thus an objective basis for international workers' solidarity does exist'.[37]

Fourth, the underdevelopment school portrays capitalism as *incapable* of developing the forces of production in the Third World as a whole because it is draining it of its surpluses. (Some would stress that since 1982 and the emergence of the 'debt crisis' and 'real transfer burden', the resource drain from many underdeveloped countries, notably in Latin America, may even exceed the actual surplus – a situation that cannot last indefinitely – since investment is not even keeping up with the depreciation of capital stock.) Stagnation in the Third World is seen to be the inevitable corollary of accumulation in the advanced countries.

Moreover, as we shall see in greater detail below, some members of the underdevelopment school who include agrarian political economy in their analysis (e.g. Amin) see peasants and semi-proletarianisation[38] as sources of primitive accumulation that increase the rate of profit in the modern sector. Pre-capitalist (or non-capitalist) spheres of production linked to capitalist spheres tend to be seen by this school as *functional* to the needs of capitalist accumulation, and as being *reproduced* in their symbiotic relationship with capitalism in many parts of the Third World.[39]

For their critics, the 'classical' interpretation of uneven development is more accurate. As Warren argued, 'The view that exploitation caused by foreign investment can be equalled with stagnation is absurd. Whatever imbalances such investment may cause, it is still true that under capitalism exploitation is the reverse side of the advance of productive forces'.[40] For this group, the local State and multinational corporations, the latter often associated with local capital through joint ventures and other 'new forms' of investment,[41] are key actors in the development of capitalism in the Third World today. Some authors, such as Warren and Ann Phillips, see foreign investment and export-oriented accumulation as capable of accelerating industrial growth to rates that exceed those of the advanced countries. For others, the stubborn persistence of pre-capitalist social relations can slow accumulation and even cause stagnation for extended periods, but in the long run accelerated accumulation will result from capitalist expansion in the Third World.

These authors also see pre-capitalist relations of production in the Third World more as a hindrance to capitalist development than as functional to it. Despite low real wages, they see labour costs as in fact relatively high, because of low productivity in the production of wage goods (i.e. goods required for the reproduction of labour power). They therefore see capitalism increasingly penetrating the production of wage goods, though it may advance slowly in the face of severe constraints on market expansion imposed by low wages and unemployment and under-employment. Thus, in the long run, they see capitalist expansionism working for, not against, capitalist development in the Third World – as did Marx and the classical Marxist writers on imperialism.

AGRARIAN POLITICAL ECONOMY AND THE 'MODES OF PRODUCTION' CONTROVERSY

For many Marxists, the critique of dependency and the underdevelopment school pointed up the importance of basing their understanding of social change and uneven development on analyses of the relations of production and social classes in concrete social formations, including the role of the State. Thus, as noted in Chapter 5, Laclau, in his critique of Frank, posited the existence of feudal as well as capitalist relations of production in Latin America. Of course, he did not see those feudal relations as exogenous to capitalism or as pockets of decline – he too rejected the orthodox concept of 'dualism' – but as an integral part of many social formations in the region. He in fact saw the expansion of the capitalist market, both internally and internationally, as buttressing, intensifying or even creating feudal or other pre-capitalist spheres of production in Latin America. This view in turn led to an important debate among Marxists over the significance of modes of production in the development process, i.e. in the transition to capitalism in the Third World.

An important contribution to this debate was that of the French anthropologist Pierre Philippe Rey, who, drawing his inspiration from Marx largely through Althusser,[42] focused on modes of production as a means to understand the material bases and workings of class alliances.[43] In seeking to develop an analytical framework that would cover both the European transition from feudalism to capitalism and the latter's relationship to other pre-capitalist modes of production in the Third World, Rey introduced the concept of *articulation* of modes of production.

Rey saw the process of articulation typically characterised by three stages during the transition to capitalism. First, articulation occurs in the sphere of exchange relations, with capitalism tending to *reinforce* the pre-capitalist mode of production, which remains dominant. 'The capitalist mode of production only finds a labour force and agricultural provisions thanks to the action of another ruling class'.[44] As examples Rey cited West African lineage societies, where capitalist trading of slaves and products reinforced the existing social relations. Other authors have cited a similar strengthening of pre-capitalist modes with the capitalist development of primitive accumulation and trade in Asia (e.g. Indonesia and parts of India) as well as the 'second serfdom' in Eastern Europe.[45]

In the second stage, Rey saw capitalism 'taking root', subordinating the pre-capitalist mode but still making use of it. Peasant agriculture is transformed, and local handicraft industries may be practically eliminated, although the peasants' break with the land is often partial (e.g. seasonal) and capitalism is slower to penetrate agriculture. Stage three, which the Third World has not reached and, indeed, has only been fully attained in the United States, is characterised by the total disappearance of pre-capitalist relations of production, notably in agriculture.

In addition to his analysis of the different phases typical of the transition to capitalism, one of Rey's main arguments was that while capitalism always seeks to expand and will ultimately seek to destroy other modes of production, pre-capitalist modes other than feudalism may be fiercely resistant to it. He argued that whereas European feudalism is the mode of production that gave birth to capitalism through its own self destruction, and in doing so provided a cocoon for capitalism during its early growth period, an alliance between capitalists and ruling classes in other pre-capitalist modes of production is generally not possible beyond the first stage. Rey therefore saw violence, i.e. extra-economic force, as necessary for capitalism to subordinate the pre-capitalist mode while still benefitting from it, i.e. during the transition period, stage two. This he argued leads to the implantation of transitional modes of production, in colonial and politically independent 'neo-colonial' societies. He concluded that whereas in its countries of origin capitalism 'had already taken root sufficiently at the beginning of the industrial period to destroy the old modes of production and substitute itself for them in the production of its means of production', it is only in the era of finance capital that 'a new leap can be accomplished: capitalism can take root in new social formations' – thereby ensuring that 'the production of all its means of production in no matter what social formation becomes possible'.[46]

While Rey was flawed for holding that capitalism must have recourse to extra-economic force to subordinate pre-capitalist modes other than feudalism,[47] the debate on articulation gave rise in the literature to a proliferation of modes of production never identified by Marx. Several authors posited the existence of a *colonial* mode of production. Thus, for example, the Pakistani Marxist Hamza Alavi felt that the idea of pre-capitalist and capitalist modes co-existing in the same social formation was inadequate, and posited a single mode that could be conceptualised 'not in terms of a diffuse generalised conception of world-wide capitalism' (as in Frank) nor by a dichotomy of pre-capitalist and capitalist modes, but in terms of 'their hierarchical structuration in a world-wide imperialist system' which, in India, gave rise to the colonial mode of production.[48]

Indian Marxists working in this vein have also produced a wealth of empirical studies. These include the work of A.K. Bagchi, who argues that colonialism produced 'export-led exploitation'. His work focuses on the de-industrialisation of India and Bangladesh under colonialism, emphasizing the destruction of indigenous industry (especially cotton textiles) and the transformation of agriculture from food to cash crops for export, which increased both rural and urban poverty.[49]

Other Marxists have posited the existence of a peasant mode of production – similar to Hyden's analysis of the Tanzanian experience, as we saw in Chapter 5. But unlike Hyden, these authors see a more direct relationship (articulation) between the development of capitalism on the one hand and of the peasant mode of production on the other. Many see the peasant mode appearing with the dissolution of other pre-capitalist modes, articulated to and dominated by the capitalist mode to which it surrenders an economic surplus.[50]

Thus, for example, Samir Amin and Kostas Vergopoulos see peasant agriculture as constituting 'not a pre-capitalist residual, but a form created by modern capitalism that is articulated to it in an exemplary manner'.[51] They perceive peasants as relying on family labour and producing not for profit but to ensure the survival and reproduction of the family. They thus see the peasant as an entrepreneur who continues to produce in the absence of profits or accumulation, contenting himself with the equivalent of a salary and working on piece rate. Since capitalist farmers include in their cost calculations a normal profit (interest paid and the opportunity cost of their own capital) and rent for the land, and pay market wages, it is cheaper for capitalism to produce food under the peasant mode of production than under capitalist relations of production.

The peasant mode of production is thus seen as functional to the dominant capitalist mode of production and, as such, as acquiring a stable existence in capitalist society. Indeed, the ultimate capitalist reform, they argue, which is implemented by the State notably through unfavourable terms of trade to agriculture that are adverse to the penetration of food production by capitalists (and may simultaneously weaken or destroy the rent-extracting landed oligarchy), is to put agriculture in the hands of peasants. The latter retain an appearance of autonomy but are in fact fully controlled by agribusiness and merchant capital as well as by industrial capital through policies of the State, particularly cheap food policies.

In a major study of *The Agrarian Question and Reformism in Latin America* (1981), Alain de Janvry in turn criticises those who posit the existence of a peasant mode of production. He first points up a conceptual confusion between the general inability of peasants to capture profits and *lack of desire* for profits on the part of the peasants. He clarifies, 'The only difference between a capitalist producer and a peasant one is the capacity to generate and expropriate a surplus via the use of hired labour: the closer this surplus is to the average rate of profit, the closer our producer is to capitalist production. It is not that peasants do not aim for a profit (surplus); it is that they will remain in production *even* in the face of their inability to earn a profit'.[52] Finding ample evidence in Latin America of a high degree of dependence by peasants for family income on the labour market ('semi-proletarianisation'), de Janvry argues that the relations of dominance perceived by some writers as an articulation of modes of production are in fact capitalist relations, and that it is impossible to define social relations for a specifically peasant mode of production.

Building on the concept of social and sectoral disarticulation[53] adopted from Amin (cf. Chapter 5), de Janvry nevertheless agrees with those authors who see a functional dualism in underdeveloped countries between the fully capitalist 'modern' sector (where production is by wage workers) and the 'traditional' sector (composed of semi-proletarian workers, i.e. peasants and the urban 'informal' sector). His reasoning is that because workers do not constitute a major source of home market demands for the capitalist sector in disarticulated economies, wages can be kept low by perpetuating the traditional sector, which assumes part of the cost of workers' subsistence and reproduction. Wage levels thus tend to correspond to the subsistence needs of the labour force in the capitalist sector *minus* net production in the traditional sector. Capitalists perceive wages as a variable cost just as they would if the labour force were fully proletarianised, but that cost is lower than it would be in the case of a fully proletarianised workforce because the traditional sector provides cheap food and cheap semi-proletarian labour power.

Contrary to Amin and others,[54] however, de Janvry sees disarticulated capitalism and functional dualism not as a distinct mode of production, with its own stable laws of reproduction, but as a specific stage in the development of capitalism in the Third World. Semi-proletarianised workers tend in the long run to be outcompeted for access to land by capitalist agriculture, and therefore to be increasingly proletarianised. The proletarianisation of the peasantry – which de Janvry empirically finds to be well advanced in Latin America, as noted earlier – is further accentuated by the demographic explosion (reflecting the vital importance of children in peasant families as means of production and security) and by the ecological impact of economic pressures on poor rural families to over-exploit their parcels of land, forests, unclaimed lands and other resources, which ultimately undermines their productivity. He nevertheless points out that, 'It is this extended period of primitive accumulation, in which a surplus is extracted from the traditional sector via the labour and wage-food markets and in which the traditional sector gradually decomposes while sustaining rapid accumulation in the modern sector, that can be properly labeled the development of underdevelopment'.[55]

Contrary to those Marxists who see a lower rate of surplus generation in the Third World than in the advanced countries (e.g. Bettelheim, Kay, Brenner, Weeks and Dore), de Janvry also finds considerable evidence that the proletariat is more severely exploited in disarticulated economies, i.e., that the rate of surplus generation tends to be higher in the Third World, as argued by Amin and the underdevelopment school. Multiple claims on that surplus (including the costs of maintaining the power structure and reproducing the social relations through repression, co-optation and corruption, as well as profit repatriation on foreign investment, royalty payments, interest on foreign debt, unfavourable terms of trade and capital flight) nevertheless seriously constrain savings and accumulation in disarticulated economies, as does limited market size (because wages do not contribute significantly to home market demands under disarticulated accumulation). The savings and market-size constraints are partially overcome by the increasingly regressive distribution of income, but this negates the possibility for growth to produce a 'natural' evolution from social disarticulation to articulation – contrary to the view implied by such orthodox writers as Chenery and Kuznets (cf. Chapter 1). Moreover, the low-wage logic of disarticulated accumulation tends to be reflected in state policies to hold down wage-food prices, which encourage shifts in agriculture from production of food for domestic consumption to exportables, and thus often lead to subsidised food imports on the one hand and to state-supported efforts to induce technological change (e.g. 'green revolution' production methods) and the development of capitalism in agriculture on the other. The final destruction of the peasantry, and of functional dualism, de Janvry notes, can nevertheless be a very protracted process, with much depending on the particular type of class alliance that controls the State.

The State

For many Marxists, a major weakness of much of the orthodox development literature is its tendency to ignore the political origins and realities of the State, or to treat them as somehow exogenous to the development process, and therefore to fail to explain the forces – class interests, alliances, conflict – that determine 'policy'.[56] While the more radical dependency writers often see the State as little more than the instrument of a virtually monolithic group of capitalists, a number of Marxists have sought to relate the behaviour of the State to the essentially competitive (as apposed to planned) nature of the capitalist mode of production, which can give rise to a considerable degree of autonomy of the State vis-à-vis the particular interests of individual capitalists or fractions of the bourgeoisie.

Thus, in one of the best known Marxist analyses of the capitalist state, published in 1975, Nicolas Poulantzas portrays the State as countering the threat to the unity of the capitalist class posed by competition over the appropriation of surplus value, and at the same time fragmenting the working class, chanelling its political action into economistic interest group struggles.[57] Others point out that although the power of the nation state may be weakened by the internationalisation of capital, the class struggle (competition between capital and labour) continues to be primarily nationally based, so the nation state continues to play a crucial role in the reproduction of capitalist relations of production.[58] Also, competition and conflict between different capitalists and class fractions tend, particularly in the Third World, to be reproduced within the State, leading to the 'capture' of certain parts of the state apparatus and the establishment of a large number of public bodies, each with its own specific objectives and little collaboration among them to achieve common goals.[59]

Among Marxist development writers, one of the most important analyses of the role of the State in concrete social formations is that provided by de Janvry. Looking at Latin America, he sees powerful conflicts among fractions of the bourgeoisie, notably between the 'national' bourgeoisie involved in the production and trade of wage goods – vital to the production of relative surpluses[60] – and whose interests call for the logic of socially articulated accumulation, and the 'dependent' bourgeoisie involved in the production or trade of exportables and 'luxuries', whose interests imply the logic of disarticulated accumulation. Each fraction forms alliances, with one alliance tending to dominate the other and to control the State.

In Latin America, de Janvry sees the dominant alliance from the 1850s to the 1930s as that between the dependent bourgeoisie (comprising the export-oriented agrarian oligarchy and the 'comprador' commercial bourgeoisie) and foreign capital. Expansion of the internal market was largely irrelevant to the interests of the dominant alliance and priority was given to exports and trade liberalism. Furthermore, when the international division of labour dominated by England (a food-deficit country) collapsed in 1929, import-substituting industrialisation developed in a way that preserved the dominance of the landed elites and 'comprador' bourgeoisie, who became the new industrialists. Quoting Hirschman, de Janvry thus notes, 'The fact that import substituting industrialisation can be accommodated relatively easily in the existing social and political environment is probably responsible for the widespread disappointment with the process. Industrialisation was expected to change the social order [i.e. permit the rise of the national bourgeoisie] and all it did was to supply manufactures!'[61]

De Janvry nevertheless sees the potential for establishing articulated accumulation – under which the State pursues policies that seek a balance between the development of production and consumption capacities (as opposed to the cheap-labour, cheap-food logic of disarticulated accumulation) and incorporate important segments of the working class through populist or social-democratic political arrangements – as clearly present during the initial phases of industrialisation in Latin America, roughly through the 1950s. This was because industrialisation led to a rapid growth of the urban proletariat at a time when there were still significant remnants of pre-capitalist relations of production in the countryside (created under conditions of labour scarcity and based on non-economic coercion enforced by powerful agrarian oligarchies). Industrialisation thus created a market not only for previously imported 'luxuries' but also for wage goods during this period, and several countries saw the emergence of populist governments whose policies reflected the importance of the internal market.[62]

By the late 1950s, however, import-substituting industrialisation was increasingly constrained by balance-of-payments deficits, by limited internal financing capabilities and by food crises (cf. Chapter 5), while capital in the advanced countries began to re-assert its expansive tendencies and to penetrate Latin America, notably through investment by multinational corporations. The combined result was to push accumulation increasingly toward production of exportables and 'luxuries', and away from wage goods and the logic of socially articulated accumulation. As surplus labour emerged and political pressures intensified against coercive pre-capitalist relations in the countryside, the development of capitalism in agriculture tended to follow the 'junker road':[63] land reforms accelerated the transformation of feudal estates into large capitalist estates that tended to leave the landowning elites in a dominant position and to block the development of capitalism among peasants (the 'farmer road'), thus blocking the development of a domestic market for wage goods in agriculture. Moreover, with landowning elites often controlling the State, agricultural development policies tended to promote labour-saving but not yield-increasing (land-saving) technological change – thereby contributing to the tendency for food production to stagnate. The 'dependent' fraction of the bourgeoisie and the logic of disarticulated accumulation thus tended to re-assert its dominance, rendering attempts to establish the logic of articulated accumulation and the dominance of the 'national' fraction of the bourgeoisie increasingly difficult – as illustrated by the failure of such attempts in Peru under Velasco (1968–1975), in Chile under Allende (1970–1973), in Argentina under the Peronist 'social pact' (1973–1976) and in Ecuador under Lara (1972–1977).

De Janvry nevertheless sees a persistence of strong conflicts in Latin America and argues that it would be a mistake to view the alliance centred on the dependent bourgeoisie as monolithic. At the level of the State, he sees the key contradiction as the irreconcilability of demands for market creation: the dependent fraction of the bourgeoisie requires cheap labour and regressive income distribution to boost demands for luxuries, while the national fraction requires – but can least afford – wage increases along with gains in labour productivity to create a domestic market for wage goods. Already in 1981, de Janvry noted that 'Overcoming this contradiction by state spending, however, re-creates another contradiction – the fiscal crisis – which is evidenced, in particular, by high rates of inflation and an enormous and growing foreign debt'.[64]

Returning to the Marxist view of the relative autonomy of the State, finally, and looking beyond Latin America, some authors have built on a concept of dual leadership by private capitalists and public policy makers to identify factors that explain the State's frequent capacity to act as 'senior partner' in the Third World.[65] Sometimes reminiscent of Lenin's analysis of the development of capitalism in Russia, these authors point to a weak bourgeoisie or serious internal or external threats to the bourgeoisie – the last of these often giving rise to a combination of class and 'national' concerns – as explaining why the State often has greater relative autonomy in the Third World than in the advanced countries.

Thus, for example, if conflict between fractions of the bourgeoisie becomes too intense or leads to a stalemate, the relative autonomy of the State is likely to expand (e.g. India, Egypt in the early days of Nasser). Broad powers of reorganisation and policy initiative are also likely to be given to the State if class conflict (between workers and capital) is seen to threaten seriously property relations (e.g. Indonesia in 1966, Chile in 1973). South Korea and Taiwan, on the other hand, are examples of countries where a persistent external military threat has been the basis of considerable relative autonomy of the State, and where land reform and a strong State have succeeded in imposing the logic of articulated accumulation and the dominance of a strong national bourgeoisie.

The Transition to Socialism

Just as Marx focused much of his attention on the dynamics of capitalism, so much of the postwar Marxist development literature has focused on the dynamics of capitalism in the Third World.

Nevertheless, some writers have turned to the question of the transition from capitalism to socialism, i.e. of the role of the State following a revolution that takes power in the name of socialism in an underdeveloped country.

Marx (and Engels), it should be recalled, envisaged socialism as being built on the solid foundations of highly developed forces of production and a high degree of socialisation of labour developed under capitalism.[66] As it turned out, however, revolutionary movements that succeeded in taking power in the name of socialism did so not in the advanced capitalist countries, but in underdeveloped countries where capitalism was immature and the industrial proletariat constituted only a small proportion of the labour force.[67] 'Socialism' has thus been constructed on the foundations of relative poverty and underdevelopment, contrary to what Marx foresaw.

This historical fact has led to much debate over whether the USSR, the countries of Eastern Europe, China, Cuba, etc., are (or were) socialist countries in the Marxist sense.[68] An early indictment from a Marxist perspective of the Soviet Union, for example, was that of Trotsky, who argued that socialism is not automatically attained by public ownership of the means of production. Like Marx, Trotsky did not believe socialism could be built in one country in isolation, and the poverty and underdevelopment of the forces of production in the USSR made the task virtually insurmountable without international proletarian support. He denounced Stalin's policies and argued, already in 1937, that while the country had made impressive gains, they were at tremendous cost in terms of lagging labour productivity, gross structural imbalances, poor quality of goods, bad management, growing inequalities and privileges, and a huge and stifling bureaucracy which resulted from the isolation and backwardness of the USSR.[69]

Also important was the debate launched in 1971 by Sweezy and Bettelheim over the 'backsliding' issue.[70] Parallel in some respects to the earlier debate between Sweezy and Dobb on the transition from feudalism to capitalism (see footnote 27), this debate focused on such issues as the meaning of socialism, the significance of planning versus markets, and the backsliding of erstwhile socialist countries to some form of capitalism (particularly state capitalism, at least until very recently). Whereas Sweezy initially tended to identify central planning with socialism and reliance on markets with capitalism, Bettelheim argued that since both the bourgeoisie and the proletariat (if in power) can engage in planning, and since both will use market processes to some degree, the decisive question in determining whether a country is on the road to socialism is whether the working class controls the State – the bureaucracy and the military – and thus dominates the conditions and results of its productive activity.[71]   Sweezy and Bettelheim also concluded that many underdeveloped countries lack an authentic proletarian class, which raises serious questions about the viability of socialism in such countries (and led Sweezy and Bettelheim to emphasize the importance of revolutionary movements and 'proletarian ideology' in the absence of an authentic proletariat as envisaged by Marx).

While they may have lacked an 'authentic' industrial proletariat in the Marxist sense, a number of underdeveloped countries have nevertheless been host to revolutions that took power in the name of socialism. Major difficulties never envisaged by Marx have thus been faced by 'socialist' governments. First of all, should they give immediate priority to developing the forces of production and the growth of output, as was notably the case in the USSR under Stalin and became so in post-Mao China? Or should they give top priority instead to class struggle and the transformation of the social relations of production, as was generally favoured by Mao for example? What should be the respective roles of and relationship between planning and markets? – a question that has loomed large for many governments. And what about the relationship between the capital-goods and consumer-goods sectors? – a question, of crucial importance for planners, in which Marx also took considerable interest, and on which some 'policy-oriented' work has recently been published.[72]

MONOPOLY CAPITAL IN UNDERDEVELOPED ECONOMIES

A Third Reverse of Uneven Development?

Following its critique of dependency thinking and particularly of the underdevelopment school, much of the Marxist development literature since the 1970s has focused on various aspects of the modes-of-production controversy and on the role of the State in non-socialist countries. There nevertheless remains considerable disagreement among Marxists as to the viability of capitalism as a road to development. Particularly important in this regard is the view put forward by some relatively orthodox Marxists – and at least one rather orthodox non-Marxist[73] – that the degree of concentration and centralisation of capital is now so high in many underdeveloped countries that it constitutes a major hindrance to local development under capitalism.[74]

In static (non-Marxist) terms, the argument is that the degree of monopolistic or oligopolistic concentration tends to be *relatively* higher, often markedly higher, in Third World countries than in the advanced countries. As a result, inter-capitalist competition (in terms of price competition) tends to be considerably less active in many underdeveloped countries than in the advanced countries. The development impact and impulses of capitalism are thus severely weakened in much of the Third World.

In dynamic terms, the argument is that with the internationalisation of industrial and financial capital, which emerged towards the end of the last century but has grown immensely in the postwar period, the processes of concentration and centralisation of capital have taken place in capitalism as a whole, hence in the underdeveloped as well as in the advanced countries. This 'maturing' of capitalism, i.e. the concentration and centralisation of capital on a global scale, accompanied the development of the forces of production in the advanced countries; but by the time capitalism reached its 'monopoly' phase, the dynamics of capitalism during its 'competitive' phase had already produced a significant degree of development of the productive forces (and socialisation of labour) in the advanced countries. In the Third World, by contrast, capitalism reached its 'monopoly' phase *prior* to the development (or at a much lower level of development) of the forces of production.

Quite aside from the modes-of-production controversy and the issue of relations between capitalist and pre-capitalist spheres, then, the question is whether monopoly capital produces dynamics *within* the capitalist spheres of underdeveloped countries that favour or hinder accumulation and the development of the forces of production in those countries. Following the analysis by Lenin and others of the dynamics of monopoly capital – and the orthodox models of oligopoly are consistent with this view – it is argued that compared to competitive capitalism, monopoly capital tends to slow accumulation and productivity growth in the underdeveloped countries just as it does in advanced countries. Moreover, insofar as the *relative* degree of monopolistic concentration is higher in many underdeveloped countries (i.e. relative to the level of development of the productive forces), the effects of the global processes of concentration and centralisation of capital in terms of slowing accumulation and productivity growth are often considerably more pronounced in those countries than in the advanced countries.

Schematically, the reasoning is as follows. Because of the transformation of the dominant nature of inter-capitalist competition, monopoly capital – in underdeveloped and developed countries alike – tends to retain a greater share of the benefits of increased productivity as profits rather than passing them along through falling prices. This in turn increases the mass of investable funds. But the growth of profitable domestic investment opportunities does not keep pace, partly because of increased downward pressures on the rate of profit but also because the dominant firms in a given market see further investment as undermining their monopolistic position or risking to destabilise an oligopolistic 'equilibrium'. Compared to the dynamics of 'young', i.e. competitive capitalism, which historically coincided with and gave strong impulse to the development of the forces of production in the advanced countries, under monopoly capitalism accumulation and productivity growth tend to be slower. While the slowing of productivity growth is visible, since the 1970s, in the advanced countries,[75] in many underdeveloped countries the relatively high degree of concentration and centralisation limits accumulation and productivity growth to the point of seriously inhibiting development of the forces of production.

Indeed, it is observed, the dynamics that stimulate monopoly capital in advanced countries to migrate in search of profitable investment opportunities outside areas where the capitalists who own it already enjoy monopolistic (oligopolistic) positions are clearly at work in the Third World as well. Such capital migration often occurs in waves, takes different forms in different countries and at different times, and can be directed to new areas of economic or financial activity and/or to new geographical areas. In the advanced countries, the postwar period alone has witnessed waves of capital migration in the forms of foreign direct investment,[76] corporate conglomeration, the growth of 'offshore' financial markets, 'sovereign' loans to the Third World, international lending to the US Treasury, and corporate mergers and acquisitions. In the Third World, the most obvious form of capital migration has of course been capital flight. But international capital migration from underdeveloped countries can also take the form of payments on foreign debt, remittances on direct foreign investment (both overtly and through transfer pricing), royalty payments, etc.

Whereas the school of writers in the Baran–Frank–Amin tradition sees monopoly capital in the advanced countries extracting economic surpluses from the underdeveloped countries, this more orthodox Marxist approach traces such international value transfers to the behaviour of highly concentrated and centralised capital in the underdeveloped economies themselves. Moreover, it should be stressed, this approach sees capital exports from underdeveloped countries as only one – and not necessarily the most critical – of the many 'paradoxes' that can be traced to that behaviour,[77] and whose net result is to seriously constrain the development of the forces of production in many underdeveloped countries.

For non-Marxists, the problem of excessive monopolistic concentration in developing countries calls for measures to strengthen competition in those countries. The measures they suggest often include the reduction or elimination of state monopolies through privatisation, deregulation of industry, the reduction or elimination of protection to stimulate competition from imports, the reduction or elimination of restrictions on foreign direct investment and technology imports to strengthen competition from and among foreign investors and technology suppliers (and among local technology importers as well), export-oriented industrialisation strategies to force local firms to face the pressures of world-market competition, and enhanced anti-trust and other such juridical competition policies.

From the Marxist perspective, in contrast, the concentration and centralisation of capital are global and ongoing processes that are inherent in the competitive (as opposed to planned) nature of capitalism. Essentially irreversible, they point to continued or accentuated uneven development on a global scale. With capitalism well into its mature 'monopoly' phase, and capital highly internationalised, they raise serious doubts about the ability of capitalism to overcome the constraints on accumulation, productivity growth and development in most underdeveloped countries.

Notes and References

1. Indeed, some important non-Marxist reviews of development studies not only see the dependency school as Marxist, but, even more mistakenly, portray it as the *only* Marxist approach. See for example, I.M.D. Little, *Economic Development: Theory, Policy and International Relations*, Basic Books, New York, 1982.
2. In Marx's Preface to *Capital*, 1867.
3. Kuusinen, 1928, in J. Degras, ed., *The Communist International, 1919–1943; Documents, Vol. 2, 1928–1938*, Oxford University Press, London, 1960, cited in G. Palma, 'Dependency: A Formal Theory of Underdevelopment or a Methodology for the Analysis of Concrete Situations of Underdevelopment?' in *World Development*, Vol. 6, 1978, p. 897.

4. See for example, M. Bober, *Karl Marx's Interpretation of History*, Harvard University Press, Cambridge, 1950.

5. See for example, E. Mandel, *Marxist Economic Theory*, Merlin, London, 1974; and B. Onimode, *An Introduction to Marxist Political Economy*, Zed Books Ltd., London, 1985.

6. Non-Marxists often mistakenly characterise Marx's approach as a type of technological determinism. In fact, for Marx, technological change is not independent of class relations, and the search for profits under capitalism stimulates and conditions technological innovation (see for example, N. Rosenburg, 'Marx as a Student of Technological Change' in his *Inside the Black Box: Technology and Economics*, Cambridge University Press, Cambridge, 1982).

7. A useful discussion of the salient features of the different modes of production is found in Onimode, *op. cit.*, Chapter 3, and in Mandel, *op. cit.*

8. The concept of economic surplus had its origins in the work of the English classical economists (like Smith and Ricardo) and the French physiocrats, who saw it as the difference between a nation's total output and that required to sustain the population and keep the capital stock intact. Marx's contribution, as he saw it, was simply to recognise that once labour power has been transformed into a commodity, through proletarianisation, its exchange value is determined like that of any other commodity: the labour time required under normal working conditions (given the state of technological advancement and level of accumulation and development in the economy) to produce it. Hence the notion of economic surplus could be translated into value terms, using the labour theory of value already developed by Ricardo and others, where the value of labour power is the value of commodities required by labour for its own reproduction (see footnote 64 in Chapter 5 for further clarification of the 'value' concept). The amount of 'subsistence' required to reproduce labour power, Marx further argued, depends both on the state of development of the society (of its production forces) and on the history and current state of class conflict – i.e. the extent to which the proletariat has conquered rights of access to higher consumption levels, leisure time, etc.

9. Proletarianised workers are 'free' in the double sense that (having been freed from the land and obligations to their feudal lord, historically in Europe) they are free to sell, or not sell, their labour power on the market; and they are dispossessed, i.e. free of anything else to sell but their labour power.

10. K. Marx, *Grundisse Foundations of the Critique of Political Economy*, 1859.

11. G. Palma, *op. cit.*, p. 890.

12. *ibid.*, p. 892.

13. Lenin, *The Development of Capitalism in Russia*, 1899, p. 607, cited in *ibid.*, p. 893.

14. *ibid.*

15. For an interesting empirical analysis along the lines of Luxemburg's model in pre-capitalist spheres of Peru in the 1970s, see B. Bradby, 'The Destruction of the Natural Economy' in *Economy and Society*, Vol. 4,

No. 2, May 1975. See also A. de Janvry, *The Agrarian Question and Reformism in Latin America*, Johns Hopkins University Press, Baltimore, 1981.

16.　Lenin commented on Stolypin's new policies: 'They know very well what they want, where they are going, and on what forces they can count. [Their policies] mark a new phase in the breakdown of the old semi-patriarchal and semi-feudal system of Czarism, a new movement towards its transformation into a middle-class monarchy... It would be empty and stupid...to say that the success of such a policy is 'impossible' in Russia... It is possible!' (cited in Palma, *op. cit.*, p. 894).

17.　Lenin was greatly influenced by Hilferding's 1910 study *Finance Capital: A study of the latest phase of capitalist development*, which defined finance capital as the fusion of industrial and bank capital, with the latter in the dominant position. While Hilferding's view of the dominance of bank capital over industrial capital was later criticised, by Sweezy and others, in important respects his study pioneered Marxist analysis of monopoly capitalism.

18.　Lenin, 1916, cited in de Janvry, *op. cit.*, p. 11.

19.　Along with Hilferding, another important contributor to the classic Marxist literature on imperialism is Bukharin, who argued in his 1917 study *Imperialism and World Economy* that the basic contradiction of finance capital, i.e. of monopoly capitalism, was between the international expansion of the forces of production and continued national appropriation of surplus value.

20.　Kuusinen, 1928, cited in de Janvry, *op. cit.*, p. 12.

21.　P. Baran, *The Political Economy of Growth*, Monthly Review Press, New York, 1957, p. 148 (1968 Modern Reader Paperback Edition).

22.　*ibid.*, p. 163.

23.　See especially M. Kalecki, *Essays in the Theory of Economic Fluctuations* (1939) and *Studies in Economic Dynamics* (1943), combined and revised in *Theory of Economic Dynamics* (1954). As Joan Robinson as well as Baran and Sweezy have pointed out, Kalecki's work has received little of the attention it deserves. He was the leader in reintegrating micro and macro theories, and 'not only discovered the *General theory* [of Keynes] independently, but also was the first to include what he called the 'degree of monopoly' in his overall model' (Baran and Sweezy, *Monopoly Capital*, Monthly Review Press, Penguin Book edition, 1966, p. 66).

24.　Cf. J. Steindl, *Maturity and Stagnation in American Capitalism*, 1952.

25.　P. Baran and P. Sweezy, *Monopoly Capital*, Monthly Review Press, New York, 1966, p. 105.

26.　One of the few empirical studies of whether developing countries exported surpluses during the 19th century, considered to be the high period of European imperialism, is a 1980 book by J.R. Hanson. While he reports that only one third of his sample of 34 countries provide even rough illustrations of significant surplus transfers, these include what is now India, Pakistan, Bangladesh, Indonesia in the 19th century and Mexico, Peru and Bolivia in an earlier period. Lloyd Reynolds, in a 1985 empirical study of economic growth in the Third World, also found an income drawn from many colonies. Cf. J.R. Hanson, *Trade in*

Transition: *Exports from the Third World, 1840–1900*, Academic Press, 1980; and L.G. Reynolds, *Economic Growth in the Third World, 1850–1980*, Yale University Press, New Haven, 1985.

27. Cf. P. Sweezy and M. Dobb, *et al., The Transition from Feudalism to Capitalism*, Science and Society, New York, 1967. Dobb saw internal factors, notably the rise of capitalist peasants hiring wage labour, as largely responsible for the decline of feudalism. Sweezy, on the other hand, saw external factors, notably the emergence of urban markets on the margin of feudalism, as the fundamental cause of the decline of the feudal mode of production.

28. A. de Janvry, *op. cit.*, p. 16. The writings of Regis Debray also contributed to thinking on the 'foco' strategy (cf. R. Debray, *Révolution dans la révolution. Lutte Armée et lutte politique en Amérique Latine*, Maspéro, Paris, 1967; and *Strategies for Revolution: Essays on Latin America*, essays written between 1965-1969, in R. Blackburn, ed., *Ideology in Social Sciences*, Fontana, London, 1972).

29. de Janvry, *op. cit.*, pp. 19–21.

30. R. Brenner, 'The Origins of Capitalist Development: A critique of Neo-Smithian Marxism' in *New Left Review*, No. 104, 1977.

31. In addition to Frank (cited in Chapter 5) see for example, P. Jalée, *The Pillage of the Third World*, Monthly Review Press, New York, 1967.

32. In the period 1958–1968, only 20 per cent of the funds used by US subsidiaries in Latin America originated from net capital inflows from the parent company, the remaining 80 per cent coming from local sources (about 40 per cent from retained profits and depreciation and 40 per cent borrowed from local sources). Cf. R. Newfarmer and W. Mueller, 'Multinational Corporations in Brazil and Mexico', Report to the Subcommittee on Multinational Corporations, US Senate, Washington, D.C., 1975.

33. See for example, C. Vaitsos, *Inter-Country Income Distribution and Transnational Enterprises*, Oxford University Press, Oxford, 1974.

34. See for example, G. Kay, *Development and Underdevelopment: A Marxist Analysis*, St. Martin's Press, New York, 1975; and J. Weeks and E. Dore, 'International Exchange and the Causes of Backwardness' in *Latin American Perspectives*, Vol. 6, No. 2, 1979.

35. Kay, *ibid.*

36. In addition to the writings of Warren (cf. Chapter 5), see for example, A. Phillips, 'The Concept of 'Development'' in *Review of African Political Economy*, No. 8, 1977.

37. Marxists espousing this position include C. Bettelheim, in his 'Theoretical Comments' appendix to Emmanuel's *Unequal Exchange* (1969), *op. cit.*; G. Kay (1975), *op. cit.*; C. Palloix, 'The Internationalisation of Capital and the Circuit of Social Capital' in H. Radice, ed., *International Firms and Modern Imperialism*, Penguin Books, 1975; and E. Mandel, *Late Capitalism*, New Left Books, London, 1976.

38. 'Semi-proletarians' are labourers who retain direct access to parcels of land that are nevertheless insufficient to provide full family subsistence.

39. In addition to Amin, writers who have adopted this position include P.P. Rey, *Les Alliances de Classes*, Maspéro, Paris, 1973; K. Vergopoulos, 'El

Capitalismo Disforme' in S. Amin and K. Vergopoulos, eds., *La Cuestión Campesina y el Capitalismo*, Mexico, 1975; and R. Stavenhagen, *Social Classes in Agrarian Societies*, Doubleday, New York, 1975. For an excellent theoretical and empirical analysis, see A. de Janvry, *op. cit.*

40.   B. Warren, 'Imperialism and Capitalist Industrialisation' in *New Left Review*, No. 81, 1973, p. 37.

41.   For a non-Marxist analysis of such investment, see C. Oman, *New Forms of Investment in Developing Country Industries: Mining, Petrochemicals, Automobiles, Textiles, Food*, OECD Development Centre, Paris, 1989.

42.   See in particular, L. Althusser and E. Balibar, *Reading Capital*, London, 1970.

43.   P.P. Rey, *Les Alliances de Classes*, Maspero, Paris, 1973. For an extensive summary of Rey, see B. Bradby, *op. cit.* See also A. Foster-Carter, 'The Modes of Production Controversy' in *New Left Review*, No. 107, 1978.

44.   Rey, *ibid.*

45.   See for example A. Richards, *Development and Modes of Production in Marxian Economics: a Critical Evaluation*, Harwood, London, 1986.

46.   Rey, *op. cit.*, pp. 137, 138, cited in Foster-Carter, *op. cit.*, p. 61.

47.   See in particular Bradby, *op. cit.*, and Foster-Carter, *ibid.*

48.   H. Alavi, 'India and the Colonial Mode of Production' in *Economic and Political Weekly*, Vol. 10, No. 33-35, 1975. See also N. Banaji 'For a Theory of Colonial Modes of Production' in *Economic and Political Weekly*, Vol. 7, No. 52, 1972.

49.   A.K. Bagchi, 'De-Industrialistion in India in the Nineteenth Century: Some Theoretical Implications' in *Journal of Development Studies*, Vol. 12, No. 2, 1976; and A.K. Bagchi, *The Political Economy of Underdevelopment*, Cambridge University Press, 1982.

50.   These authors include H. Diaz Polanco, *Teoría Marxista de la Economía Campesina*, Juan Pablos Editor, Mexico, 1977; F. Rajas and V. Moncayo, *La Producción Parcelaria y el Modo de Producción Capitalista*, ASIAS, Bogota, 1978; M. Gutelman, *Structures et reformes agraires*, Maspéro, Paris, 1974; and K. Post, *Arise, Ye Starvelings: The Jamaican labour rebellion of 1938 and its aftermath*, cited in A. Foster-Carter (1978), *op. cit.*

51.   S. Amin and K. Vergopoulos, eds., *La Question paysanne et le capitalisme*, Anthropos, Paris, 1974; and K. Vergopoulos, 'Capitalism and Peasant Productivity' in *Journal of Peasant Studies*, Vol. 5, No. 4, 1978.

52.   A. de Janvry, *op. cit.*, p. 152.

53.   De Janvry explains that under *sectoral* disarticulation, forward linkages in the production of raw materials (plantation and mining) and backward linkages in industrial production (import-substituting or for export) are weak or do not exist. Industrialisation under sectoral disarticulation thus implies external dependency for the import of capital goods and technology and places equilibrium in the balance of payments as a necessary constraint on the capacity to produce. The performance of the export sector and the nature of the terms of trade on the international market are determinants of accumulation in the modern sector.

Under *social* disarticulation, the necessary relation between production and consumption capacities does not translate into a similar relationship between return to capital and return to labour. In export-enclave economies, the modern sector's capacity to produce is determined by the return to capital that creates the derived demand for capital goods for the production of exportables; the capacity to consume is developed externally by the demand for exports. The return to capital (and to property in general, including land rents) also sustains the import of luxury consumption goods. And equilibrium in the balance of payments establishes the necessary relation between production and consumption capacities. In import-substituting economies, the modern sector's capacity to produce is created by the return to capital; the industrial sector's capacity to consume also derives from the return to capital, while that of the external sector is created by the demand for exports. Satisfying the necessary relation betwen production and consumption capacities thus now implies (1) creation of a home market for industry through consumption of part of the surplus value (the other part sustaining the development of production capacity) and (2) satisfaction of the balance-of-payments constraint by expanding the production of exportables to sustain the development of the capacity to produce.

In both export-enclave and import-substitution economies, the return to labour creates the demand for wage goods. In a highly simplified model, wage goods may be assumed to be produced by the traditional sector. In de Janvry's more realistic model, the modern sector has three branches of production (a wage-goods sector as well as the external and luxury-goods sectors) and the traditional sector also produces wage goods (see also footnote 60 below). Cf. *ibid.*, especially pp. 32–49.

54. Cf. S. Amin, *Unequal Development*, Monthly Review Press, New York, 1976; and R. Bartra, *Estructura Agraria y Clases Sociales en Mexico*, Ediciones Era, Mexico, 1974.

55. de Janvry, *op. cit.*, p. 37.

56. An important, if partial, exception is the 'collective choice' school of political economy. See for example, M. Olsen, *The Logic of Collective Action: Public Goods and the Theory of Groups*, Harvard University Press, Cambridge, 1965, and *The Rise and Decline of Nations: Economic Growth, Stagflation, and Social Rigidities*, Yale University Press, New Haven, 1981; A. Krueger, 'The Political Economy of Rent-Seeking Society' in *American Economic Review*, Vol. 64, No. 3, 1974; and R. Bates, *Markets and States in Tropical Agriculture: The Political Basis of Agricultural Policies*, University of California Press, Berkeley, 1981, and *Essays on the Political Economy of Rural Africa*, Cambridge University Press, Cambridge, 1983.

   A major non-Marxist study of the origins of the State is B. Moore Jr., *Social Origins of Dictatorship and Democracy: Lord and Peasant in the Making of the Modern World*, Beacon Press, Boston, 1966.

57. N. Poulantzas, 'Internationalisation of capitalist relations and the nation-state' in *Economy and Society*, 1975.

58. See for example, R. Murray, 'The internationalisation of capital and the nation state' in H. Radice, ed., *International Firms and Modern*

Imperialism, Penguin, 1975, cited in R. Jenkins, *Transnational Corporations and Uneven Development: The Internationalisation of Capital and The Third World*, Methuen, London, 1987.

59.   For example, T. Evans, *El Estado en la Periferia Capitalista*, Siglo XXI, Mexico, 1979, cited in R. Jenkins, *ibid.* See also G. O'Donnell, 'Comparative historical formations of the State apparatus and socio-economic change in the Third World' in *International Social Science Journal*, Vol. 32, 1980; and F. Block, 'Marxist theories of the state in world systems analysis' in B. Kaplan, ed., *Social Change in the Capitalist World Economy*, Sage, Beverly Hills, 1978.

60.   In the advanced capitalist countries where capitalist relations of production have become generalised, Marx saw the major way in which the rate of surplus value (s/v) is increased to be through productivity increases in industries producing wage goods, i.e. goods which enter into the value of labour power (v). This is what Marx described as increasing *relative* surplus value. It implies that for a given standard of living, fewer hours of socially necessary labour time are required to produce the goods consumed by workers (v), thus increasing the part of the working day which is available for producing surplus value (s). If productivity in wage-goods production is stagnant, the rate of surplus value can only be increased by lengthening the working day or increasing the intensity of labour (speed ups, etc.), which Marx described as increasing *absolute* surplus value. Physical limits nevertheless prevent absolute surplus value from being increased beyond a certain level. When pre-capitalist relations are dominant in the production of wage goods (notably wage foods) the drive for increased productivity, characteristic of capitalism, tends to be absent, and the tendency for relative surplus value to increase is therefore weak.

61.   A. Hirschman, 'The Political Economy of Import-Substituting Industrialisation in Latin America' in *Quarterly Journal of Economics*, Vol. 82, No. 1, February 1968, cited in de Janvry, *op. cit.*, p. 43.

62.   These include the Getulio Vargas regime in Brazil (1930–1945), Betancourt in Venezuela (1945–1948) and Perón in Argentina (1946–1955).

63.   Capitalism can penetrate agriculture and transform existing social relations in a variety of ways that result in different class and land-tenure configurations. In analysing rent, Marx described the emergence of a rural bourgeoisie in England through expropriation of peasants from the large landholdings and their replacement by capitalist tenant farmers. This led to the formation of a gentry that leased out its estates for a cash rent, capitalist farmers who gained access to the land through rental but also increasingly through direct ownership, and rural workers who originated in the dispossessed peasantry. Marx also noted, however, that this form could become the general rule, 'only in those countries that dominated the world market in the period of transition from the feudal to the capitalist mode of production' (Marx, *Capital*, Vol. 3, cited in de Janvry, *op. cit.*, p. 107).
        Lenin identified two other roads through which capitalism can develop in agriculture: the 'junker' and the 'farmer' roads. The junker road,

which refers to the historical experience of Prussia, is one where feudal estates are transformed into large capitalist enterprises, the feudal landlords become capitalist entrepreneurs and a majority of the peasants are expropriated and transformed into semi-proletarian or landless wage workers. Politically, the junker road leaves the landowning elites in a dominant position at the level of the State, and hence tends to perpetuate the existence of absolute rent in agricultural production, while the massive dispossession of the peasants implies the need for strong political control. The development of capitalism among peasants is blocked by the superiority of the large farms, income distribution tends to be highly regressive, the development of a domestic market for wages goods in agriculture is therefore limited, and non-democratic forms of government tend to prevail.

The 'farmer' or 'American' road originates from a proliferation of small farmers or free peasants who emerge either from the violent elimination of the feudal landowning class or land reform, or through the colonisation and homesteading of new lands. The peasant or small farmer becomes the predominant agent of agriculture and evolves into the capitalist farmer free from all feudal constraints. For Lenin, the farmer road is economically and politically superior to the junker road because it tends to enlarge the domestic market while freeing the creative initiative of the masses, and since the emerging rural bourgeoisie cannot gain hegemonic control of the State, this road prevents the existence of absolute rent and thus cheapens food prices. De Janvry further notes that by fomenting the emergence of a national bourgeoisie, the farmer road favours, but in no way ensures, articulated patterns of accumulation and democratic forms of government.

While de Janvry finds the junker road dominant in Latin America, especially in those areas with a strong legacy of latifundio domination and a relatively weak peasantry, he finds evidence of the farmer road in Mexico after 1934, in Peru after 1969, in Chile between 1967 and 1973, in the Dominican Republic and in Costa Rica. He also identifies two other roads: the 'merchant' and 'contract farmer' roads. The former results, e.g. in parts of Colombia, from the investment of local capital generated in mercantile or other urban activities (notably by professionals, military and technocrats) in the purchase of agricultural land, thereby establishing urban control over rural enterprises characterised by absentee management and heavy reliance on wage labour or relatively modern, medium-sized farms. The other road of capitalist development which is found increasingly in Latin America is that of contract farming or other types of lease arrangements in which multinational agribusiness firms assert considerable control over agricultural production through contracts with local producers – as analysed in considerable detail in C. Oman (1989), *op. cit.*, Chapter 6. (Cf. de Janvry, *op. cit.*, especially pp. 106–109, 169 and 202–223.)

64. *ibid.*, p. 44. For a recent non-Marxist analysis of the fiscal problem in Latin America, see H. Reisen and H. van Trotsenburg, *Developing Country Debt: The Budgetary and Transfer Problem*, OECD Development Centre, Paris, 1988.

65. See for example, A. Richards, *Development and Modes of Production in Marxian Economics: A critical Evaluation*, Harwood, London, 1986.

66. K. Marx and F. Engels, *The German Ideology*, 1846; and K. Marx, *The Communist Manifesto*, 1848.

67. This turn of events has been explained by some writers along Leninist lines: the emergence of monopoly capitalism after Marx's time gave rise to a global capitalist system in which the more backward countries and areas became the weakest links, and these links were broken by nationalist and socialist revolutions against the dominant centres of imperialism (see for example, L.S. Stavrianos, *Global Rift: The Third World Comes of Age*, William Morrow, New York, 1975).

68. See K. Griffin and J. Gurley, 'Radical Analyses of Imperialism, The Third World, and the Transition to Socialism: A Survey Article' in *Journal of Economic Literature*, Vol. XXIII, September 1985, for a summary review of this debate.

69. L. Trotsky, *The Revolution Betrayed*, 1937.

70. P. Sweezy and C. Bettelheim, *On the Transition to Socialism*, Monthly Review Press, New York, 1971.

71. Based on this criterion, both Sweezy and Bettelheim concluded that the Soviet Union was not on the road to socialism. In his later work on the USSR, Bettelheim emphasized that proletarian political power and nationalisation do not automatically produce socialism. That requires protracted class struggles which the Bolsheviks did not carry out because they had a very narrow revolutionary base and hardly any influence in the countryside, did not have the resources to replace the bourgeois bureaucracy and industrial managers, and lacked understanding and experience in facing such complex problems as world war and foreign interventions, civil war, economic disasters and isolation in the world. As a consequence, Bettelheim argues, a new ruling class emerged in the USSR, a state bourgeoisie. (C. Bettelheim, *Class Struggles in the USSR* (two volumes covering 1917–1923 and 1923–1930, respectively), Monthly Review Press, New York, 1976 and 1978, reported in Griffin and Gurley (1985), *op. cit.*)

72. See for example, E.V.K. Fitzgerald and R. Wuyts, eds., *The Market Within Planning: Socialist Economic Management in the Third World*, Frank Cass, London, 1988. Other recent 'policy-oriented' analyses from a Marxist perspective include G. Hyden, *No Shortcuts to Progress: African Development Management in Perspective*, Heinemann, London, 1985.

73. Nathaniel Leff, in his 1979 article, 'Monopoly Capitalism and Public Policy in Developing Countries' in *Kyklos*, Vol. 32.

74. Lauro Ferraz, Brazilian economist and politician, in private conversations.

75. For a non-Marxist analysis of the slowdown of productivity growth, see for example S. Englander and A. Mittelsladt, 'Total Factor Productivity: Macroeconomic and Structural Aspects of the Slowdown' in *OECD Economic Studies*, No. 10, 1988. See also A. Maddison, *Phases of Capitalist Development*, Oxford University Press, Oxford, 1982, and

'Growth and Slowdown in Advanced Capitalist Economies: Techniques of Quantitative Assessment' in *Journal of Economic Literature*, No. 25, 1987.

76. For a very useful review of Marxist and non-Marxist views on foreign direct investment and multinational corporate involvement in the Third World, see R. Jenkins, *Transnational Corporations and Uneven Development: The Internationalisation of Capital and the Third World*, Methuen, London, 1987.

77. Thus, to cite another example of a 'paradox' that can be traced to the dynamics of monopoly capital, one finds persistent acute excess industrial capacity (i.e. underutilisation of installed capacity) alongside persistent acute capital scarcity in many underdeveloped countries. Another example is the relative insensitivity of production technologies to relative factor prices (often reflected in highly capital-intensive production techniques).

Bibliography

ADELMAN, I., 'South Korea' in H.B. Chenery, *et al.*, 1974.

ADELMAN, I., 'Growth, Income Distribution, and Equity-Oriented Development Strategies' in *World Development*, Vol. 3, No. 1 and 2, 1975.

ADELMAN, I., 'Beyond Export-led Growth' in *World Development*, vol. 12, No. 9, 1984.

ADELMAN, I., M. HOPKINS, S. ROBINSON, G. RODGERS and R. WERY, 'A Comparison of Two Models for Income Distribution Planning' in *Journal of Policy Modelling*, Vol. 1, No. 1, 1979.

ADELMAN, I. and C.T. MORRIS, *Economic Growth and Social Equality in Developing Countries*, Stanford University Press, 1973.

ADELMAN, I, and J.E. TAYLOR, *Changing Comparative Advantages in Food and Agriculture: A Case Study of Mexico*, OECD Development Centre, Paris, 1990.

AHAMAD, S., 'On the Theory of Induced Innovation' in *Economic Journal*, Vol. 76, June 1966.

AHLUWALIA, M.S., 'Inequality, Poverty and Development' in *Journal of Development Economics*, Vol. 3, 1976.

AHLUWALIA, M.S., 'Rural Poverty and Agricultural Growth in India' in *Journal of Development Studies*, April 1978.

AHLUWALIA, M.S., N.G. CARTER and H.B. CHENERY, 'Growth and Poverty in *Developing Countries'* in *Journal of Development Economics*, September 1979.

AITIMER, O., 'The Extent of Poverty in Latin America', *World Bank Staff Working Paper No. 522*, World Bank, Washington D.C., 1982.

AKINO, M. and Y. HAYAMI, 'Agricultural Growth in Japan, 1880-1965' in *Quarterly Journal of Economics*, August 1974.

ALAVI, H., 'India and the Colonial Mode of Production' in *Economic and Political Weekly*, Vol. 10, No. 33-35, 1975.

ALEXANDRATOS, N., *World Agriculture: Towards 2000*, Belhaven Press, London, 1988.

ALIER, J.M., *Haciendas, Plantations and Collective Farms*, Frank Cass, London, 1977.

ALTHUSSER, L. and E. BALIBAR, *Reading Capital*, London, 1970.

AMIN, S., *L'accumulation à l'échelle mondiale*, Anthropos, Paris, 1970.

AMIN, S., *Unequal Development*, Monthly Review Press, New York, 1976.

AMIN, S, and K. VERGOPOULOS, eds., *La Question paysanne et le capitalisme*, Anthropos, Paris, 1974.

AMIN, S. and K. VERGOPOULOS, *La Cuestión Campesina y el Capitalismo*, Mexico, 1975.

AMSDEN, A., *Asia's New Giant: South Korea and Late Industrialisation*, Oxford University Press, New York, 1989.

ARROW, K., H.B. CHENERY, B. MINHAS and R. SOLOW, 'Capital-Labour Substitution and Economic Efficiency' in *Review of Economic Studies*, 1961.

ATHUKORALA, P. and F.C.H. HUYNH, *Export Instability and Growth: Problems and Prospects for Developing Economies*, Croom Helm, London, 1987.

AXLINE, W., *Caribbean Integration: The Politics of Regionalism*, Frances Pinter, London, 1979.

AZIZ, S., ed., *Hunger, Politics and Markets*, New York University Press, 1975.

BACHA, E., 'La Inercia y el Conflicto: el Plan Cruzado y sus desafios' in *Estudios Economicos*, El Colegio de Mexico, 1987.

BAER, W. and I. KERSTENETZKY, eds., *Inflation and Growth in Latin America*, Richard Irwin, Homewood, 1964.

BAER, W. and M. GILLES, eds., *Export Diversification and the New Protectionism*, Bureau of Economic and Business Research, University of Illinois, 1981.

BAGCHI, A.K., 'De-Industrialistion in India in the Nineteenth Century: Some Theoretical Implications' in *Journal of Development Studies*, Vol. 12, No. 2, 1976.

BAGCHI, A.K., *The Political Economy of Underdevelopment*, Cambridge University Press, 1982.

BAGU, S., *Economias de la Sociedad Colonial*, Ateneo, Buenos Aires, 1949.

BALASSA, B., 'Trade Creation and Trade Diversion in the European Common Market' in *Economic Journal*, March 1967.

BALASSA, B., *The Structure of Protection in Developing Countries*, Johns Hopkins University Press, Baltimore, 1971.

BALASSA, B., 'A Stages Approach to Comparative Advantage', paper presented at the Fifth World Congress of the International Economic Association, Tokyo, 1977.

BALASSA, B., 'Exports and Economic Growth' in *Journal of Development Economics*, Vol. 5, No. 2, June 1978.

BALASSA, B., *The Newly Industrialising Countries in the World Economy*, Pergamon, New York, 1981.

BALASSA, B. and Associates, *Development Strategies in Semi-industrial Economies*, Johns Hopkins University Press, Baltimore, 1982.

BALDWIN, R.E., *et al.*, *Trade Growth and Balance of Payments*, North Holland, Amsterdam, 1965.

BALOGH, T., *Unequal Partners*, Basil Blackwell, Oxford, 1963.

BALOGH, T., 'Failures in the Strategy Against Poverty' in *World Development*, Vol. 6, No. 1, 1978.

BANAJI, N., 'For a Theory of Colonial Modes of Production' in *Economic and Political Weekly*, Vol. 7, No. 52, 1972.

BARDHAN, P., 'Interlocking Factor Markets and Agrarian Development: A Review of the Issues' in *Oxford Economic Papers*, March 1980.

BARAN, P., *The Political Economy of Growth*, Monthly Review Press, New York, 1957.

BARAN, P., and P. SWEEZY, *Monopoly Capital*, Monthly Review Press, New York, 1966.

BARMA, T., ed., *The Structural Interdependence of the Economy*, John Wiley & Sons, New York, 1956.

BARTRA, R., *Estructura Agraria y Clases Sociales en Mexico*, Ediciones Era, Mexico, 1974.

BASTER, N., *Measuring Development*, Frank Cass, London, 1972.

BATES, R., *Markets and States in Tropical Agriculture: The Political Basis of Agricultural Policies*, University of California Press, Berkeley, 1981.

BATES, R., *Essays on the Political Economy of Rural Africa*, Cambridge University Press, Cambridge, 1983.

BAUER, P.T. and B.S. YAMEY, *Markets, Market Control and Marketing Reform*, London, 1968.

BECKFORD, L., *Persistent Poverty: Underdevelopment in Plantation Economies of the Third World*, Oxford University Press, Oxford, 1972.

BECKMAN, B., 'Imperialism and Capitalist Transformation: Critique of a Kenyan Debate' in *Review of African Political Economy*, No. 16, 1980.

BERGSMAN, J., 'Income Distribution and Poverty in Mexico' in *World Bank Staff Working Paper No. 395*, Washington, D.C., World Bank, 1980.

BERRY, R.A., and W.R. CLINE, *Agrarian Structure and Productivity in Developing Countries*, Johns Hopkins University Press, Baltimore, 1979.

BERTHELEMY, J.C., and C. MORRISON, 'Manufactured Goods Supply and Cash Crops in Subsaharan Africa' in *World Development*, Vol. 15, No. 10/11, 1987.

BETTELHEIM, C., 'Theoretical Comments' appendix to A. Emmanuel, 1972.

BETTELHEIM, C., *Class Struggles in the USSR* (two volumes covering 1917-1923 and 1923-1930, respectively), Monthly Review Press, New York, 1976 and 1978.

BHADURI, A., 'Agricultural Backwardness under Semi-Feudalism' in *Economic Journal*, Vol. 83, March 1973.

BHADURI, A., 'On the Formation of Usurious Interest Rates in Backward Agriculture' in *Cambridge Journal of Economics*, 1977.

BHAGWATI, J.N., *Trade, Balance of Payments and Growth*, North-Holland, Amsterdam, 1971.

BHAGWATI, J.N., *Anatomy and Consequences of Trade Control Regimes*, NBER, New York, 1978.

BHAGWATI, J., 'Export-Promoting Trade Strategy: Issues and Evidence' in *World Bank Research Observer*, Vol. 3, No. 1, 1988.

BIANCHI, A., 'Adjustment in Latin America, 1981-86' in V. Corbo, *et. al.*, eds., 1987.

BINSWANGER, H.P. and M.R. ROSENZWEIG, 'Behavioural and Material Determinants of Production Relations in Agriculture' in *Journal of Development Studies*, Vol. 22, No. 3, 1986.

BIRD, R.M., 'Land Taxation and Economic Development: The Model of Meiji Japan' in *Journal of Development Studies*, Vol. 13, No. 2, 1977.

BIRD, R., and L. De WULF, *Taxation and Income Distribution in Latin America: A Critical Review of Empirical Studies*, International Monetary Fund Staff Papers, 20, No. 3, 1973.

BISWAS, A.K., 'Agricultural Development and the Environment' in *Mazingira*, No. 11, 1979.

BITAR, S., 'Neo-Conservatism versus neo-structuralism in Latin America' in *CEPAL Review*, No. 34, April 1988.

BLACKBURN, R., ed., *Ideology in Social Sciences*, Fontana, London, 1972.

BLITZER, C.R., P.B. CLARK and L. TAYLOR, *Ecnomy-Wide Models and Development Planning*, Oxford University Press, Oxford, 1975.

BLOCK, F., 'Marxist theories of the state in world systems analysis' in B. Kaplan, ed., 1978.

BLOMSTRÖM and B. HETTNE, *Development Theory in Transition*, Zed, London, 1984.

BOBER, M., *Karl Marx's Interpretation of History*, Harvard University Press, Cambridge, 1950.

BOEKE, J.H., *Economics and Economic Policy of Dual Societies as Exemplified by Indonesia*, Institute of Pacific Relations, New York, 1953.

BONELLI, R. and P. VIEIRA DA CUNHA, 'Distribucao da renda e padroes de crescimento: un modelo dinamico da economia brasileii ι' :n *Pesquisa e Planejamento Economico*, Vol. III, No. 1, 1983.

BORLANG, N.E., 'Using Plants to Meet World Food Needs' in R.G. Woods, ed., 1981.

BOSERUP, E., *Woman's Role in Economic Development*, St. Martin's Press, New York, 1980.

BOYCE, K., *Agrarian Impasse in Bengal: Institutional Constraints to Technological Change*, Oxford University Press, Oxford, 1987.

BRADBY, B., 'The Destruction of the Natural Economy' in *Economy and Society*, Vol. 4, No. 2, May 1975.

BRANDER, J. and B. SPENCER, 'Tariffs and the Extraction of Foreign Monopoly Rents and Potential Entry' in *Canadian Journal of Economics*, No. 14, August 1981.

BRANDER, J. and B. SPENCER, 'Export Subsidies and International Market Share Rivalry' in *Journal of International Economics*, 1985.

BRANDT, W., *North–South: The Report of the Independent Commission on International Development Issues Under the Chairmanship of Willy Brandt*, Pan Books, London, 1980.

BRANSON, W., ed., *Trade and Structural Change in Pacific-Asia*, University of Chicago Press, Chicago, 1987.

BRENNER, R., 'The Origins of Capitalist Development: A Critique of Neo-Smithian Marxism' in *New Left Review*, No. 104, 1977.

BRETT, E.A., 'Reaching the Poorest: Does the World Bank Still Believe in Redistribution with Growth' in *Recovery in the Developing World*, World Bank, Washington, D.C., 1986.

BROMLEY, B.W., 'The Role of Land Reform in Economic Development: Comment' in C.K. Eicher and J.M. Staatz, eds., 1984.

BRUNO, M., et. al., *Inflation Stabilisation: The Experience of Israel, Argentina, Brazil, Bolivia, and Mexico*, MIT Press, Cambridge, 1988.

BRUTON, H., 'The Two Gap Approach to Aid and Development: A Comment' in *American Economic Review*, 1969.

BUKHARIN, N.I., *Imperialism and World Economy*, 1917.

BUVINIC, M. and L. MCGREEVEY, eds., *Women and Poverty in the Third World*, Johns Hopkins University Press, Baltimore, 1983.

BYERLEE, D., 'Rural–Urban Migration in Africa: Theory, Policy and Research Implications', in *International Migration Review*, 1974.

BYRES, T.J., 'Of Neopopulist Pipedreams: Daedalus in the Third World and the Myth of Urban Bias' in *Journal of Peasant Studies*, Vol. 6, No. 2, 1979.

BYRES, T.J., 'Class Formation and Class Action in the Indian Countryside' in *Journal of Peasant Studies*, Vol. 8, No. 4, July 1981.

BYRES, T.J., *et al., The Green Revolution in India*, Open University Press, London, 1983.

CARDOSO, F.H., 'El proceso de desarrollo en América Latina: Hipótesis para una interpretación sociológica', ILPES, Santiago, November 1965, reported by M. Blomstrom and B. Hettne, 1984.

CARDOSO, F.H., 'The Originality of a Copy: CEPAL and the Idea of Development' in *CEPAL Review*, Second half of 1977.

CARDOSO, F.H. and E. FALETTO, *Dependency and Development in Latin America*, University of California Press, Berkeley, 1979.

CARNOY, M., ed., *Industrialisation in a Latin American Common Market*, Brookings Institution, Washington, D.C., 1972.

CARRÉ, O., 'Utopies socialisantes en terre arabe d'orient' in *Revue Tiers-Monde*, Vol. XIX, no. 75, 1978.

CASSEN, R.H., *India: Population, Economy and Society*, MacMillan, London, 1978.

CASSEN, R., *et al., Does Aid Work? Report of an Intergovernmental Task Force*, Clarendon Press, Oxford, 1986.

CENTRE D'ETUDES PROSPECTIVES ET D'INFORMATION INTER-NATIONALES, *Economie Mondiale : La Montée des Tensions*, Economica, Paris, 1983.

CEPAL, *Introducción a la técnica de programación*, Santiago, 1975.

CEPAL/FAO, 'Una política agrícola para accelerar el desarrollo economíco de América Latina' in *Boletín Económico de América Latina*, Vol. 6, No. 2, October 1961.

CHAMBERS, R. and J. JIGGINS, 'Agricultural Research for Resource Poor Farmers: A Parsimonious Paradigm' *IDS Discussion Paper 220*, University of Sussex, Brighton, 1986.

CHENERY, H.B., 'Inter-regional and International Input-Output Analysis' in T. Barma, ed., 1956.

CHENERY, H.B., *et al., Redistribution With Growth*, Oxford University Press, London, 1974.

CHENERY, H.B. and M. BRUNO, 'Development Alternatives in an Open Economy: the Case of Israel' in *Economic Journal*, Vol. 72, 1962.

CHENERY, H.B. and T.N. SRINIVASAN, eds., *Handbook of Development Economics*, Vols. I and II, Elsevier Science Publishers, North Holland, 1988 (Vol.I) and 1989 (Vol. II).

CHENERY, H.B. and A. M. STROUT, 'Foreign Assistance and Economic Development' in *American Economic Review*, September 1966.

CHOKSI, A.M. and D. PAPAGEORGIOU, eds., *Economic Liberalisation in Developing Countries*, Basil Blackwell, Oxford, 1987.

CHOUCRI, N., 'International Political Economy: A Theoretical Perspective' in O.R. Holsti, R. Siverson and A.L. George, eds., 1980.

CIBOTTI, R. and E. SIERRA, *El sector público en la planificación del desarrollo*, Siglo XXI, Mexico, 1970.

CIDA, *Tenencia de la Tierra y Desarrollo Socio-Economico del Sector Agricola; Peru*, Washington, D.C., Pan-American Union, 1965.

CIDA, *Land Tenure Conditions and Socio-Economic Development of the Agricultural Sector: Brazil*, Washington, D.C., Organisation of American States, 1966.

CLEAVER, H.M., 'The Contradictions of the Green Revolution' in *American Economic Review*, May 1972.

CLIFFE, L. and J. SAUL, eds., *Socialism in Tanzania*, Vols. I and II., East Africa Publishers, 1972/1973.

CLINE, W., *Potential Effects of Income Redistributions on Economic Growth: Latin American Cases*, Praeger, New York, 1972.

CLINE, W., ed., *Policy Alternatives for A New International Economic Order*, Praeger, New York, 1979.

CLINE, W.R., 'Can the East Asian Model of Development be Generalised?' in *World Development*, Vol. 10, No. 2, 1982.

CLINE, W.R. and S. WEINTRAUB, eds., *Economic Stabilisation in Developing Countries*, Brookings Institution, Washington D.C., 1981.

COLLIER, P., 'Migration and Unemployment: A Dynamic General Equilibrium Analysis Applied to Tanzania' in *Oxford Economic Papers*, July 1979.

COQUERY-VIDROVITCH, C., *Afrique Noire: Permanences et Ruptures*, Payot, Paris, 1985.

CORBO, V., et al., eds., *Growth-Oriented Adjustment Programs*, Proceedings of a Symposium held in Washington, D.C., 25th-27th February 1987, International Monetary Fund and The World Bank, Washington, D.C., 1987.

CORDEN, W.M., *The Theory of Protection*, Oxford University Press, London, 1971.

CORDEN, W.M., 'The Effects of Trade on the Rate of Growth' in J.N. Bhagwati, *et al.*, 1971.

CORNIA, G., R. JOLLY and F. STEWART, *Adjustment with a Human Face*, Oxford University Press, 1987.

COWEN, M., 'The British State and Agrarian Accumulation in Kenya after 1945,' mimeo, CDS Swansea, 1980.

CROOK, N., 'On the Management of Urban Migration and Residence: An Economic Approach' in *Asian Journal of Public Administration*, 1983.

DADONE, A. and L. DIMARCO, 'The Impact of Prebisch's Ideas on Modern Economic Analysis' in L. Dimarco, ed., 1972.

DAG HAMMARSKJOLD Report, 'What Now: Another Development', *Development Dialogue*, 1/2, 1975.

DAHLMAN, C., B. ROSE-LARSON and L. WESTPHAL, *Managing Technological Development: Lessons from Newly Industrialising Countries*, World Bank Staff Working Paper No. 717, Washington D.C., 1985.

DAHLMAN, C. and L. WESTPHAL, 'Technological Effort in Industrial Development' in F. Stewart and J. James, eds., 1982.

DATTA-CHAUDHURI, M., 'Industrialisation and Foreign Trade: The Development Experiences of South Korea and the Philippines' in E. Lee, ed., 1981.

DEBRAY, R., *Révolution dans la révolution. Lutte Armée et lutte politique en Amérique Latine*, Maspéro, Paris, 1967.

DEBRAY, R., *Strategies for Revolution: Essays on Latin America*, essays written between 1965-1969, in R. Blackburn, ed., 1972.

DEGRAS, J., ed., *The Communist International, 1919–1943; Documents, Vol. 2, 1928–1938*, Oxford University Press, London, 1960.

DE JANVRY, A., *The Agrarian Question and Reformism in Latin America*, Johns Hopkins University Press, Baltimore, 1981.

DE JANVRY, A. and F. KRAMER, 'The Limits of Unequal Exchange' in *Review of Radical Political Economy*, Vol. 11, No. 4, 1979.

DE JANVRY, A. and E. SADOULET, 'Investment Strategies to Combat Rural Poverty: A proposal for Latin America' in *World Development*, Vol. 17, No. 8, 1989.

DEMAS, G., *The Economics of Development in Small Countries with Special Reference to the Caribbean*, McGill University Press, Montreal, 1965.

DE SOTO, H., *The Other Path: the Invisible Revolution in the Third World*, Harper and Row, New York, 1989 (first published in Spanish in collaboration with E. Ghers, M. Ghibellini and the Instituto Libertad y Democracia, *El Otro Sendero: La Revolución Informal*, Instituto Libertad y Democracia, 1987).

DERVIS, K., J. DE MELO and S. ROBINSON, *General Equilibrium Models for Development Policy*, Cambridge University Press, 1982.

DESAI, M. and D. MAZUMDAR, 'A Test of the Hypothesis of Disguised Unemployment' in *Economica*, Vol. 37, 1975.

DIAZ-ALEJANDRO, C., 'Delinking North and South: Unshackled or Unhinged?' in A. Fishlow, *et al.*, 1978.

DIAZ POLANCO, H., *Teoría Marxista de la Economía Campesina*, Juan Pablos Editor, Mexico, 1977.

DIMARCO, L., ed., *International Economics and Development*, Academic Press, New York, 1972.

DIXIT, A.K., 'Optimal Development in the Labour Surplus Economy' in *Review of Economic Studies*, January 1968.

DIXIT, A.K,, 'Themes of the Dual Economies: A Survey' in J. Mirrlees and N. H. Stern, eds., 1971.

DIXIT, A.K., 'Trade Policy: An Agenda for Research' in P. Krugman, ed., 1986.

DIXIT, A.K, 'Issues of Strategic Trade Policy for Small Countries' in *Scandinavian Journal of Economics*, Vol. 89, No. 3, 1987.

DOMAR, E.D., 'Capital Expansion, Rate of Growth and Employment' in *Econometrica*, April 1946.

DORNBUSCH, R., 'Stabilisation Policies in Developing Countries: What Have we Learned?' in *World Development*, Vol. 10, No. 9, 1982.

DORNBUSCH, R., 'Mexico: Stabilisation, Debt and Growth' in *Economic Policy*, No 7, October 1988.

DORNBUSCH, R. and S. EDWARDS, 'Macroeconomic Populism in Latin America', NBER Working Paper No. 2986, Cambridge, May 1989.

DORNER, P., *Land Reform and Economic Development*, Penguin, Harmondsworth, 1972.

DOS SANTOS, T., 'The Structure of Dependence' in *American Economic Review*, Vol. 60, No. 2, 1970.

DUESENBERRY, J.S., *Income, Saving and the Theory of Consumer Behaviour*, Cambridge, 1949.

DUPRIEZ, H., ed., *Economic Progress*, Louvain, 1955.

DUTCH SCHOLARS, *Indonesian Economics: The Concept of Dualism in Theory and Policy*, Van Hoeve Publishers, The Hague, 1961.

ECKSTEIN, S., G. DONALD, D. HORTON, and T. CARROLL, 'Land Reform in Latin America: Bolivia, Chile, Mexico, Peru and Venezuela' in *World Bank Staff Working Paper*, No. 275, 1978.

ECLA, *The Economic Development of Latin America and its Principal Problems*, 1950.

ECLA, *Economic Survey for Latin America, 1949*, 1951.ECLA, La distribución del ingreso en América Latina, September 1970.

EDWARDS, S., 'The Order of Liberalisation of the External Sector in Developing Countries' in *Princeton Essays in International Finance*, No. 156, Princeton University Press, Princeton, 1984.

EDWARDS, S.,'On the Sequencing of Structural Reforms', OECD Department of Economics and Statistics Working Paper No. 70, Paris, September 1989.

EICHER, C.K. and J.M. STAATZ, *Agricultural Development in the Third World*, Johns Hopkins Univerity Press, Baltimore, 1984.

EICHER, C.K. and L. WITT, eds., *Agriculture in Economic Development*, McGraw-Hill, New York, 1964.

EKSTEIN, A., ed., *Comparison of Economic Systems*, University of California Press, Berkeley, 1971.

ELLIS, H. and H. WALLICH, eds., *Economic Development for Latin America. Proceedings of a Conference held by the International Economic Association*, St. Martin's Press, New York, 1961.

ELLSWORTH, P.T., 'The Terms of Trade between Primary Producing and Industrial Countries' in *Inter-American Economic Affairs*, Vol. 10, 1956.

EMMANUEL, A., *Unequal Exchange: A Study of the Imperialism of Trade*, Monthly Review Press, New York, 1972 (originally published in French in 1969).

EMMERIJ, L., 'A Comment' in *Regional Development Dialogue*, Vol. 1, No. 1, 1980, p. 122.

EMMERIJ, L., 'Basic Needs and Employment-oriented Strategies Reconsidered' in *Development and Peace*, Vol. 2, Autumn 1981, p. 152.

EMMERIJ, L., 'The Neo-Conservatism in the West', *Third World Quarterly*, July 1982.

EMMERIJ, L., ed., *One World or Several*, papers and proceedings of the OECD Development Centre's 25th Anniversary Symposium, OECD Development Centre, Paris, 1989.

ENGLANDER, S. and A. MITTELSLADT, 'Total Factor Productivity: Macroeconomic and Structural Aspects of the Slowdown' in *OECD Economic Studies*, No. 10, 1988.

ENOS, J., and W.H. PARK, *The Adoption and Diffusion of Imported Technology in the Case of Korea*, Croom Helm, 1987.

EVANS, D., 'Emmanuel's Theory of Unequal Exchange: Critique, Counter Critique and Theoretical Contribution', IDS, University of Sussex, Discussion Paper 149, 1980.

EVANS, D. and P. ALIZADEH, *Price Distortions, Efficiency and Growth*, IDS, University of Sussex, 1985.

EVANS, P., *Dependent Development. The Alliance of Multinational, State, and Local Capital in Brazil*, Princeton University Press, Princeton, 1979.

EVANS, T., *El Estado en la Periferia Capitalista*, Siglo XXI, Mexico, 1979.

FARAG, E.A., 'The Latin American Free Trade Area' in *Inter-American Economic Affairs*, Vol. 17, No. 1, Summer 1963.

FARMER, B.H., 'Perspectives on the Green Revolution in South Asia' in *Modern Asian Studies*, Vol. 20, No. 1, 1986.

FAO, *Progress in Land Reform: Sixth Report*, United Nations, New York, 1976.

FAO, *Agriculture: Towards 2000*, Rome, 1981.

FAO, *World Food Report*, 1984.

FEDER, G., 'On Exports and Economic Growth' in *Journal of Development Economics*, Vol. 12, 1983.

FEDER, G. and G.T. O'MARA, 'Farm Size and the Diffusion of Green Revolution Technology' in *Economic Development and Cultural Change*, Vol. 30, No. 1, October 1981.

FEDER, G. and S. ZILBERMAN, 'Adoption of Agricultural, Innovations in Developing Countries: A Survey' in *Economic Development and Cultural Change*, January 1985.

FEI, J., G. RANIS, and S.W.Y. KUO, *Equity with Growth: The Taiwan Case*, Oxford University Press, London, 1979.

FERGUSON, C.E., *The Neoclassical Theory of Production and Distribution*, Cambridge University Press, Cambridge, 1969.

FERNANDEZ, R. and J. GLAZER, 'Why Haven't Debtor Countries Formed a Cartel?', NBER Working Paper No. 2980, Cambridge, May 1989.

FIELDS, G.S., *Poverty, Inequality and Development*, Cambridge University Press, 1980.

FINDLAY, R., 'Growth and Development in Trade Models' in R.W. Jones and P.B. Kenen, eds., 1984.

FISCHER, S., 'Economic Growth and Economic Policy' in V. Corbo, *et al.*, eds., 1987.

FISHLOW, A., 'Empty Economic Stages?' in *Economic Journal*, March 1965.

FISHLOW, A., 'Brazilian Size Distribution of Income' in *American Economic Review*, Vol. LX, No. 3, May 1972.

FISHLOW, A., *et al.*, *Rich and Poor Nations in the World Economy*, McGraw-Hill, New York, 1978.

FISHLOW, A., 'Comment', in G. Meier and D. Seers, eds., 1984.

FISHLOW, A., 'El Estado de la ciencia económica en América Latina' in *Progreso Economico y Social en America Latina. Deuda Externa: Crisis y Ajuste*, Interamerican Development Bank, Washington, D.C., 1985.

FITZGERALD, E.V.K. and R. WUYTS, eds., *The Market Within Planning: Socialist Economic Management in the Third World*, Frank Cass, London, 1988.

FOSTER-CARTER, A., 'The Modes of Production Controversy' in *New Left Review*, No. 107, 1978.

FOXLEY, A., *Latin American Experiments in Neo-Conservative Economics*, University of California Press, Berkeley, 1983.

FRANK, A.G., *Capitalism and Underdevelopment in Latin America: Historical Studies of Chile and Brazil*, Monthly Review Press, New York, 1969.

FRANK, A.G., 'North–South and East–West: Keynesian Paradoxes in the Brandt Report' in *Third World Quarterly*, Vol. 2, No. 4, October 1980.

FRITSCH, W and G. FRANCO, *Foreign Direct Investment and Industrial Restructuring in Brazil*, OECD Development Centre, Paris, forthcoming.

FURTADO, C., *Economic Growth of Brazil*, University of California Press, Berkeley, 1963.

FURTADO, C., *Development and Underdevelopment*, University of California Press, Berkeley, 1965.

FURTADO, C., *Subdesarrollo y Estancamiento en América Latina*, C.E.A.L., Buenos Aires, 1966.

GALENSON, W., 'Economic Growth, Poverty, and the International Agencies' in *Journal of Policy Modeling*, Vol. 1, No. 2, 1979.

GALENSON, W. and H. LEIBENSTEIN, 'Investment Criteria, Productivity and Economic Development' in *Quarterly Journal of Economics*, August 1955.

GERSCHENKRON, A., 'Economic Backwardness in Historical Perspective' in B. Hoselitz, ed., 1952.

GERSCHENKRON, A., 'Social Attitudes, Entrepreneurship, and Economic Development' in *Explorations in Entrepreneurial History*, October 1953.

GERSCHENKRON, A., 'Notes on the Rate of Industrial Growth in Italy, 1881-1913' in *The Journal of Economic History*, December 1955.

GERSCHENKRON, A., *Economic Backwardness in Historical Perspective*, Harvard University Press, Cambridge, 1962.

GHAI, D. and S. RADWAN, eds., *Agrarian Policies and Rural Poverty in Africa*, ILO, Geneva, 1983.

GHOSE, A.K., ed., *Land Reform in Contemporary Developing Countries*, Croom Helm, London, 1983.

GHOSH, P.K., ed., *New International Economic Order*, Greenwood Press, 1984.

GIERSCH, H., 'Stages and Spurts of Economic Development' in H. Dupriez, ed., 1955.

GIRVAN, N. and O. JEFFERSON, eds., *Readings on the Political Economy of the Caribbean*, New World, Kingston, 1971.

GIRVAN, N., *Foreign Capital and Economic Underdevelopment in Jamaica*, ISER, Kingston, 1972.

GOLDIN, I. and G. CASTRO DE REZENDE, *Agriculture and Economic Crisis' Lessons from Brazil*, OECD Develpment Centre, Paris, 1990.

GRABOWSKI, R., 'The Implications of an Induced Innovation Model' in *Economic Development and Cultural Change*, July 1979.

GRIFFIN, K., *Underdevelopment in Spanish America*, Allen and Unwin, London, 1969.

GRIFFIN, K. 'Foreign Capital, Domestic Savings and Economic Development' in *Oxford Bulletin of Economics and Statistics*, 1970.

GRIFFIN, K., ed., *Financing Development in Latin America*, MacMillan, London, 1971.

GRIFFIN, K., *The Green Revolution: An Economic Analysis*, UNRISD, Geneva, 1972.

GRIFFIN, K., *The Political Economy of Agrarian Change: An Essay in the Green Revolution*, MacMillan, London, 1974.

GRIFFIN, K., *Land Concentration and Rural Poverty*, MacMillan, London, 1976.

GRIFFIN, K., *International Inequality and National Poverty*, Holmes and Meier, New York, 1978.

GRIFFIN, K., 'Growth and Impoverishment in the Rural Areas of India' in *World Development*, April/May 1979.

GRIFFIN, K., *The Political Economy of Agrarian Change*, (2nd ed.), MacMillan, London, 1979.

GRIFFIN, K., 'On Misreading Development Economics' in *Third World Quarterly*, April 1984.

GRIFFIN, K., *Alternative Strategies of Economic Development*, MacMillan in association with the OECD Development Centre, London, 1989.

GRIFFIN, K. and J. GURLEY, 'Radical Analyses of Imperialism, The Third World, and the Transition to Socialism: A Survey Article' in *Journal of Economic Literature*, Vol. XXIII, September 1985.

GRIFFIN, K. and J. JAMES, *The Transition to Egalitarian Development: Economic Policies for Structural Change in the Third World*, MacMillan, London, 1981.

GRILLI, E. and M.C. YANG, 'Primary Commodity Prices, Manufactured Goods Prices, and the Terms of Trade of Developing Countries: What the Long-run Shows' in *World Bank Economic Review*, Vol. 2, No. 1, 1988.

GRUBEL, H.G., 'The Case Against the New International Economic Order' in *Weltwirtschaftliches Archive* Band 113, Heft 2, 1977.

GUTELMAN, M., *Structures et Reformes Aguaires*, Maspéro, Paris, 1974.

HABERLER, G., 'Some Problems in the Pure Theory of International Trade' in *Economic Journal*, June 1950.

HABERLER, G., *International Trade and Economic Development*, National Bank of Egypt, Cairo, 1959.

HABERLER, G., 'Terms of Trade and Economic Development' in H. Ellis and H. Wallich, eds., 1961.

HALLAK, J. and F. CAILLODS, eds., *Education, Work and Employment*, UNESCO, Paris, 1980.

HANSON, J.R., *Trade in Transition: Exports from the Third World, 1840–1900*, Academic Press, 1980.

HAQUE, W., N. METHA, A. RAHMAN, and P. WIGNARAJA, 'Micro-level Development: Design and Evaluation of Rural Development Projects' in *Development Dialogue*, Vol. 2, 1977.

HARBERGER, A.C., 'The Cost-Benefit Approach to Development Economics' in *World Development*, Vol. 11, No. 10, 1983.

HARRIS, J. and M. TODARO, 'Migration, Unemployment and Development: A Two Sector Analysis' in *American Economic Review*, March 1970.

HARROD, R.F., 'An Essay in Dynamic Theory' in *Economic Journal*, April 1939.

HASAN, P., 'Growth and Equity in East Asia' in *Finance and Development*, Vol. 15 No. 2, June 1978.

HAYAMI, Y. and V.W. RUTTAN, *Agricultural Development: An International Perspective*, Johns Hopkins University Press, Baltimore, 1971.

HAYTER, T., *The Creation of World Poverty: An Alternative View to the Brandt Report*, Pluto Press, London, 1981.

HECKSCHER, E.F., 'The Effect of Foreign trade on the Distribution of Income' in *Readings in the Theory of International Trade*, American Economic Association, 1950 (translated from Swedish original, 1919).

HELLER, P.S. and R.C. PORTER, 'Exports and Growth: An Empirical Reinvestigation' in *Journal of Development Economics*, Vol. 5, 1978.

HERRERA, A., *et al., Catastrophe or New Society? A Latin American Model*, International Development Research Centre, Ottawa, 1976.

HEWITT de ALCANTARA, C., *Modernising Mexican Agriculture: Socio-Economic Implications of Technical Change, 1940–70*, UNRISD, Geneva, 1976.

HICKS, J.R., *The Theory of Wages*, MacMillan, London, 1932.

HICKS, J.R., 'An Inaugural Lecture' in *Oxford Economic Papers*, Vol. 5, No. 2, June 1953.

HICKS, N., 'Growth v. Basic Needs: Is There a Trade Off?' in *World Development*, 1979.

HICKS, N. and P. STREETEN, 'Indicators of Development: The Search for a Basic Needs Yard Stick', *World Development*, June 1979.

HIGGINS, B., 'The Dualistic Theory of Underdeveloped Areas' in *Economic Development and Cultural Change*, January 1956.

HIGGINS, B., *Economic Development*, Norton, New York, 1968.

HIGGINS, B., 'The Disenthronement of Basic Needs? Twenty Questions' in *Regional Development Dialogue*, Vol. 1, No. 1, 1980.

HILFERDING, R., *Finance Capital: A study of the latest phase of capitalist development*, 1910.

HIRSCHMAN, A.O., *The Strategy of Economic Development*, Yale University Press, New Haven, 1958.

HIRSCHMAN, A.O., 'The Political Economy of Import-Substituting Industrialisation in Latin America' in *Quarterly Journal of Economics*, Vol. 82, No. 1, February 1968.

HIRSCHMAN, A.O., *Essays in Trespassing: Economics to Politics and Beyond*, Cambridge University Press, New York, 1981.

HIRSCHMAN, A.O., 'A Dissenter's Confession: The Strategy of Economic Development Revisited' in Meier and Seers, eds., 1984.

HOFFMEYER, E., 'The Leontief Paradox Critically Examined' in *The Manchester School of Economic and Social Studies*, Vol. 26, May 1958.

HOLSTI, O.R., R. SIVERSON and A.L. GEORGE, eds., *Change in the International System*, Westview Press, Boulder, 1980.

HOPPER, W.D., 'Allocation Efficiency in Traditional Indian Agriculture', in *Journal of Farm Economics*, August 1965.

HOSELITZ, B., ed., *The Progress of Underdeveloped Areas*, Chicago, 1952.

HOUTHAKKER, H.S. 'On Some Determinants of Savings in Developed and Underdeveloped Countries' in *Problems of Economic Development*, International Economic Association, 1965.

HUEG, W.F. and C.A. GANNON, eds., *Transforming Knowledge into Food in a Worldwide Context*, Miller Publishing Co., Minneapolis, 1978.

HUNGER PROJECT, *Ending Hunger: An Idea Whose Time Has Come*, Praeger, New York, 1985.

HYDEN, G., *Beyond Ujamaa in Tanzania*, Heinemann, 1980.

HYDEN, G., *No Shortcuts to Progress: African Development Management in Perspective*, Heinemann, London, 1985.

IDS, 'Developmental States in East Asia: Capitalist and Socialist' in *IDS Bulletin*, Vol. 15, No. 2, April 1984.

ILLICH, I.D., *Deschooling Society*, Harper and Row, New York, 1971.

ILO, *Towards Full Employment: A Programme for Colombia*, Geneva, 1970.

ILO, *Matching Employment Opportunities and Expectations: A Programme of Action for Ceylon*, Geneva, 1971.

ILO, *Employment, Incomes and Equality: A Strategy for Increasing Productive Employment in Kenya*, Geneva, 1972.

ILO, *Strategies for Employment Promotion*, Geneva, 1973.

ILO, *Employment, Growth and Basic Needs: A One World Problem*, Report of the Director General of the ILO to the Tripartite World Conference on Employment, Income Distribution and Social Progress, and the International Division of Labour, Geneva, 1976.

ILO, *Meeting Basic Needs: Strategies for Eradicating Mass Poverty and Unemployment*, Geneva, 1976.

ILO, *Poverty and Landlessness in Rural Asia*, Geneva, 1977.

ILPES, *Discussiones sobre planificación*, Siglo XXI, Mexico, 1966.

ISENMAN, P., 'Basic Needs: The Case of Sri Lanka' in *World Development*, Vol. 8, March 1980.

JALÉE, P., *The Pillage of the Third World*, Monthly Review Press, New York, 1967.

JEFFERSON, O., *The Postwar Economic Development of Jamaica*, ISER, Kingston, 1972.

JENKINS, R., *Transnational Corporations and Uneven Development: The Internationalisation of Capital and The Third World*, Methuen, London, 1987.

JOHNSON D.W., and J.S.Y. CHIN 'The Savings-Income Relation in Underdeveloped and Developed Countries' in *Economic Journal*, June 1968.

JOHNSON, H.G., 'The Gains from Freer Trade with Europe: An Estimate' in *The Manchester School*, September 1958.

JOHNSON, H.G., 'Optimal Trade Intervention in the Presence of Domestic Distortions' in R.E. Baldwin, *et al.*, 1965.

JOHNSTON, B.F. and J.W. MELLOR, 'The Role of Agriculture in Economic Development' in *American Economic Review*, September 1961.

JOHNSTON, B.F. and J. COWNIE, 'The Seed Fertilizer Revolution and Labour Force Absorption', in *American Economic Review*, 1969.

JOHNSTON, B.F. and W.C. CLARK, *Redesigning Rural Development: A Strategic Perspective*, Johns Hopkins University Press, Baltimore, 1982.

JOLLY, R., *et al.*, *Third World Employment: Problems and Strategy*, Penguin, 1973.

JONES, L.P. and I. SAKONG, *Government, Business and Entrepreneurship in Economic Developemnt: The Korean Case*, Harvard University Press, Cambridge, 1980.

JONES, R.W., 'Factor Proportions and the Heckscher–Ohlin Theory' in *Review of Economic Studies*, January 1956.

JONES, R.W., and P.B. KENEN, eds., *Handbook of International Economics*, North-Holland, Amsterdam, 1984.

JORGENSON, D., 'The Development of a Dual Economy' in *Economic Journal*, Vol. 71, 1961.

JORGENSON, D., 'Surplus Agricultural Labour and the Development of the Dual Economy', in *Oxford Economic Papers*, Vol. 19, No. 3, 1967.

JOUVE, E., ed., *Pour un nouvel order mondial*, Berger-Levrault, Paris, 1985.

KALECKI, M., *Essays in the Theory of Economic Fluctuations*, 1939.

KALECKI, M., *Studies in Economic Dynamics*, 1943.

KALECKI, M, *Theory of Economic Dynamics*, 1954.

KAPLAN, B., ed., *Social Change in the Capitalist World Economy*, Sage, Beverly Hills, 1978.

KAPLINSKY, R., 'Capitalist Accumulation in the Periphery - the Kenyan Case Reexamined' in *Review of African Political Economy* No. 16, 1980.

KATZ, J., ed., *Technology Generation in Latin American Manufacturing Industries*, MacMillan, London, 1987.

KAVOUSSI, R.M., 'International Trade and Economic Development: The Recent Experience of Developing Countries' in *The Journal of Developing Areas*, April 1985.

KAY, G., *Development and Underdevelopment: A Marxist Analysis*, St. Martin's Press, New York, 1975.

KELLY, A.C., G. WILLIAMSON and R.J. CHEETHAM, *Dualistic Economic Development: Theories and History*, University of Chicago Press, Chicago, 1972.

KENEN, P., ed., *International Trade and Finance: Frontiers for Research*, Cambridge University Press, Cambridge, 1975.

KIERZKOWSKI, H., ed., *Monopolistic Competition and International Trade*, Clarendon Press, Oxford, 1984.

KILLICK, T., ed., *The Quest for Economic Stabilisation: The IMF and the Third World*, Heinemann, London, 1984.

KILLICK, T., 'Twenty-five years in Development: The Rise and Impending Decline of Market Solutions' in *Development Policy Review*, Vol. 4, No. 2, 1986.

KINDLEBERGER, C., ed., *The International Corporation*, MIT Press, Cambridge, 1970.

KIRKPATRICK, C.H. and F.I. NIXSON, eds., *The Industrialisation of Less Developed Countries*, Manchester University Press, 1983.

KITCHING, G., *Development and Underdevelopment in Historical Perspective*, Methuen, London, 1982.

KRAVIS, I.B., 'International Differences in the Distribution of Income' in *Review of Economics and Statistics*, Vol. 45, November 1960.

KRAVIS, I.B., 'Trade as a Handmaiden of Growth: Similarities between the Nineteenth and Twentieth Centuries' in *Economic Journal*, December 1970.

KRENIN, M.E. and J.M. FINGER, 'A Critical Survey of the New International Economic Order' in *Journal of World Trade Law*, Vol. 10, No. 6, Nov/Dec 1976.

KRUEGER, A.O., 'Some Economic Costs of Exchange Control: The Turkish Case' in *Journal of Political Economy*, October 1966.

KRUEGER, A.O, 'The Political Economy of Rent-Seeking Society' in *American Economic Review*, Vol. 64, No. 3, 1974.

KRUEGER, A.O., *Liberalisation Attempts and Consequences*, NBER, New York, 1978.

KRUEGER, A.O., 'Trade Policy as an Input to Development' in *American Economic Review*, papers and proceedings, May 1980.

KRUEGER, A.O., 'Comparative Advantage and Development Policy 20 Years Later' in M. Syrquin, L. Taylor and L.E. Westphal, eds., 1984.

KRUGMAN, P., 'Increasing Returns, Monopolistic Competition and International Trade' in *Journal of International Economics*, Vol. 9, No. 4, 1979.

KRUGMAN, P., 'Import Protection as Export Promotion: International Competition in the Presence of Oligopoly and Economies of Scale' in H. Kierzkowski, ed., 1984.

KRUGMAN, P., ed., *Strategic Trade Policy and the New International Economics*, MIT Press, Cambridge, 1986.

KRUGMAN, P., 'New Trade Theory and the Less-Developed Countries', paper prepared for 'Debt, Stabilisation and Development', a conference in memory of Carlos Diaz-Alejandro, Helsinki, 23rd–25th August, 1986.

KRUGMAN, P., 'Strategic Sectors and International Competition' in R. Stern, ed., 1987.

KUUSINEN, O., 1928, in J. Degras, ed., 1960.

KUZNETS, S., 'Economic Growth and Income Inequality' in *American Economic Review*, Vol. 45, March 1955.

KUZNETS, S., 'Quantitative Aspects of the Economic Growth of Nations', parts I-X, in *Economic Development and Cultural Change*, various issues, 1956-1966.

KUZNETS, S., *Economic Growth and Structure*, Heinemann, London, 1965.

KUZNETS, S., 'Notes on the Stages of Economic Growth as a System Determinant' in A. Eckstein, ed., 1971.

LACLAU, E., 'Feudalism and Capitalism in Latin America' in *New Left Review*, No. 67, May/June 1971.

LAL, D., *The Poverty of Development Economics*, Institute of Economic Affairs, London, 1983.

LALL, S., 'Is Dependence a Useful Concept in Analysing Underdevelopment' in *World Development*, Vol. 3, No. 11, 1975.

LALL, S., 'Conflicts of Concepts: Welfare Economics and Developing Countries' in *World Development*, Vol. 4, No. 3, 1976, p. 181.

LALL, S., *Learning to Industrialise*, MacMillan, London, 1987.

LALL, S., *Building Industrial Competitiveness: New Technologies and Capabilities in Developing Countries*, OECD Development Centre, Paris, 1990.

LALL, S. AND P. STREETEN, *Foreign Investment, Transnationals and Developing Countries*, MacMillan, 1977.

LANGDON, S., 'The State and Capitalism in Kenya' in *Review of African Political Economy*, No. 8, 1977.

LARSEN, R. and R. JOLLY, eds., *Rich Country Interests and Third World Development*, St. Martin, London, 1982.

LARSON, D.A. and W.T. WILFORD, 'The Physical Quality of Life Index: A Useful Social Indicator?' in *World Development*, Vol. 7, No. 6, 1979.

LEAMER, E., *Sources of International Comparative Advantage: Theory and Evidence*, MIT Press, 1984.

LECAILLON, J., F. PAUKERT, C. MORRISSON, and D. GERMIDIS, *Income Distribution and Economic Development: An Analytical Survey*, ILO, Geneva, 1984.

LECAILLON, J. and C. MORRISSON, *Politiques Economiques et Performances Agricoles: le cas du Burkina Faso, 1960–83*, OECD Development Centre, Paris, 1985.

LECOMTE, B.J., *Project Aid*, OECD Development Centre, Paris, 1986.

LEE, G., ed., *Export-led Industrialisation and Development*, ILO, Geneva, 1981.

LEE, T.H., *Intersectoral Capital Flows in the Economic Development of Taiwan*, Cornell University Press, 1971.

LEFF, N.H., 'Monopoly Capitalism and Public Policy in Developing Countries' in *Kyklos*, Vol. 32, 1979.

LEFF, N.H., 'The Use of Policy Science Tools in Public Sector Decision making: Social Cost Benefit Analysis in the World Bank' in *Kyklos*, Vol. 38, Fasc 1, 1985.

LEIPZIGER, D.M., *Basic Needs and Development*, Oelgeschlager, Gunn and Hain, Cambridge, 1981.

LENIN, V.I., *The Development of Capitalism in Russia*, 1899.

LEONTIEF, W., *The Structure of the American Economy 1919–1929*, Harvard University Press, Cambridge, 1941.

LEWIS, J.P. and V. KALLAB, eds., *Development Strategies Reconsidered*, Overseas Development Council, Washington, D.C., 1986.

LEWIS, W.A., 'Industrial Development in Puerto Rico' in *Caribbean Economic Review*, Vol. 1, Nos. 1-2, 1949.

LEWIS, W.A., 'Industrialisation of the British West Indies' in *Caribbean Economic Review*, Vol. 2, No. 1, 1950.

LEWIS, W.A., 'Economic Development with Unlimited Supplies of Labor', in *The Manchester School of Economic and Social Studies*, May 1954.

LEWIS, W.A., *Theory of Economic Growth*, Allen and Unwin, London, 1955.

LEWIS, W.A., 'Unlimited Labour: Further Notes' in *The Manchester School of Economic and Social Studies*, January 1958.

LEWIS, W.A., 'The Slowing Down of the Engine of Growth' in *American Economic Review*, September 1980.

LEWIS, W.A., 'Development Economics in the 1950s' in G. Meier and D. Seers, eds., 1984.

LEYS. C., *Underdevelopment in Kenya: The Political Economy of Neo-Colonialism*, Heinemann, London, 1975.

LEYS, C., 'Capital Accumulation, Class Formation and Dependency – The Significance of the Kenyan Case' in *Social Register*, 1978.

LEYS, C., 'Kenya: What does Dependency Explain?' in *Review of African Political Economy*, No. 16, 1980.

LIM, H.C., 'Dependent Development in the World System: The case of South Korea, 1963–1979' Ph.D. Dissertation, Department of Sociology, Harvard University, 1982.

LIPTON, M., *Why the Poor Stay Poor: A Study of Urban Bias in World Development*, Temple Smith, London, 1977.

LIPTON, M., 'Inter-Farm, Inter-regional and Farm–Non-farm Income Distribution: The Impact of the New Cereal Varieties' in *World Development*, March 1978.

LITTLE, I.M.D., *The Experiences and Causes of Rapid Labour-intensive Development in Korea, Taiwan, Hong Kong and Singapore and the Possibilities of Emulation*, International Labour Office Working Paper, ILO, Bangkok, 1979.

LITTLE, I.M.D., *Economic Development: Theory, Policy and International Relations*, Basic Books, New York, 1982.

LITTLE, I.M.D. and J.A. MIRRLEES, *Manual of Industrial Project Analysis in Developing Countries*, Vols. I and II, OECD Development Centre, Paris, 1968 and 1969.

LITTLE, I.M.D. and J.A. MIRRLEES, *Project Appraisal and Planning for Developing Countries*, Heinemann, London, 1974.

LITTLE, I.M.D., T. SCITOVSKY and M.F.G. SCOTT, *Industry and Trade in Some Developing Countries*, Oxford University Press for the OECD Development Centre, London, 1970.

LOCKWOOD, J., ed., *The State and Economic Enterprise in Japan*, Princeton University Press, New Jersey, 1965.

LOEB, G.A., 'Capital Shortage and Labour Surplus in the United States' in *Review of Economics and Statistics*, Vol. 36, August 1954.

LONG, D., 'Development and Repression in South Korea' in *Jomo*, 1983.

LUSTIG, N., *Distribución del ingreso y crecimiento en México: Un análisis de las ideas estructuralistas*, El Colegio de Mexico, 1981.

LUSTIG, N., 'Del Estructuralismo al Neoestructuralismo: la busqueda de un paradigma heterodoxo' in *Colección Estudios CIEPLAN*, No. 23, 1988.

MacNAMARA, R.S., 'Annual Speech to the Board of Governors', World Bank, Washington, D.C., various years.

MADDISON, A., *Phases of Capitalist Development*, Oxford University Press, Oxford, 1982.

MADDISON, A., 'Growth and Slowdown in Advanced Capitalist Economies: Techniques of Quantitative Assessment' in *Journal of Economic Literature*, No. 25, 1987.

MADDISON, A., *The World Economy in the 20th Century*, OECD Development Centre, Paris, 1989.

MAHALANOBIS, P.C., 'Some Observations on the Process of Growth of National Income' in *Sankhya*, Vol. 12, Pt. 4, September 1953.

MAHALANOBIS, P.C., 'The Approach of Operational Research to Planning in India' in *Sankhya*, Vol. 16, Pts. 1 and 2, December 1955.

MANDEL, E., *Marxist Economic Theory*, Merlin, London, 1974.

MANDEL, E., *Late Capitalism* (Revised edition), New Left Books, London, 1976.

MANLEY, M., *The Politics of Change: A Jamaican Testament*, André Deutsch, London, 1974.

MANLEY, M., *A Voice at the Workplace: Reflections on Colonialism and the Jamaican Worker*, A. Deutsch, London, 1975.

MARINI, R.M., 'Dialéctica de la dependencia: la economía exportadora' in *Sociedad y Desarrollo*, No. 1, 1972.

MARINI, R.M., 'Brazilian Sub-imperialism' in *Monthly Review*, No. 9, February 1972.

MARX, K. and F. ENGELS, *The German Ideology*, 1846.

MARX, K., *The Communist Manifesto*, 1848.

MARX, K., *Grundisse: Foundations of the Critique of Political Economy*, 1859.

MARX, K., *Capital*, 1867.

MARTINER, G., *Planificación y presupuesto por programas*, Siglo XXI, Mexico, 1967.

MAYOBRE, J., 'Global Programming as an Instrument of Economic Development Policy' in H. Ellis and H. Wallich, eds., 1961.

McKINNON, R.I., *Money and Capital in Economic Development*, Brookings Institution, Washington D.C., 1973.

MEIER, G., *International Trade and Development*, Harper and Row, New York, 1963.

MEIER, G. and D. SEERS, eds., *Pioneers in Development*, Oxford University Press for the World Bank, New York, 1984.

MELLOR, J.W., 'Agricultural Development and the Intersectoral Transfer of Resources' in C.K. Eicher and J.M. Staatz, eds., 1984.

MELLOR, J.W., 'Agriculture on the road to Industrialisation' in J.P. Lewis and V. Kallab, eds., 1986.

MELLOR, J.W., 'Global Food Balances and Food Security', in *World Development*, Vol. 6, No. 9, 1988.

MELLOR, J.W., C. DELGADO and M.J. BLACKIE, eds., *Accelerating Food Production Growth in Sub-Saharan Africa*, Johns Hopkins University Press, Baltimore, 1985.

MELLOR, J.W. and B.F. JOHNSTON, 'The World Equation: Interrelationship Among Employment and Food Consumption' in *Journal of Economic Literature*, June 1984.

MICHAELY, M., 'Exports and Growth: An Empirical Investigation' in *Journal of Development Economics*, Vol. 4, 1977.

MIKESELL, R.F., *The Economics of Foreign Aid*, Weidenfeld and Nicolson, London, 1968.

MIKESELL, R.F., 'Appraising IMF Conditionality: Too Loose, Too Tight or Just Right?' in J. Williamson, ed., 1983.

MIRRLEES, J. and N.H. STERN, eds., *Models of Economic Growth*, MacMillan, London, 1971.

MOONEY, P.T., 'The Law of the Seed: Another Development and Plant Genetic Resources' in *Development Dialogue*, 1983: 1-2.

MOORE, B. Jr., *Social Origins of Dictatorship and Democracy: Lord and Peasant in the Making of the Modern World*, Beacon Press, Boston, 1966.

MORAN, T. and contributors, *Investing in Development: New Roles for Private Capital?* Transaction Books for the Overseas Development Council, New Brunswick, 1986.

MORAWETZ, D., 'Employment Implications of Industrialisation in Developing Countries', *Economic Journal*, Vol. 84, September 1976.

MORAWETZ, D., *Twenty-five Years of Economic Development, 1950-75*, World Bank, Washington, D.C., 1977.

MORGAN, T., 'The Long-run Terms of Trade between Agriculture and Manufacturing' in *Economic Development and Cultural Change*, Vol. 3, No. 1, 1959.

MORRIS, M.D., *Measuring the Condition of the World's Poor: The Physical Quality of Life Index*, Pergamon, New York, 1979.

MURPHY, K.M., A. SCHLEIFER and R. VISHNY, 'Industrialisation and the Big Push' and 'Income Distribution, Market Size and Industrialisation', NBER Working Papers No. 2708 and No. 2709, 1988.

MURRAY, R., 'The Internationalisation of Capital and the Nation State' in H. Radice, ed., 1975.

MUSSA, M., 'Macroeconomic Policy and Trade Liberalisation: Some Guidelines' in *World Bank Research Observer*, January 1987.

MYER, J., 'A Crown of Thorns: Cardoso and the Counter Revolution' in *Latin American Perspectives*, Issue IV, Vol. 2, No. 1, 1975.

MYINT, H., *The Economics of the Developing Countries*, Hutchinson University Library, London, 1964.

MYINT, H., 'The Place of Institutional Changes in International Trade Theory in the Setting of Underdeveloped Economies' in B. Ohlin *et al.*, 1979.

MYRDAL, G., *An International Economy: Problems and Prospects*, Harper, New York, 1956.

MYRDAL, G., *Rich Lands and Poor*, Harper, New York, 1957.

MYRDAL, G., *Asian Drama: An Inquiry into the Poverty of Nations*, Pantheon, New York, 1968.

MYRDAL, G., *The Challenge of World Poverty*, Penguin, 1970.

NAKAMURA, J.I., 'Growth of Japanese Agriculture 1875-1920', in W. Lockwood, ed., 1965.

NAOROJI, D., *Poverty and Un-British Rule in India*, Government of India, Delhi, 1901.

NAOROJI, D., *The Drain Theory, Papers read at the Indian Economic Conference*, Popular Prakash, Bombay, 1970.

NEWFARMER R. and W. MUELLER, 'Multinational Corporations in Brazil and Mexico', Report to the Subcommittee on Multinational Corporations, US Senate, Washington, D.C., 1975.

NICHOLLS, W.H., 'The Place of Agriculture in Economic Development' in C.K. Eicher and L.W. Witt, eds., 1964.

NURKSE, R., 'Some International Aspects of the Problem of Economic Development' in *American Economic Review*, May 1952.

OBERAI, A.S., *State Policies and Internal Migration*, St. Martin's Press, New York, 1983.

O'DONNELL, G., 'Comparative Historical Formations of the State Apparatus and Socio-Economic Change in the Third World' in *International Social Science Journal*, Vol. 32, 1980.

OECD, *Twenty-Five Years of Development Cooperation*, Chairman's Report, Development Assistance Committee, Paris, 1985.

OHKAWA, K., *Differential Structure and Agriculture: Essays on Dualistic Growth*, Hitotsubashi University Press, Tokyo, 1972.

OHLIN, B., *Interregional and International Trade*, Harvard University Press, Boston, 1933.

OHLIN, B. *et al.*, *The International Allocation of Economic Activity*, MacMillan, London, 1979.

OHLIN, G., 'Reflections on the Rostow Doctrine' in *Economic Development and Cultural Change*, July 1961.

OLSEN, M., *The Logic of Collective Action: Public Goods and the Theory of Groups*, Harvard University Press, Cambridge, 1965.

OLSEN, M., *The Rise and Decline of Nations: Economic Growth, Stagflation, and Social Rigidities*, Yale University Press, New Haven, 1981.

OMAN, C., *New Forms of International Investment in Developing Countries*, OECD Development Centre, Paris, 1984.

OMAN, C., ed., *New Forms of International Investment in Developing Countries: The National Perspective*, OECD Development Centre, Paris, 1984.

OMAN, C., *New Forms of Investment in Developing Country Industries: Mining, Petrochemicals, Automobiles, Textiles, Food*, OECD Development Centre, Paris, 1989.

ONIMODE, B., *An Introduction to Marxist Political Economy*, Zed Books Ltd., London, 1985.

OSHIMA, H.T., 'The International Comparison of Size Distribution of Family Incomes with Special Reference to Asia' in *Review of Economics and Statistics*, Vol. 34, August 1962.

OUIZON, J. and H.P. BINSWANGER, 'Modeling the Impact of Agricultural Growth and Government Policy on Income Distribution in India' in *World Bank Economic Review*, Vol. 1, No. 1, September 1986.

OVERSEAS DEVELOPMENT INSTITUTE, 'Commodity Prices: Investing in Decline', Briefing Paper, March 1988.OWEN, W.F., 'The Double Developmental Squeeze on Agriculture' in *American Economic Review*, March 1966.

OZAWA, T., *Recycling Japan's Surpluses for Developing Countries*, OECD Development Centre, Paris, 1989.

PACK, H. and L. WESTPHAL, 'Industrial Strategy and Technological Change: Theory versus Reality' in *Journal of Development Economics*, Vol. 21, 1986.

PALLOIX, C., 'The Internationalisation of Capital and the Circuit of Social Capital' in H. Radice, ed., 1975.

PALMA, G., 'Dependency: A Formal Theory of Underdevelopment or a Methodology for the Analysis of Concrete Situations of Underdevelopment?' in *World Development*, Vol. 6, 1978.

PALMER, I., *The New Rice in the Philippines*, UNRISD, Geneva, 1975.

PEARSE, A., *Seeds of Plenty, Seeds of Want*, Oxford University Press, 1980.

PEARSON, L.B., *Partners in Development*, Report of the Commission on International Development, Praeger, New York, 1969.

PEEK, P. and P. ANTOLINEZ, 'Migration and the Urban Labour Market: The Case of San Salvador' in *World Development*, April 1977.

PERES NÚÑEZ, W., *Foreign Direct Investment and Industrial Restructuring in Mexico*, OECD Development Centre, Paris, 1990.

PERKINS, D., 'Meeting Basic Needs in the People's Republic of China' in *World Development*, Vol. 6, No. 5, 1977.

PERROUX, F., 'Note on the Concept of Growth Poles', *Economie Appliquée*, Vol. 8, 1955.

PERROUX, F., *L'economie du XXè siecle*, Presses universitaires de France, Paris, 1961.

PHILLIPS, A., 'The Concept of 'Development'' in *Review of African Political Economy*, No. 8, 1977.

PINTO, A., 'Naturaleza e implicaciones de la 'heterogeneidad estructural' de la America Latina' in *El Trimestre Económico*, No. 145, January–March 1970.

POLLAK, J., *Financial Policies and Development*, OECD Development Centre, Paris, 1989.
POST, K., *Arise, Ye Starvelings: The Jamaican Labour Rebellion of 1938 and its Aftermath*, cited in A. Foster-Carter, 1978.
POULANTZAS, N., 'Internationalisation of Capitalist Relations and the Nation-State' in *Economy and Society*, 1975.
PREBISCH, R., *Problemas teóricos y pr cticos del crecimiento económico*, 1951.
PREBISCH, R., 'La Cooperación internacional en la política de desarollo latinamericano', ECLA, Santiago, 1954.
PREBISCH, R., 'Commercial Policy in the Underdeveloped Countries' in *American Economic Review*, Papers and Proceedings, May, 1959.
PREBISCH, R., *Hacia una din mica del desarrollo latinoamericano*, Fondo de Cultura Económica, Mexico, 1963.
PREBISCH, R., *A New Trade Policy for Development*, report to UNCTAD, 1964.
PREBISCH, R., *Transformación y desarrollo, la gran tarea de América Latina*, Fondo de Cultura Económica, Mexico, 1970.
PREBISCH, R., 'Five Stages in my Thinking on Development' in G. Meier and D. Seers, eds., 1984.
PREEG, G.H., 'Hard Bargaining Ahead: US Trade Policy and the Developing Countries', Overseas Development Council, Washington D.C., 1983.
PYATT, F.G. and J. ROUND, *Social Accounting Matrices: A basis for Planning*, The World Bank, Washington, D.C., 1985.
QUIBRIA, M.G. and S. RASHID, 'The Puzzle of Sharecropping: A Survey of Theories' in *World Development*, Vol. 12, No. 2, 1984.
RADICE, H., ed., *International Firms and Modern Imperialism*, Penguin Books, 1975.
RAJ, K.N., 'Linkages in Industrialisation and Development Strategy: Some Basic Issues' in *Journal of Development Planning*, No. 8, 1975.
RAJAS, F. and V. MONCAYO, *La Producción Parcelaria y el Modo de Producción Capitalista*, ASIAS, Bogota, 1978.
RAMASWANI, V.K., ed., *Trade and Development*, Allen and Unwin, London, 1971.
RAMASWAMI, V.K. and T.N. SRINIVASAN 'Optimal Subsidies and Taxes when some Factors are Traded', *Journal of Political Economy*, Vol. 76, 1968.
RANIS, G., 'Challenges and Opportunities Posed by Asia's Super Exporters: Implications for Manufacured Exports from Latin America' in W. Baer and M. Gilles, eds., 1981.
RANIS, G., 'Comment on Cline' in *World Development*, Vol. 13, No. 4, 1985.
RANIS, G. and J. FEI, 'A Theory of Economic Development' in *American Economic Review*, September 1961.
RANIS, G. and J. FEI, *Development of the Labour Surplus Economy: Theory and Practice*, Irwin, Homewood, 1964.
RAO, C.H. Hanumantha, 'Alternative Explanations of the Inverse Relationship between Farm Size and Output per Acre in India', in *Indian Economic Review*, Vol. 1, No. 2, Oct. 1966.
REISEN, H, and A. VAN TROTSENBURG, *Developing Country Debt: The Budgetary and Transfer Problem*, OECD Development Centre, Paris, 1988.

RENAUD, B., *National Urbanisation Policy in Developing Countries*, 1979.

REY, P.P., *Les Alliances de Classes*, Maspero, Paris, 1973.

REYNOLDS, L.G., *Economic Growth in the Third World, 1850–1980*, Yale University Press, New Haven, 1985.

RHODA, R., 'Rural Development and Urban Migration: Can We Keep Them Down on the Farm?' in *International Migration Review*, Vol. 17, No. 61, 1983.

RICHARDS, A., *Development and Modes of Production in Marxian Economics: a Critical Evaluation*, Harwood, London, 1986.

RIEDEL, J., 'Trade as the Engine of Growth in Developing Countries, Revisited' in *Economic Journal*, Vol. 94, 1984.

RIMMER, D., 'The Abstraction from Politics: A Critique of Economic Theory and Design with Reference to West Africa' in *Journal of Development Studies*, Vol. 5, No. 3, 1969.

ROBSON, P., *The Economics of International Integration*, London, 1972.

RODGERS, G.B., 'A Conceptualisation of Poverty in Rural India' in *World Development*, Vol. 4, No. 4, April 1976.

RODNEY, W., *How Europe Underdeveloped Africa*, Tanzania Publishing House, Dar es Salaam, 1972.

RODRIGUEZ, O., 'Sobre la concepción del sistema centro-periferia' in *CEPAL Review* 1977.

RODRIGUEZ, O., *La Teoría del Subdesarrollo de la CEPAL*, Siglo XXI, Mexico, 1980.

RONDINELLI, D.A., *Development Projects as Policy Experiments*, Methuen, London, 1983.

ROS, J., 'On Models of inertial inflation', WIDER, mimeo, July 1987.

ROSENBURG, N., 'Marx as a Student of Technological Change' in his *Inside the Black Box: Technology and Economics*, Cambridge University Press, Cambridge, 1982.

ROSENSTEIN-RODAN, P.N., 'Industrialisation of Eastern and South Eastern Europe' in *Economic Journal*, Vol. 53, 1943.

ROSENSTEIN-RODAN, P.N., 'Notes on the Theory of the Big Push' in H. Ellis and H. Wallich, eds., 1961.

ROSENSTEIN-RODAN, P.N., ed., *Capital Formation and Economic Development*, MIT Press, Cambridge, 1964.

ROSENSTEIN-RODAN, P.N., 'Natura Facit Saltum: Analysis of the Disequilibrium Growth Process' in Meier and Seers, eds., 1984.

ROSTOW, W.W., 'The Take Off into Self-Sustained Growth' in *Economic Journal*, March 1956.

ROSTOW, W.W., *The Stages of Economic Growth: A Non-Communist Manifesto*, Cambridge University Press, Cambridge, 1960.

ROY, P., 'Transition in Agriculture: Empirical Indicators and Results' in *Journal of Peasant Studies*, Vol. 8, No. 2, January 1981.

RUTTAN, V.W., 'The Green Revolution: Seven Generalisations' in *International Development Review*, December 1977.

RUTTAN, V.W, 'Integrated Rural Development Programmes: A Historical Perspective' in *World Development*, Vol. 12, No. 4, 1984.

RWEYEMAMU, J., 'International Trade and the Developing Countries' in *Journal of Modern African Studies*, Vol. III, No. 2, 1969.

RWEYEMAMU, J., 'The Political Economy of Foreign Private Investment in the Underdeveloped Countries' in *The African Review*, Vol. 1, 1971.

RWEYEMAMU, J., *Underdevelopment and Industrialisation in Tanzania*, Oxford University Press, Oxford, 1973.

SACHS, J., 'Trade and Exchange-Rate Policies in Growth-Oriented Adjustment Programs' in Corbo, *et al.* eds., 1987.

SAITH, A.,'Development and Distribution: A Critique of the Cross-Country U Hypothesis' in *Journal of Development Economics*, Vol. 13, 1983.

SAMUELSON, P.A. 'International Trade and the Equalisation of Factor Prices' in *The Economic Journal*, Vol. LVIII, No. 230, London, June 1948.

SAMUELSON, P.A. 'International Factor - Price Equalisation Once Again' in *The Economic Journal*, Vol. LIX, No. 234, London, June 1949.

SCARF, H. and J. SHOVEN, eds., *Applied General Equilibrium Analysis*, Cambridge University Press, 1984.

SCHNEIDER, H., *Meeting Food Needs in a Context of Change*, OECD Development Centre, Paris, 1984.

SCHULTZ, T.W., 'Capital Formation by Education' in *Journal of Political Economy*, December 1960.

SCHULTZ, T.W., *Transforming Traditional Agriculture*, Yale University Press, New Haven, 1964.

SCHULTZ, T.W.,'The Doctrine of Agricultural Labour of Zero Value' in his *Transforming Traditional Agriculture*, Yale University Press, New Haven, 1964.

SCHULTZ, T.W., 'Education Investments and Returns' in H.B. Chenery and T.N. Srinivasan, eds., 1988.

SCITOVSKY, T., 'Two Concepts of External Economies' in *Journal of Political Economy*, April 1954.

SEERS, D., 'What are we trying to measure' in N. Baster, ed., 1972.

SEN, A.K., 'Surplus Labour in India: A Critique of Schultz's Statistical Test' (with reply and rejoinder) in *Economic Journal*, March 1967.

SEN, A.K., 'Peasants and Dualism with or without Surplus Labour', in *Journal of Political Economy*, October 1966.

SEN, A.K., *Employment, Technology and Development*, London, 1975.

SEN, A.K., 'Poor, Relatively Speaking' in *Oxford Economic Papers*, Vol. 35, No. 1, 1983.

SHAPIRO, K., 'Efficiency Differentials in Peasant Agriculture and their Implications for Development', contributed papers read at the 16th International conference of Agricultural Economists, University of Oxford Institute of Agricultural Economics, Oxford, 1977.

SHIVJI, I., 'Tanzania – The Silent Class Struggle' in *Cherche*, 1970.

SHIVJI, I., 'Capitalism Unlimited. Public Corporations in Partnership with Multinational Corporations' in *The African Review*, Vol. 3, 1973.

SHIVJI, I., *Class Struggles in Tanzania*, Heinemann Press, 1975.

SIMMONS, J.,'Education for Development Reconsidered' in *World Development*, Nov./Dec. 1979.

SINGER, H.W., 'The Distribution of Gains between Investing and Borrowing Countries' in *American Economic Review*, May, 1950.

SINGER, H.W., 'Dualism Revisited: A New Approach to the Problems of the Dual Society in Developing Countries' in *Journal of Development Studies*, Vol. 17, No. 1, October 1970.

SINGER, H.W., 'Industrialisation: Where Do We Stand? Where Are We Going?' in *Industry and Development*, No. 12, 1984.

SINGER, H.W. and P. ALIZADEH, 'Import Substitution Revisited in a Darkening External Environment' in *Imspannungsfeld von Wirtschaft Technik and Politik*, Gunter Olzog Verlag, Munich, 1986.

SINGH, A., 'The Basic Needs Approach to Development vs the New International Economic Order: The Significance of Third World Industrialisation' in *World Development*, Vol. 7, No. 6, 1979.

SOLIGO, R. and J.S. STERN, 'Tariff Protection; Import Substitution and Investment Efficiency' in *Pakistan Development Review*, Summer, 1965.

SOZA, H., *Planificación del desarrollo industrial*, Siglo XXI, Mexico, 1966.

SPENCER, B. and J. BRANDER, 'International R&D Rivalry and Industrial Strategy' in *Review of Economic Studies*, No. 5, 1983.

SPITZ, P., 'Silent Violence: Famine and Inequality', in *International Social Science Journal*, Vol. 30, No. 4, 1978.

SPRAOS, J., 'The Statistical Debate on the Net Barter Terms of Trade Between Primary Commodities and Manufactures' in *Economic Journal*, Vol. 90, No. 357, 1980.

SPRAOS, J., *Inequalising Trade? A Study of Traditional North–South Specialisation in the Context of Terms of Trade Concepts*, Oxford University Press, Oxford, 1983.

STARK, O., 'Migrants and Markets', Migration and Development Program Discussion Paper No. 37, Harvard University, 1988.

STAVENHAGEN, R., *Social Classes in Agrarian Societies*, Doubleday, New York, 1975.

STAVRIANOS, L.S., *Global Rift: The Third World Comes of Age*, William Morrow, New York, 1975.

STEGEMANN, K., 'Policy Rivalry Among Industrial States: What Can We Learn from Models of Strategic Trade Theory?' in *International Organisation*, Vol. 43, No. 1, Winter 1989.

STEINBERG, D.T., 'Foreign Aid and the Development of the Republic of Korea: The Effectiveness of Concessional Assistance' in *US Aid Special Study*, No. 42, October 1985.

STEINDL, J., *Maturity and Stagnation in American Capitalism*, Blackwell, Oxford, 1952.

STERN, N., 'The Economics of Development: A Survey' in *Economic Journal*, Vol. 99, September 1989.

STERN, R.M., 'Testing Trade Theories in International Trade and Finance' in P. Kenen, ed., 1975.

STERN, R., ed., *US Trade Policies in a Changing World Economy*, MIT Press, Cambridge, 1987.

STEWART, F., 'Limitations of the Neoclassical Approach to Development: A Review of Deepak Lal: 'The Poverty of Development Economics'', *SOAS/UCL Development Seminar Paper 64*, 1984, reprinted in *Journal of Development Studies*, 1985.

STEWART, F. and J. JAMES, eds., *The Economics of New Technology in Developing Countries*, Frances Pinter, London, 1982.

STREETEN, P., 'Balanced versus Unbalanced Growth' in *Economic and Political Weekly*, April 20, 1973.

STREETEN, P., 'The Distinctive Features of a Basic Needs Approach to Development' in *International Development Review*, Vol. 19, No. 3, 1977.
STREETEN, P., 'A Comment' in *Regional Development Dialogue*, Vol. 1, No. 1, 1980.
STREETEN, P., *et al., First Things First: Meeting Basic Human Needs in the Developing Countries*, Oxford University Press, New York, 1981.
STREETEN, P., *Development Perspectives*, MacMillan, London, 1981.
STREETEN, P., 'A Cool Look at Outward Oriented Strategies for Development' in *World Economy*, Vol. 5, September 1982.
STREETEN, P., 'Basic Needs: Some Unsettled Questions' in *World Development*, Vol. 12, No. 9, 1984.
STREETEN, P., 'Development Dichotomies' in Meier and Seers, eds., 1984.
STREETEN, P. and S.J. BURKI, 'Basic Needs: Some Issues' in *World Development*, Vol. 6, No. 3, 1978.
SUNKEL, O., 'National Development Policy and External Dependency in Latin America' in *Journal of Development Studies*, Vol. 1, No. 1, 1969.
SUNKEL, O., 'Big Business and Dependency' in *Foreign Affairs*, Vol. 24, no. 1, 1972.
SUNKEL, O., 'Transnational Capitalism and National Disintegration in Latin America' in *Social and Economic Studies*, Vol. 22, No. 1, 1973.
SUNKEL, O., 'Transnationalisation and its National Consequences' in J. Villamil, ed., 1979.
SWAINSON, N., 'The Rise of a National Bourgeoisie in Kenya' in *Review of African Political Economy*, No. 8, 1977.
SWAINSON, N., *The Development of Corporate Capitalism in Kenya, 1918–1977*, Heinemann, New York, 1980.
SWAMINATHAN, M.S., 'The Green Revolution Can Reach the Small Farmer' in S. Aziz, ed., 1975.
SWEEZY, P. and C. BETTELHEIM, *On the Transition to Socialism*, Monthly Review Press, New York, 1971.
SWEEZY, P. and M. DOBB, *et al., The Transition from Feudalism to Capitalism*, Science and Society, New York, 1967.
SYRQUIN, M., L. TAYLOR and L.E. WESTPHAL, eds., *Economic Structure and Performance*, Academic Press, New York, 1984.
TAVARES, M.C., 'Auge y declinación del proceso de sustitució'n de importaciones en el Brasil' in *Boletin Económica de América Latina*, Vol. 9, No. 1, March 1964.
TAYLOR, L., 'IS/LM in the Tropics: Diagrammatics of the New Structuralist Macro Critique' in W. Cline and S. Weintraub, eds., 1981.
THOMAS, C., *Dependence and Transformation. The Economics of the Transition to Socialism*, Monthly Review Press, New York, 1972.
TINBERGEN, J., *et al., Reshaping the International Order, A Report of the Club of Rome*, E.P. Dutton, New York, 1976.
TINBERGEN, J. and H. C. BOS, 'A Planning Model for the Education Requirements of Economic Growth' in OECD, *Econometric Models of Education*, Paris, 1965.
TOYE, J., 'Dirigisme and Development Economics' in *Cambridge Journal of Economics*, Vol. 9, No. 1, 1985.
TROTSKY, L., *The Revolution Betrayed*, 1937.

TUN WAI, U., 'Interest Rates Outside the Organised Money Markets in Underdeveloped Economies', in *IMF Staff Papers*, Vol. VI, No. 1, November 1957.

TURNHAM, D. and I. JAEGER, *The Employment Problem in Less Developed Countries: A Review of Evidence*, OECD Development Centre, Paris, 1971.

UL HAQ, M., *The Poverty Curtain: Choices for the Third World*, Columbia University Press, New York, 1976.

UNITED NATIONS, *Measures for the Economic Development of Under-Developed Countries*, 1951.

UNCTAD, *Trade and Development Report*, New York, 1983.

UNCTC, *Transnational Corporations in World Development Trends and Prospects*, United Nations, New York, 1988.

UNIDO, *Guidelines for Project Evaluation*, United Nations, New York, 1972.

UNIDO, *Industry and Development: Global Report 1985*, New York, 1985.

UNIDO, *International Comparative Advantage in Manufacturing: Changing Profiles of Resources and Trade*, Vienna, 1986.

UNRISD, *Contents and Measurements of Socio-economic Development*, Geneva 1979.

VAITSOS, C., *Inter-Country Income Distribution and Transnational Enterprises*, Oxford University Press, Oxford, 1974.

VAITSOS, C., 'Crisis in Regional Cooperation among Developing Countries: A Survey' in *World Development*, Vol. 6, 1978.

VALAVANIS-VAIL, S., 'Leontief's Scarce Factor Paradox' in *Journal of Political Economy*, Vol. 54, December 1954.

VALDERRAMA, M. and P. LUDMANN, *La Oligarquia Terrateniente Ayer y Hoy*, Universidad Católica del Perú, Lima, 1979.

VAN de LAAR, A., 'The World Bank and the World's Poor' in *World Development*, Vol. 4, No. 10/11, 1976.

VERGOPOULOS, K., 'El Capitalismo Disforme' in S. Amin and K. Vergopoulos, eds., 1975.

VERGOPOULOS, K., 'Capitalism and Peasant Productivity' in *Journal of Peasant Studies*, Vol. 5, No. 4, 1978.

VERNON, R., *Sovereignty at Bay: the Multinational Spread of US Enterprises*, Basic Books, New York, 1971.

VILLAMIL, J., ed., *Transnational Capitalism and National Development: New Perspectives on Dependence*, Harvester Press, Sussex, 1979.

VINER, J., *The Customs Union Issue*, Carnegie Endowment for International Peace, New York, 1950.

VINER, J., *International Trade and Economic Development*, the Free Press, 1952.

VINER, J., *International Trade and Economic Development*, Clarendon Press, Oxford, 1953.

VITALE, L., 'América Latina: feudal o capitalista?' in *Estrategia*, No. 3, 1966.

VON PISCHKE, J.D., D.W. ADAMS and G. DONALD, eds., *Rural Financial Markets in Low-Income Countries: Their Use and Abuse*, Johns Hopkins University Press, Baltimore, 1983.

VUSKOVIC, P., 'Distribución del ingreso y opciones de desarrollo' in *Cuadernos de la Realidad Nacional* (Santiago), No. 5, September 1970.

WARD, B., 'The Decade of Development – A Study in Frustration' (A lecture delivered at the Overseas Development Institute on May 3, 1965), Overseas Development Institute, London, 1965.

WARREN, B., 'Imperialism and Capitalist Industrialisation' in *New Left Review*, No. 81, 1973.

WARREN, B., *Imperialism: Pioneer of Capitalism*, New Left Books, London, 1980.

WARRINER, D., 'Land Reform and Economic Development', in *National Bank of Egypt, Fiftieth Anniversary Commemoration Lectures*, Cairo, 1955.

WEEKES-VAGLIANI, W., *The Integration of Women in Development Projects*, OECD Development Centre, Paris, 1985.

WEEKS, J. and E. DORE, 'International Exchange and the Causes of Backwardness' in *Latin American Perspectives*, Vol. 6, No. 2, 1979.

WEISSKOPF, T., 'Dependence as an Explanation of Underdevelopment: A Critique,' M.S. University of Michigan, 1976, reported in Blomström and Hettne, 1984.

WELLS, J., 'The Diffusion of Durables in Brazil and its Implications for Recent Controversies Concerning Brazilian Development' in *Cambridge Journal of Economics*, No. 1, 1977.

WESTPHAL, L., Y.W. KHEE and G. PURSELL, 'Foreign Influences on Korean Industrial Development' in *Oxford Bulletin of Economics and Statistics*, November 1979.

WHITE, J., *The Politics of Foreign Aid*, London, 1974, Chapter VI.

WIGNARAJA, G., 'Industrialisation and Social Development: Some Comparisons of South Asia with the East Asian NICs' in P. Wignaraja, *et al.*, 1990.

WIGNARAJA, P., *et al., Participatory Development: Learning from South Asia*, Oxford University Press, Oxford and Karachi, 1990.

WILLIAMS, G., *The Brandt Report: A Critical Indroduction*, Third World First, London, 1980.

WILLIAMSON, J., ed., *IMF Conditionality*, Institute for International Economics, Washington, D.C., 1983.

WILLIAMSON, J.G., 'Regional Inequality and the Progress of National Development: A Description of Patterns' in *Economic Development and Cultural Change*, July 1965.

WILLIAMSON, J.G., 'Migration and Urbanisation' in H.B. Chenery and T.N. Srinivasan, eds., 1988.

WILLIAMSON, O., *Markets and Hierarchies*, Free Press, New York, 1975.

WOLFGANG, W., 'The Infant-Export Industry Argument' in *Canadian Journal of Economics*, Vol. 17, 1984.

WOODS, R.G., ed., *Future Dimensions of the World Food Problem*, Westview Press, Boulder, 1981.

WORLD BANK, *Towards Sustained Development in Sub-Saharan Africa: A Joint Program of Action*, Washington, D.C., 1984.

WORLD BANK, *The Assault on World Poverty*, Washington, D.C., 1975.

WORLD BANK, *Rural Development*, Sector Policy Paper, Washington D.C., February 1975.

WORLD BANK, *World Development Report*, Washington, D.C., 1977 and 1979.

WORLD BANK, *World Development Report*, Washington, D.C., 1980.

WORLD BANK, *Recovery in the Developing World: The London Symposium on the World Bank's Role*, Washington, D.C., 1986.

WUYTS, M., *On the Nature of Underdevelopment: An analysis of Two Views on Underdevelopment*, ERB, University of Dar es Salaam, 1976.

WYNN, S., 'The Taiwanese 'Economic Miracle" in *Monthly Review*, Vol. 30, No. 11, 1982.

YAGCI, F., 'Protection and Incentives in Turkish Manufacturing: An Evaluation of Policies and their Impact in 1981' in World Bank Staff Working Paper No. 660, Washington D.C., 1984.

YOTOPOULOS, P.A. and J.B. NUGENT, *Economics of Development*, Harper and Row, New York, 1976.

YUDELMAN, M., 'Integrated Rural Development Projects: The Bank's Experience' in *Finance and Development*, Vol. 14, No. 1, March 1977.

Index

ALL ABOUT ME AND THE THINGS I CAN DO, NOW THAT

I AM FIVE!

SO-CWS-724

Words by
Peter Jarrette and
Dorothy Rose

Pictures by
Anthony Rao

Little Simon
Published by Simon & Schuster, New York

Text copyright © 1982 by Little Simon,
a Simon & Schuster Division of Gulf & Western Corporation.
Simon & Schuster Building, 1230 Avenue of the Americas, New York, New York 10020.
Illustrations copyright © 1982 by Anthony Rao. Printed in U.S.A. 0-671-44469-7
10 9 8 7 6 5 4 3 2 1

I just couldn't wait for this day to arrive,

Today is my birthday—
Hooray, I am five!

The friends that I made
Since I started in school,

Came over to play and to splash in the pool.

We try to decide which direction to go,

Let's all climb a tree, if the branches are low.

We're up in the tree,
Not too far from the ground,

We're in our own spaceship and flying around.

Our ride is all finished,
We're back in the yard,

We rest in the shade,
Because space rides are hard.

It's fun playing games, I like musical chairs,

And prowling the attic in search of some bears.

Some friends that I play with
Are ones I've made up,
My favorite's Harry, a little blue pup.

I'm helping my parents
And they think it's fine,
We work very hard to make everything shine.

In school we all draw
With our pencils and pens,

Giraffes, cows, and pigs,
And some horses and hens.

I'm learning to read words
Like "cat", "dog" and "look",
And soon I'll be able
To read this whole book.

Both large ones and small ones,
All numbers are fun,
I count up 'til twenty,
Without skipping one.

Each day that I'm five
Brings a new bag of tricks,
I hardly can wait
'Til the day I am six!